MW01697856

Five Aspects of Woman

A Biblical Theology of Femininity

Volume Two

Barbara Mouser

Copyright © 1992, 1993, 1994, 1995, 1997, 2002, 2008, 2011, 2012 International Council for Gender Studies, Inc. Published by the International Council for Gender Studies, Inc. (ICGS), PO Box 702, Waxahachie, Texas 75168.

All rights reserved. This publication is the sole property of the International Council for Gender Studies, Inc. of Waxahachie, Texas. No part of this publication may be reproduced, translated, or transmitted in any form or by any means—electronic or mechanical, including photocopying, recording, or any information storage and retrieval system—without permission in writing from the publisher.

Scripture, unless noted, is taken from the New American Standard Bible (NASB), copyright © 1960, 1963, 1968, 1971, 1973, 1975, 1977, 1995 by The Lockman Foundation.

Scripture quotations in "The Womanliness of Deborah" supplement are from The Holy Bible, English Standard Version, copyright © 2001 by Crossway Bibles, a division of Good News Publishers. Used by permission. All rights reserved.

Front and back covers:
Design—Julie Handel
Text—Janet Niblack
Photography—Mariette Hart
Models—Amanda Walke and Karuss Ferchau

Book:
Icons, diagrams, page layout—Priscilla Fisher

Printed in the United States by Snowfall Press, Monument, Colorado.

ISBN: 978-1-929656-27-1

ISBN set (*Volume One* and *Volume Two* together): 978-1-929656-28-8

For more information about ICGS, the *Five Aspects of Woman* course, the *Five Aspects of Man* course, and other materials available from ICGS, please write the publisher, call 800-317-6958, or see websites:
http://www.fiveaspects.org
http://www.5aspects.org

6/2013

Table of Contents — *Volume Two*

Five Aspects of Woman

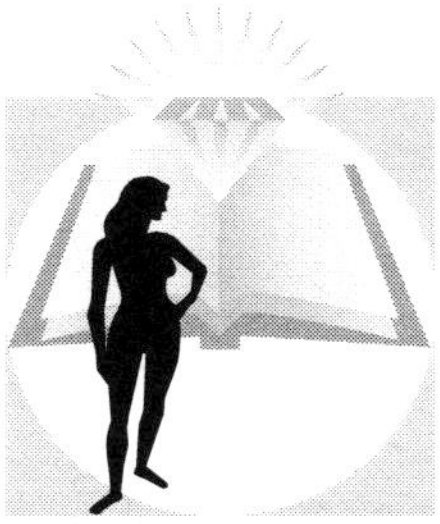

Five Aspects of Woman is one course, published in two volumes for the convenience of our students. Neither *Volume One* nor *Volume Two* is a stand-alone study. *Volume Two* should be studied after *Volume One*, in accord with the guidelines provided.

Five Aspects of Woman*—Volume Two*

Lady of Wisdom

Woman, skill, and insight. *Woman, like wisdom, reproves, counsels, teaches, and sponsors others.*

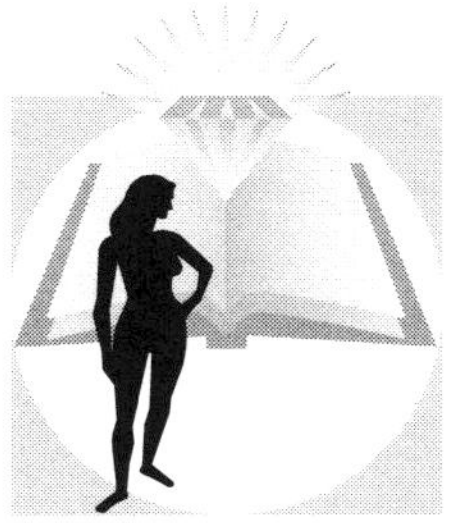

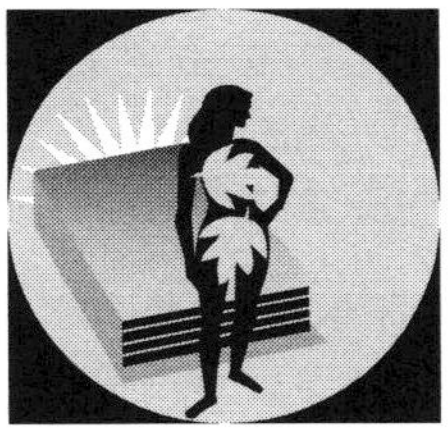

God created woman to be Lady of Wisdom.

Wisdom has built her house, she has hewn out her seven pillars; she has prepared her food, she has mixed her wine; she has also set her table; she has sent out her maidens, she calls from the tops of the heights of the city: "Whoever is naive, let him turn in here!" To him who lacks understanding she says, "Come, eat of my food, and drink of the wine I have mixed. Forsake your folly and live, and proceed in the way of understanding." PROVERBS 9:1-6 *The fear of the LORD is the beginning of wisdom...* PROVERBS 9:10a *Charm is deceitful and beauty is vain, but a woman who fears the LORD, she shall be praised.* PROVERBS 31:30

LESSON 14 : Lady of Wisdom – *created*

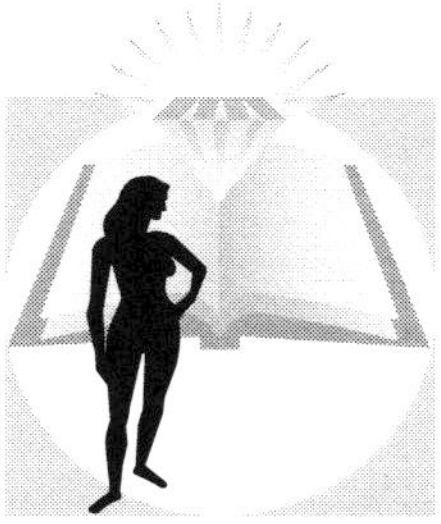

1. Who is "lady" wisdom?

The first three aspects are as simple as one, two, three—Mistress of the Domain in Genesis 1, Helper-Completer in Genesis 2, and Lifegiver in Genesis 3. To find our fourth definitive view of woman, however, we must turn many pages in the Old Testament to the Wisdom Literature. Many passages between Genesis 3 and Proverbs amplify the first three aspects and introduce the last two; but, in my view, there is not a new, definitive passage in these pages. In Proverbs, however, we see femininity not only in a new light, we meet "the first feminine," a femininity that existed even before Eve. Wisdom is personified in Proverbs 1-9 as a great lady who is the helper and companion of God and the teacher and counselor of man. This personification and the subsequent feminine role models offered in the book of Proverbs provide a fourth view of womanhood, the **wisdom** aspect.

1.1 Wisdom in Proverbs is not Christ.

Some people find this aspect difficult. These passages and concepts may be unfamiliar, or what I explain may contradict something you have learned before. Many teach that the feminine wisdom figure in Proverbs is Christ; feminists increasingly teach that she is the goddess Sophia who is to be worshiped. I do not believe either of these interpretations is correct. So first we must ask, who or what is feminine wisdom?

In the prologue of Proverbs, chapters 1-9, Solomon urges his readers that all of life is a choice between wisdom and folly. He presents both as women. "Lady" wisdom gives life through discipline and training; "woman" folly leads us to death through deceit and worldly pleasures.

Wisdom personified as a woman speaks in chapters 1, 8, and 9. She speaks of her origins in Proverbs 8:22-26: *"The LORD possessed me at the beginning of His way, before His works of old. 23 From everlasting I was established, from the beginning, from the earliest times of the earth. 24 When there were no depths I was brought forth, when there were no springs abounding with water. 25 Before the mountains were settled, before the hills I was brought forth; 26 while He had not yet made the earth and the fields, nor the first dust of the world."* If this passage is teaching anything, it is certainly teaching that whoever this is, she existed before this material world. Over and over she emphasizes that she was before the water, the earth, the mountains—all the material creations of God.

KEY Wisdom–*created*
person–FEMALE FIGURE ("clothed" in nakedness according to her untested, unashamed, sinless standing before God)
character–SQUARE (untested, sinless)
femininity–CIRCLE (untested, sinless)
role/work–SPARKLING JEWEL (woman is embodiment of wisdom); OPEN BOOK (learning)

Some say this entity must be Christ. They remember that John says the world was created through Christ and Paul says Christ is our wisdom. Therefore, they reason, this is Christ. However, that interpretation is not faithful to the context of Proverbs. This entity clearly has a beginning; she is not eternal. In Proverbs 8:22 , the verb usually rendered *brought forth* or *possessed* is well translated *created*. If there is any doubt, verses 24 and 25 say this entity was *brought forth*; that is, she was *given birth*. This entity is not God Himself; rather, it is the first of God's creative acts as is clearly stated in verse 22. Before creation, Christ was eternal God. He has no beginning in eternity. His only beginning as a creature came inside history 2,000 years ago in the womb of Mary.[1]

1. Refer to Supplement B for an extensive discussion of the exegetical and theological issues surrounding the feminine personification of wisdom in Proverbs and its relationship to the rest of Scripture.

1.2 Wisdom is the body of creation principles.

Wisdom in Proverbs is a body of principles (not Christ, and certainly not a goddess). Like the great Architect and Artist He is, God first created His blueprint, the plan for His universe. In His mind He established or appointed (v. 8:23) the principles that were to give substance and structure to His universe. This is the wisdom that He brought forth before His first creative acts. We will mention two examples of such creation or wisdom principles, the physical and the moral.

Natural laws

Physics is the study of the principles which order the physical world, principles such as gravity, electromagnetic energy, and nuclear power. These forces are basic to the structure of creation. Galileo said that mathematics is the alphabet of God. Math describes the underlying principles of how the universe works—energy, matter, light, time, and so forth. God developed the design principles of the physical universe before He built it. In Job 40 and 41, God asks Job some 70 questions about the universe, especially its natural laws—none of which Job could possibly answer. God's point is that the wisdom and power which frame the universe are finally His alone.

In Proverbs, wisdom is not actually a woman, a goddess, or Jesus. Wisdom is the body of creation principles by which God created and sustains His universe.

Moral patterns

Just as with physics and nature, there are moral principles which undergird the design of life. "Whatever a man sows, he will reap." Is that a Christian principle? Is it a Jewish principle? Versions of this proverb exist all over the world. What about "pride comes before a fall?" Or, "to guard your life, guard your tongue"? We could go through many maxims. Just as physicists codify the principles that order the physical world, wisdom teachers codify in pithy sayings the principles that govern human society. This is what the couplets of Proverbs are.

Wisdom is not actually a woman. She is actually the body of creation principles by which God created the universe, and with which He sustains it. Since the fall, principles of death and chaos have been added. But even though the curse is here, the creation has been sustained in the rocks and planets, in the plants and animals, and in the moral patterns of human society. God created and maintains these wisdom principles which give the creation its order, beauty, and structure.

2. How is wisdom like a lady?

Literally, wisdom is the body of God's creation principles. Figuratively, she is personified as a woman. Wisdom and women share feminine roles toward God and men. Does this femininity mean anything? **Masculinity is rooted in the Godhead. Femininity is rooted in the creation. This is the central answer given in this study about the essential roots of masculinity and femininity.** We will go deeper into this essential truth in future lessons. For now, let us pursue a more in-depth understanding of wisdom and why it is personified as a woman.

2.1 Wisdom: Companion and glorifier of God

In Proverbs 8:30, wisdom says, *"Then I was beside Him* [God]*, as a master workman; and I was daily His delight, rejoicing always before Him, rejoicing in the world, His earth, and having my delight in the* *sons of men."* In eternity past, before anything else was, the masculine Trinity—Father, Son, and Holy Spirit—existed in love and glory. Before They created the material universe, They created wisdom—the scientific, natural, and moral principles that would govern and give beauty to the whole creation. As a body, these principles took feminine roles toward God, acting as His helper, companion, and glorifier. With God in His work, wisdom delighted in Him and in what He was doing.

2.2 Wisdom as inviter and hostess

What are wisdom's roles to humanity? How does she act toward human beings? Proverbs 8 describes her activity this way:

> Proverbs 8:1-8—*Does not wisdom call, and understanding lift up her voice? 2 On top of the heights beside the way, where the paths meet, she takes her stand; 3 beside the gates, at the opening to the city, at the entrance of the doors, she cries out: 4 "To you, O men, I call, and my voice is to the sons of men. 5 O naive ones, understand prudence; and, O fools, understand wisdom. 6 Listen, for I will speak noble things; and the opening of my lips will reveal right things. 7 For my mouth will utter truth; and wickedness is an abomination to my lips. 8 All the utterances of my mouth are in righteousness; there is nothing crooked or perverted in them."*

Wisdom calls to humanity in chapters 1, 8, and 9. She calls out in the street, in the high places, and sends out her maidens as well.

> Proverbs 9:1-6—*Wisdom has built her house, she has hewn out her seven pillars; 2 She has prepared her food, she has mixed her wine; she has also set her table; 3 she has sent out her maidens, she calls from the tops of the heights of the city; 4 "Whoever is naive, let him turn in here!" To him who lacks understanding she says, 5 "Come, eat of my food, and drink of the wine I have mixed. 6 Forsake your folly and live, and proceed in the way of understanding."*

The picture is of a great and regal woman standing on the edge of her estate with her grand palace behind her, a lavish banquet prepared within. She and her maidens go out to invite people from the highways and byways to come in and learn of her and partake of her riches. Most people do not turn in. Most people go on down the broad road to destruction.

One might say, "I do not see any women standing on the street corners. What is Solomon talking about?" He is talking about the **general revelation** in creation which continually proclaims God's truth to us and calls us to make moral choices. **Special revelation** is the written and verbal truth communicated in the Bible. General revelation is what we see of God and His truth in the creation every day. Romans 1:20 says, *For since the creation of the world His invisible attributes, His eternal power and divine nature, have been clearly seen, being understood through what has been made, so that we are without excuse.* There is a continual revelation going on, the great and moral structure of the universe calling out to us on every street corner. Solomon describes this revelation as a great lady and her maidens calling out to us, inviting us to her banquet.

2.3 Wisdom's scorn

Wisdom calls out to fools with whom she is displeased.

> Proverbs 1:22-26—*"How long, O naive ones, will you love being simple-minded? And scoffers delight themselves in scoffing and fools hate knowledge? 23 Turn to my reproof, behold, I will pour out my spirit on you; I will make my words known to you. 24 Because I called and you refused, I stretched out my hand and no one paid attention; 25 and you neglected all my counsel and did not want my reproof; 26 I will also laugh at your calamity; I will mock when your dread comes,..."*

Wisdom's absolute rejection of the fool in his folly is an evidence that this personification of Proverbs is not Christ. God often forgives and extends grace to fools even in their dying hour, as He did with Samson and the thief on the cross. The prodigal son truly played the fool, nevertheless, his father received him with joy upon his return.

Wisdom, on the other hand, is not a person; she is an impersonal body of principles, not unlike the wheels of justice themselves. The moral principles of God's universe roll on, even when He graciously and personally forgives us. Samson's last prayer was answered, but still he died as a blind prisoner in a heathen temple. The thief on the cross still died by crucifixion for his crimes. The prodigal, though graciously received and forgiven by his father, still had squandered his inheritance and his youth.

Suppose you take a course in Greek and don't study all semester. You are lazy and miss class repeatedly. When you get to the final exam, guess what? It's Greek to you! At this point, you might pray, "Oh Jesus, I am sorry that I did not study my Greek." Jesus will forgive you, but wisdom won't. Language wisdom will not magically perch on your shoulder and give you all the answers. You rejected discipline when she beckoned all during the semester, and now she rejects you. Or, perhaps you forget to put money in the bank, but keep writing checks. All of a sudden they take on a rubbery quality, and you receive a notice declaring "insufficient funds." You say, "Oh dear, I am sorry I forgot to put money in the bank." It's good that you are sorry, but still there is no money in the bank; and the gas and lights go off anyway. Wisdom and the wheels of justice keep going.

I know a young man who was very upset the first time he read about wisdom's rejection of the fool in Proverbs 1. He thought this meant God would be mad at him forever. Proverbs 1 is not about Christ rejecting repentant fools. Proverbs 1 is about wisdom's rejecting the fools who reject her. There is a time to pursue knowledge and discipline; if we reject that invitation, we will reap what we sow and be satiated with our own folly. Wisdom's students are the only ones she helps at the time of testing.

2.4 Wisdom: Reprover and teacher

Wisdom is a hostess who invites everyone; she is also an equal-opportunity reprover. She tells young fools where they are wrong and what they need to do to be right. A strict disciplinarian, she is the mother who spanks her children, the teacher who does not smile until Thanksgiving, and the nurse who expects you to take your medicine. As Biblical Christians, we rightly strive to defend woman's role of quiet submission; however, we must not neglect woman's role as reprover of young fools. Wise women rule their domains with the sword of the spirit and sometimes a rod of wood (Prov. 22:15; 23:13-14). Peace and freedom come to children, not only from their mother's lifegiving kindness, but also through her wise and steady discipline.

2.5 Wisdom: Counselor, protectress, patron, friend

For all her strictness, wisdom has a beautiful and soft side seen only by those who pursue her, turning away from folly. Listen to Proverbs 4 as the father extols the benefits of wisdom to his son:

> Proverbs 4:5-12 (NKJV)—*"Get wisdom! Get understanding! Do not forget, nor turn away from the words of my mouth. 6 Do not forsake her, and she will preserve you; love her, and she will keep you. 7 Wisdom is the principal thing; therefore get wisdom. And in all your getting, get understanding. 8 Exalt her, and she will promote you; she will bring you honor, when you embrace her. 9 She will place on your head an ornament of grace; a crown of glory she will deliver to you. 10 Hear, my son, and receive my sayings, and the years of your life will be many. 11 I have taught you in the way of wisdom; I have led you in right paths. 12 When you walk, your steps will not be hindered, and when you run, you will not stumble."*

What an amazing wealth of benefits is ascribed to wisdom! Consider this list of blessings promised in Proverbs 1-9 to those who seek wisdom and accept her reproofs. She gives profit better than silver, gain more precious than gold, long life, riches, honor, pleasant ways, peace, happiness, life to the soul, adornment, security, sweet sleep, fearlessness, and exaltation. If you accept her teaching and learn her ways, she will become your patron and benefactress. She will shower you with her bounty, and do everything she can to smooth your way. Finally, she will exalt and glorify you.

2.6 An illustration of wisdom's roles

Wisdom invites all; she reproves and rebukes fools; she teaches and counsels her students; she protects and befriends all who pursue her. She is the benefactress and glorifier of wise men. Following is a fictional story which will illustrate wisdom's roles and their progression.

THE STORY OF SOPHIA REGENT
An Illustration of a Woman in Wisdom's Roles

Sophia Regent had always loved music. In her small hometown, a teacher taught her the basics and encouraged her to pursue her studies. She went on to university and earned a scholarship to an excellent conservatory. She even played several fine concerts in major halls. Later, as circumstance would have it, Sophia found herself in another small town with her own music studio. Her perennial ad read, "Will teach piano and basic repertoire. Come prepared to work. Instruction will be terminated if practice hours are not maintained." She actually did this last part about dismissing students who did not practice and was poorer for it. She maintained her standards, and that seemed more important to her.

And the would-be Van Cliburns would traipse through, some with pigtails and loads of freckles, others with butch haircuts and patches on the patches of their Levis. A few were reserved and even wore Sunday clothes. Most of them were musical washouts. The ones easiest to get rid of were the ones who had neither talent nor desire for music. Most of those were gone in three weeks. The next to go were the ones with some talent but no heart, that is, no love or respect for the material or the teacher. She hated to see the talent wasted, but she had learned to let them go. The hardest were those with good, sweet natures and absolutely no talent. It hurt to tell their parents that their child would learn the piano.

But then one day it happened. A boy had been coming for three weeks. He looked no different from scores of others. He was not rude, but he was not overly polite. She had been amazed in the previous weeks how quickly he had mastered his initial lessons. But now, today, here he was, presenting with fine execution and feeling a learner's piece she usually worked on for six weeks. And there was something else. His manner, which usually reminded her of someone lazing out at third base chewing gum, was different when he played. What was it—focus? intensity? desire?

For the first time in a long time, Sophia had to struggle for her composure. What she said was, "Thomas, the middle section needs more work. Please repeat it while I go to the kitchen for a glass of water." What she felt like doing was shouting in a loud voice, "Oh, praise the Lord! I think He has sent me a pianist!"

The next few years were difficult for Sophia and Thomas. Sophia felt strongly that her most important mission was to ground Thomas in basic technical proficiency and good musical habits. She must not allow him the luxury of relying on his giftedness at the expense of training. Their most explosive argument occurred the day before his recital when he was 13. He wanted to play a flashy piece to show off. She said, "You may not play this piece at my recital because you cannot play it properly." To which Thomas shouted, "Then I will fake it!" To which she shouted back, "That is exactly what I will not permit you to do!" He stomped out the door.

She grieved the rest of the day, wondering if she really had lost him for good. To her amazement, he came to the recital the following night, calm, but not meeting her eye. He dutifully played the piece she had chosen, if not with enthusiasm, at least with proficiency.

The next years were some of the happiest Sophia ever spent as a music teacher. She had been faithful to persevere and ground Thomas in the basic musical disciplines he would need. Now they could go on to heights of musical fellowship. They spent hours discussing composers, composition, renditions, performances. She shared her most precious insights, the ones it had taken her a lifetime as a musician to glean. Thomas went to college and studied with two good teachers. Sophia knew most of the music faculty. She used every connection she had to smooth his way, but her proudest accomplishment was helping him get into her old conservatory.

Finally the night came—Thomas' concert debut. Sophia was no longer young, or even middle-aged. But she dressed with utter care and entered the concert hall with a bearing both regal and happy. Thomas did not disappoint her or anyone. His concert was marvelous, as the thunderous standing ovation proved. The first roses to reach him were from Sophia. She had arranged for that.

This is a fictional story about a human lady of wisdom. She invited everyone, but she reproved and required excellence, which resulted in many drop-outs. When she found a true student, she required even more. After overcoming the difficulties of training, Sophia and Thomas entered into a beautiful meadow-land of fellowship, which is the special province of teachers and students who share the love and mastery of their discipline. After that, she did everything she could to further him and support his career. Finally, she became his glorifier, standing to applaud him, sending him tribute because he had earned it as a wise and skillful man.

2.7 Review of wisdom's roles

Who is "lady" wisdom?

- She is a personification of the body of creation principles which takes feminine roles.
- She is God's helper, companion, and glorifier in the creation order.
- She invites, reproves, teaches, and counsels people.
- She is the patron, benefactress, and glorifier of wise people.

3. What does the femininity of wisdom have to do with me?

3.1 Feminine strength

The femininity of wisdom is important because it models critical elements of womanhood. Many critics of traditional femininity charge that feminine women are childlike—naive, silly, frequently bored or depressed. These critics believe that such naive and depressed women will be helped only by rejecting femininity itself. According to them, femininity is weak. Strength lies only in masculinity, therefore women should seek masculine rhythms, lifestyles, and roles. Others advocate androgyny. Do away with masculinity and femininity altogether; strive to be merely humans who love and respect one another.

A woman's desire for inner strength, self-respect, and the respect of others is right and good. Too many women have thought that academic and professional titles, work in the public domain, and making money are the only keys to confidence, security, and respect. The Bible clearly teaches that it is the woman who fears the Lord who gains inner strength and outer respect. The real way a woman gains depth of character, self-respect, and honor is by becoming a woman of excellence, a truly wise woman, taking the roles of feminine wisdom in ways appropriate to her life. Weight and depth come from our core character, not our outward credits.

3.2 The virtues of wisdom

How does one become wise? What is Biblical wisdom? Wisdom, in its most simple form, is **skill**. Riding a bicycle is bicycle wisdom. Sewing with a needle or a sewing machine is sewing wisdom. Walking on a tightrope is another kind of physical wisdom. All of these wisdoms have to do with mastering the physical principles which allow you to produce with skill in a certain area. All physical skill boils down to that. The first mention of wisdom in the Bible is the skill of the women who sewed the tabernacle curtains and the metallurgy skill of the goldsmith who made its furniture. They could produce with skill because they had mastered fabric and metal working (Ex. 31:2-5; 35:25-26). This is wisdom at its most basic.

Another form of wisdom is **insight**. Wisdom principles include the natural and moral patterns of life. Wisdom seeks to penetrate the nature of what is, the mystery of this world. Why is there suffering? What is true worship? What is wisdom and wise living? What are the limitations of mortality? What is the nature of romantic love? The wisdom books of Job, Psalms, Proverbs, Ecclesiastes, and Song of Solomon address these very questions.

The first and most basic form of wisdom is practical skill in the physical world. The second form of wisdom is insight into the mysteries of life. Finally the root of all wisdom is the **fear of the Lord**. The reverential fear of the true God is the basis of all insight and morality. Unbelievers can be moral people. They can have insight into various things, and they certainly do have all kinds of practical skills. But finally, as Proverbs tells us, the root of wisdom is the reverential fear of the God who created all these principles.

4. How do we become wise?

4.1 Mastering skills

All women need to be skillful in the practical sense. It is not enough just to be sweet. It is not enough to be well-intended, as you drift along. God wants you to be a skillful person in very practical ways. When you took your inventory under Mistress of the Domain (Vol. One, pp. 37-38), I hope you identified areas in which you have already become skillful or other areas in which you intend to become skillful. You can pursue skill at the university or at a crafts session at the local community center. You can pursue Bible study skills you need but have neglected. Name anything from selling tomatoes to studying the book of John. Every discipline requires skills which must be learned.

> The first and most basic form of wisdom is practical skill in the physical world. The second form of wisdom is insight into the mysteries of life. Finally, the root of all wisdom is the fear of the Lord.

4.2 Pondering for insight

Wise women are not only workers; they are thinkers and ponderers. To make wisdom yours, you will have to study, listen to wise people, ponder, meditate, and think. Mary, the mother of Jesus, pondered everything that happened—the annunciation, the shepherds, the angels, Jesus' boyhood (Luke 1:29; 2:19, 33, 51). She took in God's great works and thought about them. She was not verbose, but when she did speak, words of value and weight came forth. Her hymn, only 133 words in length, has stood for the ages (Luke 1:46-55).

The lady-of-wisdom aspect is crucial to feminine maturity. Only the mistress and wisdom aspects focus on woman's life as an individual before God and on her duties in His world. Helper, Lifegiver, and Glory of Man focus on men, children, and others. Many women have no individual identity because they see themselves only as an extension of their husband, their children, or social group. Feminists have brought up this issue repeatedly. The answer to this weakness is not to become less relational; being relational is basic to our femininity and ministry. The answer is to be individually rooted in God, His Word, and His world. Even when all alone, the mature, godly woman has identity because at the core of her being is the fear of the Lord, insight into His ways, and skill in service. Skillful, insightful women who fear the Lord will be enthroned as valued leaders in society. This does not mean you will be a senator or queen. It does mean you will be a person of influence in your world. Your world may be a tiny community or a large and powerful social circle, but you will be respected. What you say will matter. You will be a guardian of heritage and a patron of the things that count.

5. Inner domains to guard and keep: Part Two

5.1 The feminine soul

Femininity is concerned greatly with guarding and keeping inner spaces for people. In Lifegiver—*created, we* introduced five inner domains—virginity, lovemaking, the womb, the breasts, and the home (*FAW—Vol. One*, pp. 163-167). Now let us consider three more inner domains especially related to wisdom. First, consider the inner domain of your own soul. Your own inner thoughts and feelings as a woman are a subjective kingdom in themselves. Most people agree that a woman's inner being is a world more rich and complicated than the man's. It is no mistake that Solomon wrote his great love song from the viewpoint of the woman.

Consider Hannah and Mary, great lifegivers and great women of wisdom as well. The partnership God desires with women is not just the use of their bodies for making babies. He desires the use of their minds for making intelligent praise. He is not only the Weaver in the inner space of the womb, He is the Teacher in the inner space of the soul. While God created Samuel in Hannah's womb, He constructed the knowledge of His future work in her understanding. Hannah's prayer included praise for the great acts God was yet to do in Samuel's lifetime. Hannah's prayer opened, *"My heart exalts in the Lord."* A thousand years later, Mary, carrying the King of whom Hannah sang, likewise proclaimed, *"My soul exalts the Lord."* The humble, intelligent praise that followed in Mary's Magnificat showed her to be one who had sought wisdom, heeded reproof, and inclined her heart to understanding.

The partnership God desires with women is not just the use of their bodies for making babies. He desires the use of their minds for making intelligent praise. He is not only the Weaver in the inner space of the womb, He is the Teacher in the inner space of the soul.

The womb and the mind of woman are not at war. Woman's soul is an internal garden, even as is her body, to be cultivated and filled with riches and precious treasures. Mary was not a fool who gazed only to forget immediately. She pondered experience and treasured truth. She pondered the salutation of Gabriel and treasured the shepherds' account of the angelic host. She was amazed with Joseph at the prophecies about the baby Jesus. While she did not understand all Jesus said, she treasured it all.

Sometimes our souls are like gardens completely filled with weeds of confusion, worry, fretting, and silliness. Our souls should be like beautiful gardens full of worthy things that have been pondered and treasured over the years. Many of you will give artistic expression to your inner riches through singing, writing, painting, flower arranging, or whatever your ministry is, even as Hannah and Mary did. Hannah and Mary did not make much money, they did not have high degrees, but they were wise. They had depth of character, and they expressed their worship of God with great skill in their poetry. Their works live to this day because God has honored them in the outer domains of the world where they themselves never went.

5.2 Community

A seventh inner domain for people is the **community**. We can define community as a group of people organized for life. Before focusing on the way wise women give life in community, consider Bethlehem as a template of community from the book of Ruth.

THE COMMUNITY OF BETHLEHEM

The book of Ruth is a many-faceted jewel, frequently called, with justification, the greatest short story ever written. One can meditate on it for a lifetime and continually find new and radiant facets. Most Bible students are aware that it shines forth with stories of redemption, loyalty, and romance. Consider it now as an illuminating portrait of community.

According to our definition, a community is a group of people organized for life. True life does not exist apart from justice, productivity, love, and growth. Very briefly, let us consider Bethlehem from these four perspectives. Before we do, please note that Bethlehem is not only a gendered society; it is a classed society. Four classes are represented: The landowner (represented by Boaz), the manager (he answered to Boaz and directed the workers in Ruth 2:5-7), the workers reaping in the fields (Ruth 2:4,15-16, 21), and the disenfranchised poor (Ruth and Naomi).

Justice. Without good men to enforce law and order, there is no justice. Sexual molestation was known in Bethlehem, as was theft of grain, and the neglect of poor widows. In every one of these cases, injustices were blocked because Boaz actively pursued justice: He commanded his men not to touch Ruth; he slept beside his grain to protect it from thieves; and he went straight to the gates to inform his nearest kinsman of his rights and responsibilities toward the widows.

Productivity. There was grain in Bethlehem because God had alleviated the famine, and the people worked in an organized way. Boaz was a good man on good terms with his manager and his workers: Boaz oversaw the work; the manager directed the workers; and the workers labored. Thus the harvest was garnered, and Bethlehem fulfilled its name as "house of bread."

Charity. *Love your neighbor as yourself.* The facets of love are many— fellowship, commitment, empathy, kindness, generosity, just treatment, attentiveness, promptness in service, submission to authority, gratitude, discretion, diligence, and humility. Every one of these and many more are demonstrated specifically by characters in the book of Ruth.

Growth. The book of Ruth ends with a wedding and a baby! And not just any wedding, but the wedding of the highest class—Boaz, the landowner—to the lowest class—Ruth, the Moabite gleaner. In God's economy, the classes are not bounded by rigid barriers of self-righteous pride, but rather, are positions on the community team, flexible and responsive to God's guidance at every turn. (Just so, productivity is not a stingy and selfish amassing of wealth, but is rather a stewardship with generosity, as Boaz so beautifully demonstrated.)

That which is truly living grows and goes forward into the future. Bethlehem, this living community with its justice, productivity, and love, grows and goes forward through the wedding of Boaz and Ruth and through Obed their son, not only into the future of the tenth century B.C., but into the history of the world!

Community life has an outer, public side and an inner, personal side. Leading men are primarily responsible for the first, and leading and prominent women are primarily responsible for the latter.

In God's plan, the women of each family, church, and city are to be the major players and God's key partners in caring for people. In the U.S. government, the Department of Human Resources has usurped the responsibility for the health, education, and welfare of the American people. How much better off we would be if our communities relied primarily on local, wise women for health, education, and welfare rather than on a monstrous and impersonal government bureaucracy!

Now let us compare how the wise women of Bethlehem gave life personally in community, as the wise men provided public structure. The women of Bethlehem greeted Naomi when she returned from Moab; Naomi felt free to tell them the truth about her grievous condition. At the end of the story, the same women, who heard her grief, shared her joy. They gave Naomi a private blessing of intimate details and personal focus (Ruth 4:14-15), even as the elders gave Ruth a public blessing of historic reference and regional dimensions (Ruth 4:11-12). Study the chart on the following page to compare and contrast these blessings. All people need to be blessed both in public and private, thus wise men and wise women are needed in every community.

Moving forward 11 centuries to the book of Acts, we find two more revealing references to the place of women in the inner domain of community life. Acts 13:50—*But the Jews incited the devout women of prominence and the leading men of the city* [Pisidian Antioch] *and instigated a persecution against Paul and Barnabas, and drove them out of their district.* Four chapters later we read: Acts 17:11-12—*Now these were more noble-minded than those in Thessalonica, for they received the word with great eagerness, examining the Scriptures daily to see whether these things were so. 12 Therefore many of them believed, along with a number of prominent Greek women and men.*

Notice the role of *prominent women* in these communities. The unbelieving Jews who wanted Paul and Barnabas to be rejected in Pisidian Antioch *incited the devout women of prominence and the leading men of the city.* On a happier note, it is cited that *prominent Greek women and men* accepted the Gospel in Berea. For the good and the bad, the destiny of these communities was linked not just to the city fathers, but to the prominent women as well. Such women must be women of wisdom, if they are to guide their communities into blessing as in Berea. Women of folly, on the other hand, will lead whole cities to death, as in Pisidian Antioch.

5.3 Civilization

The heart of the kingdom

Finally, let us consider the largest of all the inner domains—civilization itself. **Human civilization** is the bounded area where humanity has conquered, ordered, built, preserved, beautified, and put down roots. It is to be contrasted with the frontier, the wilderness, and barbarism. Women have a key role to play in keeping not just their wombs, their houses, or even their souls. They are the fundamental keepers of civilization and human heritage itself. Civilization is culture in a refined and developed state, fostered by memory, morality, and manners. Such civilization endures only when it lives in the hearts and souls of its women When morals, memory, manners, art, faith, and love perish in the women of any society, then their people are dead. No matter how brave or rich its men, that civilization is dead, because there is no real life or beauty left. Brave men may defend their honor unto death, perishing for relics and stones, but they will have no real and living civilization for which to fight.

How hostesses rule

"Lady" wisdom is presented first and foremost as a hostess who invites and presides. Like her, prominent women serve in every generation as hostesses in their domains. This role is one of the most effective for advancing people and influencing society. Amaury de Riencourt,

THE PUBLIC AND PRIVATE BLESSINGS OF RUTH 4

PUBLIC, OUTER-DOMAIN BLESSING	PRIVATE, INNER-DOMAIN BLESSING
Ruth 4:11-12—*All the people who were in the court, and the elders, said, "We are witnesses. May the LORD make the woman who is coming into your home like Rachel and Leah, both of whom built the house of Israel; and may you achieve wealth in Ephrathah and become famous in Bethlehem. 12 Moreover, may your house be like the house of Perez whom Tamar bore to Judah, through the offspring which the LORD will give you by this young woman."*	Ruth 4:14-17—*Then the women said to Naomi, "Blessed is the LORD who has not left you without a redeemer today, and may his* [Obed's] *name become famous in Israel. 15 May he also be to you a restorer of life and a sustainer of your old age; for your daughter-in-law, who loves you and is better to you than seven sons, has given birth to him." 16 Then Naomi took the child and laid him in her lap, and became his nurse. 17 The neighbor women gave him a name, saying, "A son has been born to Naomi!" So they named him Obed. He is the father of Jesse, the father of David.*
Who: Elders leading the people	**Who**: Women in conversation to Naomi
Where: In the court	**Where**: Some private context, probably home
When: At the time of wedding, a public event	**When**: After the birth of Obed, a home event
What: Details of the public blessing	**What**: Details of the personal blessing
Frame of blessing: Future hopes, historic, national—Ruth to be like nation's mothers, Rachel and Leah, and clan mother, Tamar. Unborn child, yet future, called "offspring."	***Frame of blessing***: Present facts—Ruth's love, better than seven sons, and her having given birth. Son is born and personally named by the women; "Obed" means worshiper.
Purpose of blessing: To call greatness on Ruth's offspring, by praying for:	***Purpose of blessing***—To insure Naomi's personal happiness, by praying:
a. Ruth to build house like Rachel and Leah	a. Thanking God for what He had done already for Naomi personally—He has *not left you without a redeemer today*
b. Family to achieve wealth* in area/city (Ephrathah)	b. For Obed's fame in Israel (scope of women's prayer even wider than elders' prayer!)
c. Line to become famous/renowned in city (Bethlehem)	c. For Obed to be *a restorer of life and a sustainer* to Naomi personally in her old age
Result of blessing: Community prayer answered as Ruth bears a son (4:13), whose line does indeed make Bethlehem Ephrathah famous (Mic. 5:2; Matt. 1:6)!	***Results of blessing***: Personal prayer answered as Naomi receives Obed in her lap;** national prayer answered in history when Obed becomes a father of King David.

* This word *wealth* is our old friend, *chayil*. Thus the book of Ruth says in summary, may the man of *chayil* (2:1) join with the woman of *chayil* (3:11), and together may they achieve *chayil* (4:11)—wealth, nobility, and excellence!

** Thus Naomi is not *empty*, as in Ruth 1:21, but full and fulfilling her role as lifegiver to the generations.

writes this of the women who presided over the famous French salons of the seventeenth and eighteenth centuries:

> One and all, these women regulated the cultural life of the country, gave talent its due, disciplined the often tempestuous behavior of their male guests, curbed their unjustified pride, and occasionally encouraged those rare birds who were unduly humble and shy. At all times they made sure that their guests, whatever their social standing in their profession, could communicate fruitfully with one another on a plane of complete equality and perfect courtesy. They also knew how to stimulate creativity by the use of appropriate encouragement and praise. The Abbe de St. Pierre, astounded at his unexpected success and popularity in Mme. Gophren's salon, admitted that he was merely an instrument in her skillful hands.
>
> Far better psychologists than the cocksure males, and also more basically realistic and modest, hostesses spoke little and listened a great deal, knowing with their usual flair how to bring dull conversation delicately to an end. But talented men were always encouraged, and came away quite surprised to discover that they were far more witty in this kind of environment than elsewhere.[2]

This is just an example, but once again it well describes the roles of "lady" wisdom. These hostesses had mastery of the tongue, could reprove pride, encourage the shy, and exalt the wise. De Riencourt is writing about this in the context of fostering civilization itself—the arts, heritage—the things that separate us from the animals.

To close on a more epic, holy, and humble note, remember Martha of Bethany. As a humble homemaker, she greatly extended Jesus' ministry in the environs of Jerusalem through her habitual hospitality to Him and His entire entourage of disciples. Do not allow her famous over-attention to details (Luke 10:38-42) cause you to forget that her courage to sponsor this controversial "Rabbi" changed the world (John 11)! In a similar way, Lydia opened the whole continent of Europe to Paul and the Gospel through both her hospitality and her faith (Acts 16:13-16). Truly, she is an example of a wise woman influencing civilization from the "platform" of a women's prayer meeting. Thus God, who is not limited to save by many or by few, uses great queens and prominent women to guide civilization, but He just as often uses lowly maids!

Women have a key role to play in keeping not just their wombs, their houses, or even their souls. They are the fundamental keepers of civilization and human heritage itself.

6. Lesson summary

Plainly speaking, wisdom is the body of God's creation principles, the natural laws by and with which He created and runs the universe. These laws are both moral and physical. Solomon personifies this wisdom as a woman to highlight the fact that wisdom, although impersonal, takes feminine roles toward God and man. Portrayed by Solomon, "lady" wisdom is the helper, companion, and glorifier of God; she is the reprover, teacher, and counselor of men. The wisdom aspect of femininity, based on emulating "lady" wisdom and fulfilling human wisdom, is fundamental to a woman's maturity. Human wisdom is skill and insight, rooted in the fear of the Lord. Only through reverence for God, skill, and insight can a woman attain the inner strength and respect befitting her as a creature fully in God's image. As women embody the feminine roles of wisdom, they guard and keep their own souls, their communities, and civilization itself.

2. Amaury de Riencourt, *Sex and Power in History* (New York: Dell Publishing., 1975), 270-271.

Profile of Wisdom—*created*

Key Bible passages
Proverbs 9:10; 31:30

Focus on God
One to be feared above all others, wondrous Creator

Created basis of this aspect
The femininity of wisdom and the creation itself; the woman's resultant parallel roles; and her "intuitive" capacity for insight into the world around her

Roles of this aspect
Reprover, teacher, counselor, protectress, friend, patron, benefactress, lover, wife (Prov. 1:20-33; 3:13-26; 4:1-13; 9:1-6; 31:1-31); all these presuppose she herself was first a learner, heeder of reproof, and ponderer

Related Bible passages
- Sarah counsels Abraham (Gen. 21:9-13);
- Wise woman of Abel (2 Sam. 20:13-22);
- Hannah's song, Abigail's petition, and Mary's Magnificat are all wisdom pieces (1 Sam. 2:1-10; 25:18-35; Luke 1:46-55);
- The gender framework of Proverbs (especially chapters 1-9; 14:1; 19:14; 31);
- Mary as a ponderer (Luke 1:29; 2:19, 51); and
- Jesus and John the Baptist are sons of wisdom (Luke 7:33-35)

Chief drives and motives
To gain insight and skill; to learn; to reprove fools, teach, and counsel learners, exalt wisdom and wise people; to enhance culture and civilization

Focus and/or areas of application
Practical skill in living—speech, money, sex, work, friends, enemies, food, crafts, arts; insights into mysteries of life, spiritual things, psychology, and philosophy

Characteristics
Reserved, contemplative, discriminating, discerning, judicious, sensible, strict, witty, subtle, refined, cultured, accomplished, classy, elegant, mysterious, deep, prudent

Character emphasis
Humility, discipline

KEY to diagram at right

SYMBOLS OF GOD

Person–HAND–God is Creator (hand creates man). He is Spirit (hand is transparent), infinite (hand fades, as into infinity), and preeminent (hand's position–above creation; hand's size–able to hold world).

Character–SQUARE–God's character is holy (square suggests the cube of the Holy of Holies) and infinite in all His attributes (square fades, as into infinity).

Masculinity–TRIANGLE–The triangle represents the original Masculine–the Trinity. God is the Initiator who descends and enters into His creation (triangle penetrates world). His masculinity is infinite (triangle fades, as into infinity).

Words–GENESIS 1:3, PROVERBS 3:19–God creates everything from nothing through His wisdom.

Roles/work–HAND, WORDS–God is active within His creation as all-wise Creator/Sustainer.

SYMBOLS OF CREATION

Femininity–CIRCLE–The circle reflects the spherical shape of the sun/moon/world/womb. Feminine in relation to God, the creation is designed to receive her masculine Creator (pale triangle at top of world). All femininity is created and therefore finite (bounded edge doesn't fade).

Mankind's dwelling–PHOTO of EARTH–The world is man's home (peaceable place full of life). The world is finite (bounded edge) and subordinate to God (position–below God; small size–fits in God's hand).

Wisdom–SPARKLING JEWELS within EARTH–God's natural law, feminine and embedded in His feminine creation, is more precious than jewels.

Words about creation's wisdom–PROVERBS 3:15; ROMANS 1:20–God designed His creation to reveal His wisdom principles and His true nature.

SYMBOLS OF MANKIND

Persons–SEX-DISTINCT FIGURES–God created man, male and female (sex-classic silhouettes). They are "clothed" in nakedness according to their untested, unashamed, sinless standing before God. Man is finite (bounded edges).

Character–SQUARE–Man is created in the image of God (squares smaller than but reflective of God's square). Both man and woman are created in the image of God (they don't share a square). Man's character is finite in all his attributes (bounded edges).

Masculinity–TRIANGLE–Man's masculinity reflects God's, but is finite (bounded edges).

Femininity–CIRCLE–Woman's femininity reflects creation's and is likewise finite (bounded edge).

Words–ROMANS 11:33; PROVERBS 31:10–Mankind responds to God with faith and wonder. Woman and wisdom are both like precious jewels.

Feminine role/work–Lady of Wisdom–SPARKLING JEWEL, OPEN BOOK–Woman is the embodiment of wisdom.

Masculine role/work–Sage–SPARKLING JEWEL, PICK AXE, OPEN BOOK–Man is to seek wisdom (pick axe–tool to mine; open book–all learning, especially from the Bible) and be disciplined by wisdom in order to love and lead his realm wisely; he is to lead in defending Truth (refer to *FAW–Vol. Two*, p. 178).

Lady of Wisdom – *created*

"Let there be light..."

The LORD by wisdom founded the earth; by understanding He established the heavens.

God is the all-wise Creator.

He possesses the eternal attribute of wisdom.

He created the physical and moral wisdom principles which undergird His creation.

He created mankind with the ability to understand the principles of wisdom, and to relate to the all-wise God who made them.

Woman learns wisdom by submitting herself to God and His natural law, thus becoming an embodiment of wisdom and a guardian of civilization.

Man learns wisdom by submitting himself to God and His natural law, thus becoming a worthy lord of the earth.

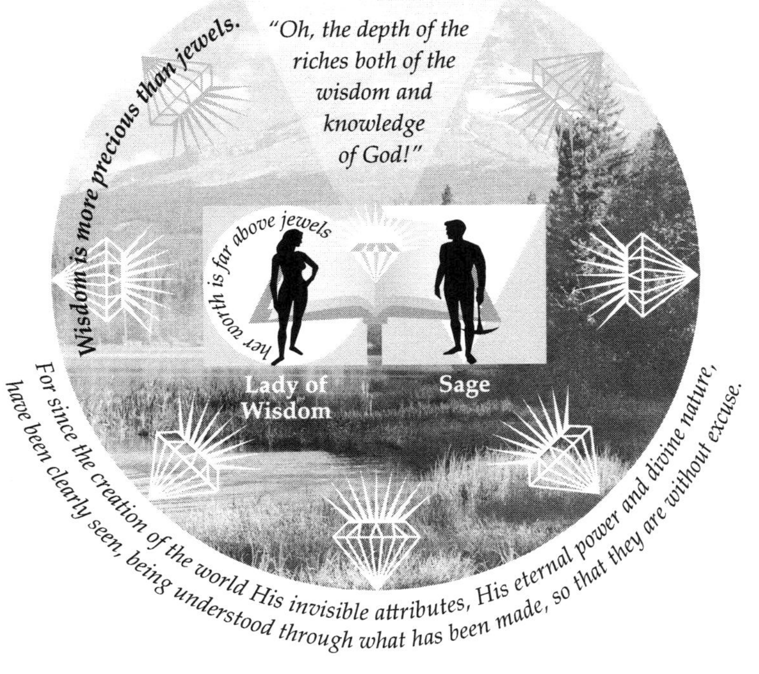

Woman emulates feminine Wisdom in her roles and ministries.

Woman, like man, becomes wise through training in skill, insight, and the fear of the Lord.

Wise women, like Wisdom, are rare, valuable, and grounded in the fear of the Lord. They are hostesses, reprovers, teachers, counselors, and patrons.

Personification of Wisdom—*created*

I am Lady Wisdom—*created.*

I am the first of all God's feminine creations. I existed even before the earth and Eve, for God made me before He made the world. I am the plan and principles by which God created His universe morally and physically. I am the principles of order, beauty, and life which help sustain the world, causing it to show forth the glory of God.

I am not really a person, yet both Solomon and Jesus spoke of me as a woman, for I take feminine roles toward God and men. I have been God's companion, responder, and glorifier since the beginning of creation.

In every corner of God's world, I call to humanity, earnestly entreating each one of them to turn to my reproof and instruction. Unfortunately, most are fools and spurn me; therefore, I spurn them. When calamity comes on fools, I give them no help. However, here and there I find willing learners who turn aside to seek me. On them I focus my utmost attention. At first I am very strict, correcting and instructing them without a hint of flattery. Then as the learners begin to understand my ways, I soften and become their protectress, benefactress, and patron. Finally, I exalt and glorify those who grow mature in wisdom. I no longer speak to them as a teacher, but rather as a counselor speaking confidentially to a friend. To the wisest, who prize and pursue me, I become as lover and wife.

Every woman should seek to incorporate my feminine roles into her individual femininity. Women should rebuke and limit the folly of fools. They should practice, teach, and sponsor that which is moral, skillful, and of finest quality. Women should be full of wise counsel. Ultimately, they should glorify and exalt God and truly wise people.

Bible Study of Wisdom—*created*

Before beginning this study, read the entire lesson, pages 4-20.

> *She* [Wisdom] *is more precious than jewels; and nothing you desire compares with her.*
>
> PROVERBS 3:15

> *An excellent wife, who can find? For her worth is far above jewels.*
>
> PROVERBS 31:10

The tenth Biblical view of woman

Created in the pattern of wisdom, woman shares wisdom's roles and relationships.

Who is "lady" wisdom?

In this, our fourth view or aspect of womanhood, we look at woman from a different perspective. The previous studies—Mistress of the Domain, Helper-Completer, and Lifegiver—are all based on definitive statements about the created nature of woman as she was designed by God. In this study we will look at an original pattern or archetype of femininity rather than at a definition (refer to *FAW—Vol. One*, p. 8.).

In order to understand "lady" wisdom, it is necessary to understand a figure of speech called personification. *Webster's Dictionary* defines **personification** as "the representation of a thing or abstraction as a person." John Bunyan's, *The Pilgrim's Progress*, is filled with personification. He transforms numerous virtues and vices into people who speak and act according to the characteristic they represent.

Centuries before Bunyan, Solomon used personification to reveal the nature of wisdom as it had never been revealed before. According to Solomon in Proverbs 1-9, wisdom is best understood as a great lady, the companion of God, the teacher and counselor of mankind. Wisdom is not actually a woman, a goddess, or Jesus. Wisdom is the body of creation principles by which God created and sustains His universe. In submission to these principles, people live and prosper.

Women and wisdom share femininity itself. By learning "lady" wisdom's principles and emulating her roles and relationships, we will find a powerful and mature aspect of our femininity.

How is wisdom like a lady?

1. Describe the roles and actions of "lady" wisdom in each of the following relationships according to the verses provided. Note the roles and responses of the partners to "lady" wisdom where appropriate.

   The relationships of "lady" wisdom:

   toward God (Prov. 3:19; 8:30-31)

   toward the fool (Prov. 1:20-32)

   toward the learner (Prov. 1:23, 33; 2:1-16)

   toward the wise man (Prov. 3:13-18; 4:8-9; 8:15-17)

2. Do you see any parallels between the way "lady" wisdom relates to God in the preceding verses and the way woman was created to relate to man (Gen. 2:18; Eph. 5:22; 1 Cor. 11:7-9)?

Points to ponder

Ideally, wisdom relates to humans in a mother-to-wife progression. Wisdom first approaches a child (when he is young and foolish) as a mother or strict school teacher. If he obeys and listens to her, he becomes an adolescent with whom deeper communication and friendship are possible. During this time wisdom acts as a teacher and patron, showering her student with knowledge and benefits. At maturity the boy becomes a man, and wisdom becomes his helper and intimate lover. She responds to him with her counsel and exalts him as he rules his domain maturely. As she has been moving from mother to wife, he has been growing from fool to king.

3. Describe a woman you know who embodies many of the actions and roles of "lady" wisdom. She might be a teacher, a friend, or perhaps your own mother.

Review

Who is "lady" wisdom? She is a personification (not a real person or being) of the body of creation principles which takes feminine roles. She is God's companion, responder, and glorifier in the creation order. She invites, reproves, teaches, and counsels people. She is the patron, benefactress, and glorifier of wise people.

How do we become like "lady" wisdom?

In the Bible, the first and simplest meaning of the word ***wisdom*** is skill. Walking is a human skill based on the mastery of the principles of gravity. When we walk, we balance our bodies against the force of gravity. As anyone who has ever watched a toddler knows, gaining this mastery is a process.

4. Name some examples of practical wisdom skills in Exodus 31:3-5 and Proverbs 31:13, 16, 19, 22.

5. What advantages does a skillful woman have in her home, her community, and in the service of God, compared to the well-meaning, but unskilled woman?

6. Wisdom is more than practical skill. It also entails insight into the complexities and mysteries of life. Such insight is gained only through experience and discernment. Match the following five wisdom books (Job, Psalms, Proverbs, Ecclesiastes, Song of Solomon) with the phrases which best describe their content:

   the true worship of God

   the ways of love

   the nature of suffering

   the vanity of this life

   the principles of success

7. Why is the Bible sufficient to provide for us an overall framework for life (2 Tim. 3:16-17)? Can you think of any major areas of thought touching on the meaning of life which are omitted in the five books of Biblical wisdom (listed in question 6)?

8. Wise women are not only skillful workers; they are thinkers and ponderers. How did Mary gain wisdom (Luke 1:29; 2:19, 33, 51)? How does she reveal her depth of insight (Luke 1:46-55)?

9. Of all the principles which wisdom includes, what is the first and most foundational principle (Prov. 1:7; 9:10)? What is the foundation of a woman's godly reputation according to Proverbs 31:30?

Points to ponder

Critics of femininity often charge that women never really grow up, but rather remain childlike, bored, or depressed most of their lives. They rightly sense that something strong, meaty, and decisive should be added to many feminine personalities. These critics often suggest masculinization or androgyny as the solution for this problem. God's provision for feminine depth and maturity is not for women to seek to become masculine. His answer is for us to recover the deep, resonating notes of true Biblical femininity. This kind of character depth is acquired through the lifelong pursuit of skill, insight, and the reverential fear of God.

Inner domains which women guard and keep: Part Two

Femininity is greatly concerned with guarding and keeping inner spaces for people. In the created lifegiver lesson, we introduced five such domains over which women have a special stewardship from God—virginity, lovemaking, the womb, the breasts, and the home. Just as the lifegiver aspect has a special relationship to these domains, so the lady-of-wisdom aspect relates to three more inner domains—the feminine soul, the community, and civilization itself.

10. Both Hannah and Mary influenced the world and all of history with their lives. Where did they enthrone God first (1 Sam. 2:1; Luke 1:46-47)? Why is this a great accomplishment in itself (Prov. 4:23-24; Luke 6:45; James 3:6-8)?

11. How does God demonstrate in both Hannah and Mary that the mind, the womb, and the spirit of woman are not at war or in competition (1 Sam. 2:1-10; Luke 1:46-55)?

12. How are your community and civilization two of your inner domains (refer to pp. 12-15)?

Becoming a lady of wisdom for others

Picturing "lady" wisdom in your life depends upon your actually possessing some wisdom. If you have not made some progress as a learner, you will have no wisdom to invite others to share. You will have no base of skill and insight from which to teach, correct, or counsel. You will have no store of riches with which you can bless and exalt others.

13. Everyone starts out as a fool, because foolishness is bound up in the heart of a child. Our response to reproof determines whether we are hardened into permanent fools or whether we become wise women.

    What are the results of rejecting or responding to reproof (Prov. 10:17; 12:1; 13:18)?

Rejecting reproof	Responding to reproof

14. How did you last respond to reproof—whether from an authority in your life, the bathroom scale, or an unbalanced checkbook?

15. What are some of your skills? How are you using these skills to enrich the lives of the people around you? If you are using your skills, do you see this as service to God? Why or why not?

16. Choose the question more appropriate for you:

a. If you are a mother, you are on the frontier of civilization. You already hold the office of "lady" wisdom for your children. As a mother, your subject matter is vast. You are seeking to teach wisdom about everything from how to brush teeth to the meaning of the universe! What have you learned about wisdom that encourages and challenges you to be a faithful lady of wisdom to your children this week?

b. If you are not a mother, what have you learned about life, suffering, rejoicing, hardship, or contentment that enables you to give counsel to others in your sphere of influence?

The only difference between soot and diamonds is heat, pressure, and time. God says a wise woman is like a jewel. Her character is of great beauty and value because she has endured the heat and pressure of testing and training over time. A lady-of-wisdom woman is like a diamond which has formed under the pressure of reproof, discipline, and self-control. She grows in authority by learning to rule with skill in God's world. Out of her wisdom flows her ministry to others.

Every woman should seek to incorporate "lady" wisdom's patterns into her individual femininity. Women should rebuke and limit the folly of fools, They should practice, teach, and sponsor that which is moral, skillful, and of finest quality. Women should be full of wise counsel. Ultimately, they should glorify and exalt God and truly wise people.

"Lady" wisdom is the first feminine thing created by God. As we understand and emulate this metaphorical woman, we will ground our own womanhood in the excellence and depth of character considered priceless by God and others.

The beginning of wisdom is: Acquire wisdom; and with all your acquiring, get understanding. Prize her, and she will exalt you; she will honor you if you embrace her. She will place on your head a garland of grace; she will present you with a crown of beauty.

PROVERBS 4:7-9

LESSON 15 : Lady of Wisdom – *fallen*

1. Who is "woman" folly?

Folly is wisdom's evil counterpart. You remember from our previous study that Solomon presents wisdom, God's creation principles, as a woman. Wisdom, he says in Proverbs 1-9, is like a great lady who invites, reproves, teaches, protects, blesses, and exalts her human children. She brings beauty, order, and life to the creation.

1.1 Folly is feminine

Solomon says that folly also is like a woman. Folly's patterns, roles, and motives are perverted distortions of the beauty and righteousness we see in wisdom. Wisdom is a personification of God's creation principles. Folly personifies the principles of the curse—pride, deceit, death, and destruction. As wisdom seeks to give life to her children, folly seeks to deceive her children and bring them down to death.

Wisdom and folly personified as women are both feminine archetypes. An **archetype**, you will remember, is an original or exemplary pattern. Over time, we as women will grow to be more like wisdom or more like folly. Since ancient times , society has operated with models both good and bad. Consciously or unconsciously, we all follow gender patterns and role models. Since the media age, the succession of these images has accelerated to a dizzying speed. Thankfully we have ageless patterns from Scripture to be our sexual guideposts. We do not have to depend upon modern media to model womanhood for us. I would much rather depend upon the Holy Spirit and Solomon to outline wise and foolish femininity for me, than to be left with the endlessly hyped and discarded vamps and tramps of the world. When our second daughter was no more than ten, she described an evil woman, "She was a Jezebel like Delilah!" My husband and I were amused, but pleased that she was getting her gender types from Scripture, and in double doses!

1.2 Wisdom and folly in Proverbs 1-9

A survey of Proverbs 1-9 will introduce the character of folly and review for us the character of wisdom. In Proverbs 1, the father warns his son against sinful companions. In verses 20-33, "lady wisdom" speaks for the first time. She calls to fools. In essence she says, "Give heed to me now. If you do not listen, and calamity comes upon you, I will not help you." We must respond to wisdom and her discipline in the day of training if we expect any help from her during the time of testing.

KEY Wisdom–*fallen*
person–FEMALE FIGURE (clothed in fig leaves according to her fallen, ashamed, guilty standing before God)
character–DARK SQUARE (polluted with sin)
femininity–DARK CIRCLE (polluted with sin)
role/work–HIDDEN JEWEL, CLOSED BOOK (woman is embodiment of folly)

In Proverbs 2-4, the father amplifies the rich and beneficial nature of wisdom. He exhorts his son repeatedly to pursue wisdom, stressing what a desirable and precious prize she is. In Proverbs 3 is a representative passage:

> Proverbs 3:13-18—*How blessed is the man who finds wisdom and the man who gains understanding. 14 For her profit is better than the profit of silver and her gain better than fine gold. 15 She is*

more precious than jewels; and nothing you desire compares with her. 16 Long life is in her right hand; in her left hand are riches and honor. 17 Her ways are pleasant ways and all her paths are peace. 18 She is a tree of life to those who take hold of her, and happy are all who hold her fast.

In the middle section, Proverbs 5-7, the focus shifts to the nature of folly and to warnings against various kinds of foolishness. In each of these chapters, a significant section is devoted to the dangers of the adulteress. Certainly adultery is a major kind of folly in and of itself, but there are many forms of foolishness—pride, indebtedness, alcoholism, laziness, babbling, and so forth. The adulteress in these verses is not merely an adulteress. She is also a picture and representative of folly itself, a greater and more comprehensive evil than merely one individual adulteress.

Proverbs 5:3-8—*For the lips of an adulteress drip honey and smoother than oil is her speech; 4 but in the end she is bitter as wormwood, sharp as a two-edged sword. 5 Her feet go down to death, her steps take hold of Sheol. 6 She does not ponder the path of life; her ways are unstable, she does not know it. 7 Now then, my sons, listen to me and do not depart from the words of my mouth. 8 Keep your way far from her and do not go near the door of her house,...*

In Proverbs 6:24-35, once again we find the same kinds of warning about the destructive results of adultery. Chapter 7 continues on the same topic, featuring a morality play starring the adulteress and the young fool, set in the street below the writer's window. The capture of the young fool by the adulteress and his subsequent destruction are described in vivid detail.

Proverbs 7:6-23—*For at the window of my house I looked out through my lattice, 7 and I saw among the naive, and discerned among the youths a young man lacking sense, 8 passing through the street near her corner; and he takes the way to her house, 9 in the twilight, in the evening, in the middle of the night and in the darkness. 10 And behold, a woman comes to meet him, dressed as a harlot and cunning of heart. 11 She is boisterous and rebellious, her feet do not remain at home; 12 she is now in the streets, now in the squares, and lurks by every corner. 13 So she seizes him and kisses him and with a brazen face she says to him: 14 "I was due to offer peace offerings; today I have paid my vows. 15 Therefore I have come out to meet you, to seek your presence earnestly, and I have found you.* [Notice how she deceives him with a false show of religion and flatters him by proclaiming him unique and special.] *16 I have spread my couch with coverings, with colored linens of Egypt. 17 I have sprinkled my bed with myrrh, aloes and cinnamon. 18 Come, let us drink our fill of love until morning; let us delight ourselves with caresses. 19 For my husband is not at home, he has gone on a long journey; 20 he has taken a bag of money with him, at the full moon he will come home." 21 With her many persuasions she entices him; with her flattering lips she seduces him. 22 Suddenly he follows her as an ox goes to the slaughter, or as one in fetters to the discipline of a fool, 23 until an arrow pierces through his liver; as a bird hastens to the snare, so he does not know that it will cost him his life.*

Proverbs 7 concludes with verses 25-27—*Do not let your heart turn aside to her ways, do not stray into her paths. 26 For many are the victims she has cast down, and numerous are all her slain. 27 Her house is the way to Sheol, descending to the chambers of death.*

We know that simple and individual adulteresses are destructive for young men. However, the claims made for this woman are larger than life. Her house is the very gate of hell. She personally takes men to the slaughter and down to death. As is made clear in Proverbs 9, this adulteress is not merely an adulteress. She represents folly itself, the one who entices all of us with flattery and worldly pleasures in an attempt to destroy us.

In Proverbs 8, wisdom gives her climactic speech, revealing her origin, nature, and her benefits for wise men. She again warns of the dire results for those who reject her. In chapter 9, Solomon brings his entire prologue into crisp focus, setting his two themes side by side in crystal contrast. In chapter 9, we have feminine wisdom (vv. 1-6) contrasted with feminine folly (vv. 13-18).

> Proverbs 9:1-6—*Wisdom has built her house, she has hewn out her seven pillars; 2 she has prepared her food, she has mixed her wine; she has also set her table; 3 she has sent out her maidens, she calls from the tops of the heights of the city: 4 "Whoever is naive, let him turn in here!" To him who lacks understanding she says, 5 "Come, eat of my food and drink of the wine I have mixed. 6 Forsake your folly and live, and proceed in the way of understanding."*

Wisdom is a great woman who makes lavish preparations in a fabulous home. She invites foolish, untaught people to come in and learn from her, promising them understanding and life. The middle section of chapter 9, verses 7-12, describes the two kinds of people who receive wisdom's invitation: Fools and scoffers on the one hand, and wise men, on the other. The contrasting presentation of folly:

> Proverbs 9:13-18—*The woman of folly is boisterous, she is naive and knows nothing.* [That is what the NASB says. Other translations say *"She knows no shame; she is shameless,"* which is probably better.] *14 She sits at the doorway of her house, on a seat by the high places of the city, 15 calling to those who pass by, who are making their paths straight: 16 "Whoever is naive, let him turn in here," and to him who lacks understanding she says, 17 "Stolen water is sweet; and bread eaten in secret is pleasant." 18 But he does not know that the dead are there, that her guests are in the depths of Sheol.*

Folly is an utter contrast to wisdom. Folly has no great house; she has made no lavish preparation. All she has to offer is bread and water, compared with the rich food of meat and wine. What is her attraction? Her hook is the illicit nature of what she offers—stolen bread eaten in secret. Many things in this world are attractive not because of their intrinsic value, but because of their illicit aura. Drugs, alcohol, promiscuous sex, gambling, and all types of dishonesty, from shoplifting to fraud, offer the tingle of the forbidden and the secret. This is folly's greatest appeal; but, it is an appeal that leads to death.

2. The roles of folly

2.1 Inviter/hunter

Folly and wisdom have at least one thing in common. They both start by calling to us. They beckon to us, inviting us to enter into life with them. But after this initial similarity, the contrasts are stark. For just below the surface of their similarity as inviters, we see a vast difference in motive. Folly is actually a hunter looking for prey. Wisdom is a teacher looking for students.

2.2 Flatterer

Wisdom is strict and reproving from the very beginning. Folly is a flatterer. Her words, it is warned repeatedly, are oily and go down like honey. While wisdom tells us all the ways we are wrong and how we need to shape up, folly tells us we are wonderful, special, and unique—that she has come looking only for us.

2.3 Seducer/deceiver

Wisdom offers instruction and counsel. Folly offers pleasure and the satisfaction of fleshly appetites. Food, wine, sex, illicit pleasures, and thrills are her stock and trade. Like the White Witch of C.S. Lewis' famous *Narnia Chronicles*, she promises Turkish Delight but gives dry bread and a stone dungeon.[1]

2.4 Captor/enslaver

While wisdom is training her students in order to free them, folly chains her students to their lower passions in order to enslave them. After short pleasures, her guests find bitter regret.

2.5 Executioner/assassin

Finally, while wisdom exalts her lovers with power, success, life, and peace, folly takes her victims down to death. Acting as an executioner for God[2] and as an assassin for the devil, folly finally kills those who come to her.

2.6 Review: The contrast between wisdom and folly

To review, the contrast and progression of wisdom's and folly's roles can be summarized in this way:

- Wisdom seeks students; folly hunts prey.
- Wisdom reproves and teaches; folly flatters and seduces.
- Wisdom counsels and trains; folly deceives and enslaves.
- Wisdom blesses and glorifies; folly takes down to death.

1. C.S. Lewis, *The Lion, The Witch, and The Wardrobe* (New York: Harper Collins Publishers, 1994), original copyright 1950; renewed copyright 1978. See chap. 4, "Turkish Delight," 35-48, and chap. 9, "In the Witch's House," 87-99.

2. God is as just and sovereign in the destruction of fools as He is in the exaltation of the humble. He kills and makes alive (1 Sam. 2:6-7). Galatians 6:7-8—*Do not be deceived, God is not mocked; for whatever a man sows, this he will also reap. 8 For the one who sows to his own flesh will from the flesh reap corruption, but the one who sows to the Spirit will from the Spirit reap eternal life.*

Notice the progressive defeminization of folly. Initially we think a seductress is more sexy or feminine than a mother figure (which is how wisdom approaches us). But, what finally could be less feminine than an executioner! On the other hand, wisdom becomes softer, richer, and more feminine to her pursuers with every passing year.

Also notice the progression of giving and taking. Folly starts out by giving. She feeds flattery to our egos and worldly delights to our lusts. In the end she takes all—our strength, health, time, and finally our very lives. Wisdom starts out requiring much—our obedience, concentration, hard work, and loyalty. But in the end she gives riches beyond what we could have imagined.

3. How to become a woman of folly

Before we look at some particular women of folly from the Scriptures, let's ask ourselves an uncomfortable question. How much are our feminine patterns like folly's? All of us are like folly to some extent, because we are sinful women; and all of us are like wisdom to some extent because, at least sometimes, we act in her righteous patterns. Suppose you wanted to excel as a woman folly. The following guidelines well cover her fundamentals. If you follow them, you will be well on your way to her likeness.

3.1 Reject authorities

To advance as a woman folly, you must disregard, disdain, and forget God. This is best done by rebelling against all human authorities in your life—parents, husband, bosses, teachers, church elders, and government officials.

3.2 Reject reproof

To be foolish, reject all reproof. To be more foolish still, turn and attack anyone who would reprove you. When corrected, a genuine fool will deny his wrongdoing and then turn and attack the one who admonished him. This is the hallmark of a true fool.

3.3 Reject rigorous training

Always be a quitter. Whenever a course or trial becomes difficult, give up immediately. Enduring rigorous training is only for those who would be wise. To be foolish, you must change your mind often, particularly regarding commitments, especially religious commitments. Double-mindedness will greatly hasten your journey on the road to folly. Standing up under trial is only for people going the other way.

3.4 Loose the tongue

Be sure to talk a lot! Chatter, babble, air your own opinions, always speak without thinking. Then to advance in destructive power, move on to lies, deceit, slander, and gossip. This will be easy to do. As someone has said, your tongue is already a ball of destructive fire (James 3:1-12), so just let it go.

4. Case studies: Women of folly

4.1 Eve

Unfortunately, the story of our first mother is in part a woman-of-folly story. Eve dwelt in innocence but became foolish when she turned away from the truth that she knew and indulged in vain speculations about the nature of the tree. Being enticed, she sinned. The Bible says Eve was deceived. What is the nature of deception? If being deceived means you don't understand what is going on, then why are you held accountable?

Nehemiah provides a clear answer to this question. Some of his enemies tried to deceive him, but he was able to resist. Nehemiah's supposed friend, Shemaiah, says to him, *"Let us meet together in the house of God, within the temple, and let us close the doors of the temple, for they are coming to kill you, and they are coming to kill you at night." 11 But I said, "Should a man like me flee? And could one such as I go into the temple to save his life? I will not go in"*(Neh. 6:10b-11).

It is unlawful for Nehemiah to go into the temple because he is not a priest. But Shemaiah, his supposed friend, says, "Your life is in danger. Come on, we have to hide in the temple. Let's close the door. They will not look for you there because you are not supposed to be in there." But Nehemiah says, "No, this is wrong. I will not do it." Notice the result in the following verse: Nehemiah 6:12—*Then I perceived that surely God had not sent him. But he uttered his prophecy against me because Tobiah and Sanballot had hired him.*

"Light obeyed brings more light. Light rejected brings the night." This is a proverb my father quoted to me in childhood which I have never forgotten. Nehemiah had some light. He knew from Scripture that he should not go into the temple. What he did not know was that Shemaiah had been hired to deceive and destroy him. Nehemiah was afraid, and he did want to hide; but in the moment of testing he stayed with the truth he knew. In refusing to go into the temple, he clung to the light he had. When he did that, he was given more light. By that new light he understood—the Scripture says he ***perceived***—that Shemaiah was a deceiver.

A similar thing might have happened with Eve. Eve might not have seen through the serpent, might not have known he was the devil incarnate, might never have fathomed what was wrong with his arguments. But had she simply held her ground with the light she had ("we must not eat of this tree"), she would not have disobeyed. It is probable that at that very moment Eve's eyes would have been opened—not to the experience of sin and guilt, but to the evil character of Satan. But, as we know, she did not hold to the light she had.

The way we keep from being deceived is to cling to whatever truth we have. Eve did not do this. She was enticed. Notice Satan is the masculine archetype of the deceiver. He uses the same tools as feminine folly—flattery and sensual pleasures. Satan told Eve she would be a god; the fruit was beautiful; it would taste good. Satan also enticed Eve to indulge in vain speculations. He questioned the truth she knew. "Hath God said?" he asks. Believing the lie, she indulged in sin and received the consequences of moral and physical death.

No sooner had she succumbed and taken the fruit, than she seeks to give it to her husband. It makes one wonder. Did Eve really think she had become a god? Is that why she wanted to get Adam involved? Or, did she have a sick feeling inside, knowing what she had done was wrong? Now in sin, did she want Adam to be guilty with her? I do not think Eve really thought she was a god. I think she knew she had stepped into sin. Being deceived, she became a deceiver and thus, an embodiment of folly.

4.2 Delilah

Of all Biblical couples, none surpasses Samson and Delilah in modeling the relationship of the fool and folly. Samson loved more than one ungodly woman; and in so doing, he rejected wisdom's calls. But Delilah was his real undoing.

We do not know when Samson realized that Delilah was a Philistine agent. I used to wonder why Samson wasn't disturbed that Delilah kept quizzing him about his secret, that she bound him to make him weak, and, most of all, that Philistines kept jumping out of her curtains. I thought, "Why does this not bother Samson? He just keeps coming back." I have concluded that he was so pridefully secure in his strength that he believed himself to be invincible. He knew who she was and what she was up to, but found this added to her illicit attraction.

This sense of prideful invincibility is characteristic of many different kinds of fools. Gamblers firmly believe they will not lose; drunks are quite sure they are not alcoholics; the promiscuous are quite sure they will never contract a terrible disease. The Philistines keep jumping out of the curtains, so to speak, but these foolish people do not flee. They think, "We can just stay with folly because nothing is going to happen to us."

Delilah is like folly in that her honeyed words and her pressuring persuasiveness win the day. Folly is persistent. Delilah kept working on Samson until she got his true heart—the truth of his secret. Then, she turned him over to his enemies. It is a gruesome picture. The first thing the Philistines did was put Samson's eyes out. The way of a fool is a path to darkness. As we follow our sin natures, we experience a process of darkening. Light obeyed brings more light; light rejected brings the night. Samson rejected the light he had, and he received the night in spirit and body. Furthermore, he was taken in chains to grind out the grain of his enemies, a slave of the lowest sort. Even though Proverbs 5 was written many years after Samson's life, this passage makes one think of Samson. Listen to these words, the words of a man who has come to his own end in folly. Proverbs 5:12-14, *"How I have hated instruction! And my heart spurned reproof! 13 I have not listened to the voice of my teachers, nor inclined my ear to my instructors! 14 I was almost in utter ruin in the midst of the assembly and congregation."*

At his end, Samson cried out to God and was heard. God did allow him to pull down the temple of the Philistines, thus killing more of his enemies at the time of his death than he had killed while living. Wisdom does not hear fools when they cry out, but God often does. He heard the thief on the cross when he was dying in his folly, and He heard Samson as well.

Wisdom will not come along and fix your dissipated life, but God will graciously save you from your sin if you ask Him. God may be gracious to you in other ways as well. However, He will not reconstruct your whole life or obliterate all the consequences of your sinful life choices. He respects our personhood too much for that. Samson died in blindness with the Philistines as an example of a fool who dies in his folly. But he also died with his prayer answered to avenge himself upon his enemies, thus significantly fulfilling his life mission.

4.3 Potiphar's wife

Finally, on a more positive note, Potiphar's wife and Joseph are a fine example of folly and the wise man. Potiphar's wife tried repeatedly to seduce Joseph, but he resisted her temptations. Genesis 39:7-9—*It came about after these events that his master's wife looked with desire at Joseph, and she said, "Lie with me." 8 But he refused and said to his master's wife, "Behold, with me here, my master does not concern himself with anything in the house, and he has put all that he owns in my charge. 9 There is no one greater in this house than I, and he has withheld nothing from me except you, because you are his wife. How then could I do this great evil and sin against God?"*

Finally Potiphar's wife actually grabs Joseph to embrace him. He runs, leaving his coat with her. This is a very literal and vivid picture of a wise man resisting and fleeing folly. Joseph did become a great and wise leader later in life. He had many years of rigorous training yet to undergo in prison; nevertheless, this decision to flee folly was an important step in building a character worthy of the exaltation he would later experience.

5. Women of folly are diverse and abounding

As you consider this material, you may be saying to yourself, "This is interesting, but it doesn't have anything to do with me because I am not a seductress. I am not like Delilah. I am not a secret enemy agent, and I do not represent a honey trap. I am not like Potiphar's wife, a bored housewife sitting in the suburbs eating chocolates and seducing the gardener. None of this really applies to me." Because you may not identify with the adulteress, I want to introduce you to several versions of feminine folly. Folly and her patterns do lurk in the sin nature of all of us, whether we know it or not.

5.1 Folly is a real danger

Proverbs emphasizes the seductress because she is a real, literal danger to the young men to whom the book was originally written. Even more, she vividly pictures the techniques of flattery and enticement in all settings. Folly has many faces. Wherever and whenever you have a woman who presents an initial message that is sweet, tantalizing, or titillating, but which leads to moral corruption and foolishness, you have a woman of folly.

5.2 Religious faces of folly

Consider three possible women of folly, deceivers who might inhabit any neighborhood Sunday school. One denies the truth and authority of the Bible, teaching the ideas of liberal theology. Another teaches legalism, replacing God's truth and grace with man's ability to keep rules. Finally, there is the simplistic, trite teacher who replaces the cold steel and rich banquet of Scripture with syrupy sentiment and banal platitudes. Foolish Sunday school teachers may propagate one or all of these errors. In so doing they set up their young hearers to reject Christianity altogether as untrue or irrelevant, or they may succeed in guiding their students to become worse Pharisees than themselves. In any case, as harmless as they may appear, these teachers are women of folly, guiding the unsuspecting to destruction.

5.3 The foolish mother

The role of mother is the most important embodiment of both wisdom and folly. According to the Biblical model, the father in every nuclear family is a king and his wife is his queen and lady of wisdom beside him. The children are little fools growing up around them, and, it is hoped, are being trained to be wise people. The mother should be a counselor to her husband, standing beside the king to give him good advice. She is a lady of wisdom to her children, leading with reproof and instruction. However, if a mother is not wise, but is careless and indulgent, she is a woman of folly. Women who never reprove, but rather coddle their children and give them no boundaries, set them up for failure and destruction.

5.4 The witch

A more obvious woman of folly is the witch. Those attracted to the occult and its practices can be Satan's tools to deceive and seduce. There are many witches in our country today—women who are deeply read and in tune with the ideas, powers, and practices of false religions and occult powers. They may be ugly and have a sign out front which says "Sophie's Palm Reading," or they may be beautiful, professionally dressed, and claim to have personal insights from "spirit guides." In either case, they are a variety of witch, true and dangerous women of folly.

5.5 The beguiling "scholar"

Another enticing woman folly can be the scholarly and humanistic humanities professor. I did not say all scholarly humanities professors are women of folly. I said "humanistic" humanities professors. Consider the example of Margaret Mead, as analyzed by Nicholas Davidson in his book, *The Failure of Feminism*. I quote here at length because Mr. Davidson well traces the methods of a skillful woman folly on a national stage,[3] and in the very area of our interest, the nature of sexuality.

> It is difficult to overrate Mead's influence on American thought. Hundreds of young Americans decided to become anthropologists after reading one or another of her many works. Mead's work remains the main transmitter of anthropological ideas to the American public. For the past 60 years, since the publication of her best selling *Coming of Age in Samoa,* she has spoken as the voice of authority to Americans on questions of sex, gender, and culture. Mead's influence on American thought has surpassed that of any other theorist, including Freud. Quite apart from her enormous prestige within the anthropological profession, she wielded an even greater direct influence on the American public to whom she was able to express herself without the intermediaries of professional consensus or journalistic reporting. …
>
> She was the great popularizer of cultural determinism, particularly as it applied to the sexes. Mead dressed the idea of cultural determinism in vivid unforgettable color and brought it to the non-anthropological public as a simple, irrefutable idea which promised a better society. It was quite a pitch. [Davidson quotes Mead:]
>
> "Many, if not all of the personality traits which we have called masculine or feminine are as lightly linked to sex as are the clothing, the manners, and the form of headdress that a society at a given period assigns to either sex. We are forced to conclude that human nature is almost unbelievably malleable, responding accurately and contrastingly to contrasting cultural conditions. The differences between individuals who are members of different cultures, like the differences between individuals within a culture, are almost entirely to be laid to differences in conditioning, especially during early childhood. And the form of this conditioning is culturally determined. Standardized personality differences between the sexes are of this order: cultural creations to which each generation, male and female, is trained to conform."

3. The celebrity TV hostess, Oprah Winfrey, would be a more modern example of a woman folly functioning at a national level, guiding the thoughts and values of an entire culture.

[Commenting on Mead, Davidson then writes:]

> Mead's most glamorous evidence came from her studies of gender in primitive societies. ... This seemed like an impressive proof that a society could, without any serious difficulty assimilate the temperaments of men and women to a unitary standard without contradiction from biological forces and thereby establish a sexual egalitarianism. Men could be feminine, women masculine. Both sexes masculine, or both sexes feminine. These different solutions, Mead argued, had their characteristic strengths and weaknesses. It was up to Americans to choose the balance that would be best for their own society. ...[4]

Davidson, continues:

> Even the phases of human psychological maturation were said to be culturally determined. The Samoan adolescent simply flowed, as it were, from an easy childhood unmarred by parental harshness into an untroubled adolescence in preparation for an undemanding adulthood. As Mead described this island paradise,
>
> "As the dawn begins to fall among the soft brown roofs and the slender palm trees stand out against a colorless, gleaming sea, lovers slip home from trysts beneath the palm trees or in the shadow of beached canoes, that the light may find each sleeper in his appointed place."
>
> What a vision! What a vision of bliss to her American adolescent readers wracked by sexual frustration, the inability to understand the opposite sex, acne, parental pressure, and the insistent demands of adult society. No wonder cultural anthropology has been so well liked in 20th century America. What other science could promise a future of love under the palm trees?[5]

I can remember from my girlhood the many "Good Housekeeping" magazines my grandmother kept on the coffee table. They almost always contained an article by Margaret Mead. This woman was a woman of folly to a whole nation. Her honeyed words, seemingly so attractive, wooed us to believe that there was no need for sexual standards. According to her, strict sexual taboos or boundaries were completely unnecessary. Enlightened people make up their sexual identities as they go along. These are the enticements of a woman of folly.

6. Lesson challenge and prayer

On a more positive note, our society has its ladies of wisdom as well as its women of folly. Many high school English teachers have embodied wisdom in wonderful ways. One's language—spoken, read, and written—is the key to much power—the power of mind, understanding, identity, and roots. Indeed, by language we conquer and function in God's world. But frequently young men play the fool and reject these wise women. They rebel and refuse to learn grammar, write research papers, and read the classics. Then what happens? They go on in life and later come to wish fervently that they were more literate. They find in the real world of work and relationships that they need to know how to read, write, and speak well. I know of one man whose wife helped him learn to write later in life. By availing himself of a second woman of wisdom, after missing out on the first ones, he was able to advance in his profession.

4. Nicholas Davidson, *The Failure of Feminism*, (Buffalo, NY: Prometheus Books, 1988), 167-169.

5. Ibid., 171.

Over the years, I have heard various responses to this material. One that comes readily to mind is a young mother in Germany who heard a one-day seminar introducing the *Five Aspects*. Coming up to me after the seminar, she commented, "This explains something I did not understand at all. I recently have had an experience with a woman who came on so sweetly. She seemed like peaches and cream, and then later I found out that, in fact, she was very mean and even vicious. On the other hand, there is another women that I have found much harder to get to know; and yet as I do, I am finding her to be a genuinely wonderful person. I have been very puzzled by this, but now I see, it is the patterns of folly and wisdom all over again."

Indeed, we all will see these patterns repeatedly. For life is truly a choice between these two women. We must pursue the one, and flee the other. Moreover, as women we must model ourselves after the one, and put to death the other.

•

God of all knowledge,

Help us to be like wisdom,

and not like folly.

Help us not to be deceived or deceiving.

Guard our tongues and our hearts

from foolish ways.

In Christ's name,

Amen.

•

KEY to diagram at right

SYMBOLS OF GOD

Person–Implied by His voice.

Character–SQUARE–God's character is holy (square suggests the cube of the Holy of Holies) and infinite in all His attributes (square fades, as into infinity).

Masculinity–TRIANGLE–The triangle represents the original Masculine–the Trinity. God is the Initiator who descends and enters into His creation (triangle penetrates world). His masculinity is infinite (triangle fades, as into infinity).

Words–GENESIS 3:17–God judges man/mankind for his disobedience by cursing his realm.

Roles/work–WORDS–God is active within His creation as all-wise Creator, defied Sovereign, and righteous Judge.

SYMBOLS OF CREATION

Femininity–CIRCLE–The circle reflects the spherical shape of the sun/moon/world/womb. Feminine in relation to God, the creation is designed to receive her masculine Creator; but now fallen and cursed, she rejects Him (darkened triangle at top of world). All femininity is created and therefore finite (bounded edge doesn't fade).

Mankind's dwelling–PHOTO of DARKENED EARTH–The world, man's home, is now fallen and cursed. The world is finite (bounded edge) and subordinate to God (position–below God; small size–fits in God's hand).

Wisdom–NON-SPARKLING JEWELS–God's natural law, embedded in creation, is cursed.

Words about folly–PROVERBS 7:26–The principles of the world's system lead to death.

SYMBOLS OF MANKIND

Persons–SEX-DISTINCT FIGURES–God created man, male and female (sex-classic silhouettes). They are clothed in fig leaves according to their fallen, ashamed, guilty standing before God. Man is finite (bounded edges).

Character–SQUARE–Man is created in the image of God (squares smaller than but reflective of God's square). Both man and woman are created in the image of God (they don't share a square). Man's character is finite in all his attributes (bounded edges), and is now polluted with sin (darkened).

Masculinity–TRIANGLE–Man's masculinity reflects God's, but is finite (bounded edges), and is now polluted with sin (darkened).

Femininity–CIRCLE–Woman's femininity reflects creation's and is likewise finite (bounded edge). Now it is polluted with sin (darkened).

Words–PROVERBS 5:12; 6:26; ROMANS 1:22, 25–Mankind responds to God with disbelief and rejection. Woman and folly both hunt and kill fools.

Feminine role/work–Woman Folly–HIDDEN JEWEL, CLOSED BOOK–Woman is the embodiment of folly.

Masculine role/work–Fool–HIDDEN JEWEL, CLOSED BOOK–Man rejects learning, wisdom, and God (refer to *FAW–Vol. Two*, p. 178).

Woman Folly

"Because you have listened to the voice of your wife, and have eaten from the tree about which I commanded you,...cursed is the ground because of you."

God is the righteous and just Judge.

He subjected the creation to futility and death, that He might set it free.

Fallen woman rejects God and His creation principles, thus destroying inner domains with folly and sin.

Fallen man rejects God and His creation principles, thus leading humanity to destruction in folly and sin.

Fallen woman emulates feminine Folly in her roles.

Woman, like man, becomes a fool by rejecting the Lord and discipline.

Foolish women, like Folly, deceive, entice, seduce, enslave, and destroy.

Personification of Woman Folly

I am Woman Folly.

I personify the deceit, corruption, and death inherent in God's curse on Adam. Originally, life and beautiful complexity governed God's world. Since the curse, however, human beings and their world system are bound and rooted in pride, deceit, decay, and death.

Like Lady Wisdom, I am not a real person. I am a body of principles. I am the sum total of all the vanity and vain things of this world. Also like Lady Wisdom, I am pictured in the Bible as a woman in various feminine roles. Witches, evil queens, and seductive adulteresses are three of my favorite personae.

I seek all humanity, even as Wisdom does. I invite, cajole, and entice each one to drink fully of me. Yet I am not actually a hostess seeking guests, nor a teacher seeking students. Actually, I am an adulteress seeking a mark, a hunter seeking prey.

Lady Wisdom, at first, seems strict and stern, but I am just the opposite. In the beginning, flattery and fleshly indulgences are my stock-in-trade. With oily, honeyed words, I puff up silly, vain people even while I satiate their carnal desires. At first my bonds are as light as a spider's web, but soon I forge them as strong as chains. After that, there is no need to flatter the stupid one, nor give him pleasures. Now he is my slave, my prisoner. I can treat him as harshly as I please. I can kill him when I want, for he is in my prison. I do not have to fear the intervention of my counterpart, Wisdom, for she does not hear the cries of those who spurned her long ago.

Every woman has the capacity to picture me, and every woman does to some extent. However, some reflect my dramatic qualities in a brilliant way. My favorite protégé from the Bible is Delilah. Now there was a woman who knew how to get the job done! Flattery, sex, manipulation, deceit, nagging, perseverance—she knew every trick in the book. And her victim—what a pretty sight he was when she was through with him—blinded, in chains, enslaved to his enemy, mocked, and finally crushed in death! Of course, that picture is somewhat marred. The victim did cry out in the end to the Only One who hears fools in bondage. Nevertheless, I took his freedom, sight, and life. Of that I am proud.

Bible Study of Wisdom—*fallen*

Before beginning this study, read the entire lesson, pages 28-40.

The woman of folly is boisterous, she is naive, and knows nothing. And she sits at the doorway of her house, on a seat by the high places of the city, calling to those who pass by, who are making their paths straight: "Whoever is naive, let him turn in here." ... But he does not know that the dead are there, that her guests are in the depths of Sheol.

PROVERBS 9:13-16, 18

The eleventh Biblical view of woman

Rebellious and deceiving, "woman" folly encourages fools along a path of destruction.

Who is "woman" folly?

We learned in our last lesson that Solomon presents wisdom, the body of God's creation principles, as a woman. Wisdom, he says in Proverbs 1-9, is like a great lady who invites, reproves, teaches, protects, blesses, and exalts her human children. She brings beauty, order, and life to the creation. Solomon says that folly is also like a woman. Folly's patterns, roles, and motives are perverted distortions of the beauty and righteousness we saw in "lady" wisdom. "Lady" wisdom is a personification of God's creation principles. "Woman" folly personifies the principles of the curse—pride, deceit, death, and destruction. As wisdom seeks to give life to her children, folly seeks to deceive hers and to bring them down to death. Over time, we women will grow to be more like "lady" wisdom or more like "woman" folly. Like them, we will bring life or death to those within our influence.

1. Solomon brings his Proverbs prologue into crisp focus with his parallel presentations of "lady" wisdom and "woman" folly in 9:1-6, 13-18. Study these passages carefully and list as many contrasts and comparisons as you can between these metaphorical women.

"lady" wisdom	"woman" folly

2. Proverbs 5:1-14 is a father's impassioned plea to his son, warning him of the dangers of the adulteress. How does the father describe folly's style, her methods, and her results? What are the son's defenses against her?

3. Proverbs 7 is a vivid morality play starring the adulteress and the young fool. Read this chapter carefully, preferably out loud. (If you are in a group, take parts: The father, vv. 1-5, 24-27; the narrator, vv. 6-13, 21-23; and the adulteress, vv. 14-20.) What specific details of the text give this adulteress individuality? How is this adulteress like the one described in chapter 5? How is she like folly presented in Proverbs 9:13-18?

4. Write a paragraph defending the following ideas:

a. Solomon writes much about adultery in Proverbs 1-9 because this is one of the most dangerous temptations a young man can face. In your answer define the *stolen water* and *secret bread* of Proverbs 9:17, in the context of adultery (Prov. 5:15-17).

b. Solomon writes much about adultery in Proverbs 1-9 because in addition to being one of the most dangerous temptations a young man can face, it is a vivid illustration of every type of folly. In your answer define the *stolen water* and *secret bread* of Proverbs 9:17 in this broader sense.

Case studies: Women of folly

Eve: Deceived and deceiving

5. What reasons did Eve give God for eating the forbidden fruit (Gen. 3:1-7, 13)? What does Paul say about this event (1 Tim. 2:14)?

6. Nehemiah had enemies who wanted to deceive him. When did he see through the deception that was placed before him by his false friends (Neh. 6:10-13)?

7. Once deceived, Eve became a deceiver (Gen. 3:6). Why do you think this happened? Has it ever happened to you?

8. Eve could have responded to her temptation in the way Nehemiah responded to his. What virtues would have guarded Eve, and will guard us, from Satan's deceptions (Rom. 1:21; 2 Thess. 2:8-12; 2 Cor. 10:5)?

Points to ponder

According to 1 Timothy 2:13-14, Eve was quite deceived, but Adam willfully and knowingly disobeyed. Created to be a cooperative follower, woman's extra leadability makes her more susceptible to deception than man. Women are often more subjective in their judgments, depending more on how things seem (feelings, nuances, appearances). The fruit looked good and appeared desirable, and Satan was like an angel of light. Man is often more logical, depending on objective facts. Adam knew all the facts and chose to disobey God in favor of pleasing his wife (Gen. 3:17). Adam had the greater responsibility and the greater culpability. Eve stood guilty as well, not for failing to see through Satan's arguments, but rather, for failing to cling to the truth she had.

Samson and Delilah: A fool and a woman of folly

9. How did Samson disregard his parents' wisdom in his early years (Judg. 14:1-9)?

10. Who was Delilah? How did she play the part of "woman" folly in Samson's life (Judg. 16)?

11. Was Samson aware of Delilah's purposes? Why do you think he chose to ignore all the signs and yield to her (Judg. 16:8-9, 12, 14; Prov. 1:32)?

12. In what ways did Samson's latter days picture the destiny of a fool (Judg. 16:21-26; Prov. 7:21-23)? How did God show His grace to Samson (Judg. 16:28-30)?

Points to ponder

Salvation is by grace, but wisdom rules by the principle *as you sow, so shall you reap*. Samson and the thief on the cross (Luke 23:39-43) both experienced the just rewards of their folly; they also found grace from God in their dying hours.

Joseph and Potiphar's wife: A wise man and a woman of folly

13. How does Potiphar's wife reveal herself to be mature and well-exercised in the ways of folly (Gen. 39:5-20)?

14. How does Joseph's response to Potiphar's wife and his subsequent career show him to be one who loved wisdom? Select some verses from Genesis 39 and Proverbs 5 and 7 to support your answer.

The pattern set by wisdom is to lead others to life through reproof and discipline. The pattern set by folly is to take others down to death through flattery and sensuality.

15. Consider how the following women might all be different versions of folly. Select one woman from the list and describe how she might lead a fool down to destruction: The indulgent mother; the scholarly but ungodly professor; the nice school teacher; the trite Sunday school teacher; or the overly protective mother.

To be or not to be a woman of folly?

16. In order to become a woman of folly, how should one respond in each of the following areas?

authorities and their guidance

discipline and reproof

commitments and trials

the use of the tongue

17. Imbibing flattery is often the first step in being deceived. Flattering others is often the first step in deceiving. Define **flattery** from the dictionary. What are its characteristics and motives (Prov. 5:3-4; 29:5; Jude 16)?

Watch over your heart with all diligence, for from it flow the springs of life. Put away from you a deceitful mouth, and put devious lips far from you.

PROVERBS 4:23-24

18. Do you consider yourself more susceptible to flattery or to being a flatterer? From material covered in this lesson, write three principles which will protect you from one or both of these sins, and which you plan to apply.

Review

- Wisdom seeks students; folly hunts prey.
- Wisdom reproves and teaches; folly flatters and seduces.
- Wisdom counsels and trains; folly deceives and enslaves.
- Wisdom blesses and glorifies; folly takes down to death.

LESSON 16 : Lady of Wisdom – *redeemed*

1. The woman of excellence: Who is she?

Here is a list of quotes from a well-known personality. Can you identify her?

"Sit up. You are slouching. It is bad for your back."
"Don't read in that dim light."
"You are driving too fast."
"Here. Take your raincoat. It is going to rain."
"Practice your piano for an hour now. Then you may go out."
"Don't eat that candy bar right before lunch. It will ruin your appetite."
"Finish your homework."
"Don't talk with your mouth full. And don't smack."
"Don't stand there with the refrigerator door open. Figure out what you want and then get it."
"You can't wear that outfit. It is almost vulgar."
"You have too much eye make-up on."
"Don't say 'can't'—'can't' never could do anything."
"Remember, pretty is as pretty does."
"If you don't get ready right now, you are going to be late."
"Don't say, 'him and me are going.' Say, 'he and I are going.'"

Who is this person? You've already guessed; it's Mother. These quotes certainly sound like my mother. They probably sound like your mother, too. I have presented this lecture more than once, and every audience has thought it's Mother. I have asked them, "Are you sure it's not Dad?" Everyone has shaken her head, "No, it's not Dad; it's Mother."

Why are we so sure? If you look at this list of quotes, you will see it is a series of commands and exhortations about the details of life, from how to sit, speak, eat, go, come, even how to look in the refrigerator! These commands and exhortations are sprinkled with proverbs— pithy little statements of wisdom like "pretty is as pretty does," or "can't never could do anything." Every mother is the primary lady of wisdom for her young children. Like the book of Proverbs, mothers are a catalog of wisdom, telling us what to do in all basic areas—including money, friends, enemies, speech, food, sex, manners, and so on.

KEY Wisdom–*redeemed*
person–FEMALE FIGURE (clothed in white robe–Christ's righteousness–according to her forgiven, redeemed standing before God)
character–GLOWING SQUARE (redeemed from sin)
femininity–DOTTED CIRCLE (redeemed from sin)
role/work–SPARKLING JEWEL ON ROBE (acquired wisdom); OPEN, RADIANT BOOK (learning with mind of Christ)

1.1 Wisdom and wise women are persistently parallel.

There is not one simple verse that says women should be like wisdom. Rather, it is the very structure and parallelisms of the book of Proverbs which present the righteous woman as an embodiment of feminine wisdom. Consider these parallelisms. Proverbs 9:1 says, *Wisdom has built her house....* The passage goes on to describe how she sets forth a lavish banquet in her beautiful mansion. Five chapters later, Proverbs 14:1 says, *The wise woman builds her house,...*

Proverbs 3:15 says that wisdom *is more precious than jewels and nothing you desire compares with her.* Proverbs 8:11 says the same thing, *For wisdom is better than jewels, and all desirable things cannot compare with her.* Job 28:12a says, *Where can wisdom be found?* Job 28:18b says, *And the acquisition of wisdom is above that of pearls.* It is in these contexts that we should read the familiar Proverbs 31:10, *Who can find the excellent wife? For her worth is far above jewels.*[1] Proverbs 9:10 says, *The fear of the Lord is the beginning of wisdom.* Proverbs 31:30 reads, *The woman who fears the Lord, she shall be praised.* The parallels between wisdom and the wise woman are powerful and deliberate:

- Both are productive in the same way—they build their houses.
- Both are of great value—they are more valuable than jewels.
- Both are rare and difficult to find—they must be sought with diligence.
- Finally, both wisdom and the wise woman have the same root virtue. They fear the Lord.

1.2 Intentional literary parallelisms

The book of Proverbs, originally written to teach young men wisdom, falls into three main sections. The first section is the prologue, chapters 1-9. In these chapters, the father introduces wisdom and folly personified as women. He urges his son to pursue wisdom and flee folly. Section 2, chapters 10-30, contains the collection of proverbs themselves, the pithy wise sayings, usually in couplet form, providing moral maxims on how to live. The third and final section, the epilogue of chapter 31, presents the words and ministry of a specific wise mother (31:1-9) and a portrait of the wise wife (31:10-31).

The wise mother and wife at the end of Proverbs are specific and deliberate human examples of the archetypal and metaphorical wisdom presented in the front of the book. Thus, the epilogue echoes and answers the prologue. The specific wise women of chapter 31 are to be heeded and treasured just as the metaphorical wisdom of chapters 1-9 is to be heeded and treasured. Young men will find archetypal wisdom by heeding, pursuing, and treasuring her human embodiments—godly mothers and wives. Even when king, Lemuel remembered the moral wisdom his mother taught him as a boy (31:1-9). When seeking a wife, a man is instructed to look first and foremost for strength of character (31:10-11, 30). Men should seek and honor wise women; we as women should make these wise women our models. We should give our children sound wisdom and be for our husbands jewels, completely worthy of their trust and appreciation.

2. The fear of the Lord

The fear of the Lord is the root virtue of the lady-of-wisdom aspect just as love is the root virtue of lifegiver. **The fear of the Lord** is reverential respect for God and His standards based on the conscious knowledge that God is God.

What is **conscious knowledge**? All people know that God is God, but many choose to suppress this knowledge, to turn away from it, putting it behind their backs. They do not want to live in the light of God's presence (Rom 1:18ff). In contrast, the person who fears the Lord chooses to keep the knowledge of God before him. Those who do not fear the Lord suppress this truth; those who fear Him live in His presence. The passages on the fear of the Lord organize themselves with clarity around "R" words: Reverence, restraint, refuge, rejoicing, and reward.

---

1. The word translated *pearls* in Job 28:18 and *jewels* in Prov. 3:15 and 31:10 is the same Hebrew word *peninim*. Robert L. Thomas, ed., *New American Standard Exhaustive Concordance of the Bible* (Nashville: Holman Bible Publishers, 1981), jewels, p. 645; pearls, p. 930; and *peninim*, p. 1582, entry 6443.

2.1 Reverence

The first "R" word, **reverence**, is in the definition itself. The fear of the Lord includes a reverential respect for God and His standards. We cannot separate God as a Person from His righteous standards. Repeatedly the Bible says the fear of the Lord is to hate evil. Evil is that which is contrary to God and His laws. If you really love and fear the Lord, you will reverence His standards, His righteousness. Therefore, you will hate evil.

2.2 Restraint

Reverence for God leads to restraint. A man said to a friend of mine recently, "I don't sleep with women because I am afraid of God." That is a fantastic reason to be pure. It is probably the best reason. The young man knows God and His laws exist. While he has a drive and desire to be promiscuous, he maintains a conscious knowledge of God and His standards. He knows God judges sinners, so he restrains himself. This is a good example of fearing the Lord.

Nehemiah provides another good example of restraint. In his time, other officials in the nation are oppressing the people and overcharging them on taxes. Nehemiah writes, *But I did not do so because of the fear of God* (Neh. 5:15). Jonah provides another interesting example. Jonah says to the sailors, "If you want this storm to stop, you must throw me overboard." The sailors did not want to be party to Jonah's drowning because they feared the Lord (Jon. 1:12-14). They did not want to kill someone. Ironically, they feared the Lord more than Jonah did. This happens more often than you would think. Some unbelievers actually fear God more than believers who are flaunting their disobedience.

The fear of the Lord restrains people from wickedness, from doing immoral and dishonest things. The fear of the Lord has greatly eroded in America; we know this because we are increasingly unrestrained morally and ethically.

2.3 Refuge

When we fear the Lord He becomes our refuge, because fearing Him is the one fear that casts out all others. The fear of the Lord conquers all other fears. It works like this. When we lock onto the greatness and awesome power of God, all other powers and forces shrink down to insignificance, even though they may be great by human standards.

For instance, Shiphrah and Puah, the midwives in Moses' day, did not kill the boy babies because they feared the Lord. Pharaoh was the great power. He had the power of life and death. But, their fear of the Lord was greater than their fear of Pharaoh (Ex. 1). In the same way, Shadrach, Meshach, and Abednego were not afraid of the fiery furnace. They would rather go into the fiery furnace than worship idols (Dan. 3:16-18). Jesus clearly articulates this truth when He says, *"Do not fear those who kill the body but are unable to kill the soul; but rather fear Him who is able to destroy both soul and body in hell"* (Matt. 10:28). Remember, this was spoken by a Man who knew He would be tortured to death.

> When we fear the Lord, He becomes our refuge, because fearing Him is the one fear that casts out all other fears.

Those who fear the Lord become fearless because God is their refuge. Not only does His greatness shrink to insignificance the fears of this life; but the Lord is, in fact, a refuge for those who fear Him. Boaz said of Ruth, who came to an unknown country where Moabites were not appreciated, *"May the LORD reward your work, and your wages be full from the LORD, the God of Israel, under whose wings you have come to seek refuge"* (Ruth 2:12). Proverbs 18:10 says, *The name of the Lord is a strong tower; the righteous runs into it and is safe.*

I was delighted once by a television interview of the Canadian pairs ice skating couple, Lloyd Eisler and Isabelle Brasseur. Lloyd had gone all over Canada looking for a partner. Well over six feet tall and very strong, he eventually chose tiny five-foot Isabelle Brasseur. The interviewer asked Isabelle to describe the try-out. She had great big eyes and was quite hilarious in manner. She said, "Oh, he was so big! I did not even want to get on the ice with him. I was scared to death he would just throw me up to the roof...." Then she paused and said, "But then I learned that with his strength he saves and protects me, and now I trust him completely."

When we contemplate God, we should be awed by His greatness and power. We should be afraid, wondering what will happen to us "if we get on the ice with God," so to speak. Then we realize as we learn His character, that His great power can and will be deployed on our behalf. That was what Isabelle learned in skating with Lloyd. The person strong enough to throw you high in the air is also the person who can catch you and keep you from falling. This is a picture of God as Refuge. We are in awe of God, and yet we come to learn that the very power we rightly fear is the source of our protection when we trust and lean upon Him.

2.4 Rejoicing

This leads to the fourth "R"—rejoicing. Unfortunately, many people associate the fear of the Lord with cowering in the corner. It is true—the more wicked people are, the more they experience terror when they face the greatness of God. But God says the fear He desires is characterized by trembling with rejoicing. This is, in fact, His command in Psalm 2:10-12, written to kings and the rulers of the earth: *Now therefore, O kings, show discernment. Take warning, O judges of the earth. 11 Worship the LORD with reverence and rejoice with trembling. 12 Do homage to the Son, that He not become angry, and you perish in the way, for His wrath may soon be kindled. How blessed are all who take refuge in Him!*

Psalm 34 is another wonderful psalm on the fear of the Lord. Notice the themes of rejoicing, radiance, and refuge for those who make the true God their God in verses 5-9: *They looked to Him and were radiant, and their faces will never be ashamed. 6 This poor man cried, and the LORD heard him and saved him out of all his troubles. 7 The angel of the LORD encamps around those who fear Him, and rescues them. 8 O taste and see that the LORD is good; how blessed is the man who takes refuge in Him! 9 O fear the LORD, you His saints; for to those who fear Him there is no want.*

> The fear of the Lord produces a striving for excellent work and the hope of reward from God.

2.5 Reward

Those who fear the Lord look to Him for their final reward. Psalm 19:9-11 says, *The fear of the LORD is clean, enduring forever; the judgments of the LORD are true; they are righteous altogether. 10 They are more desirable than gold, yes, than much fine gold; sweeter also than honey and the drippings of the honeycomb. 11 Moreover, by them Your servant is warned; in keeping them there is great reward.* The melancholy air of Moses' Psalm 90 is understandable when one considers Moses' life with the unbelieving Jews and their cursed wilderness existence. Note his concern in verses 11-12 and 16-17, at the end of his psalm: *Who understands the power of Your anger and Your fury, according to the fear that is due You? 12 So teach us to number our days, that we may present to You a heart of wisdom. ... 16 Let Your work appear to Your servants and Your majesty to their children. 17 Let the favor of the Lord our God be upon us; and confirm for us the work of our hands; yes, confirm the work of our hands.*

The fear of the Lord produces a striving for excellent work and the hope of reward from God. Just so, Proverbs 31:30-31 says, *Charm is deceitful and beauty is vain, but a woman who fears the LORD, she shall be praised. 31 Give her the product of her hands, and let her works praise her in the gates.* The fear of the Lord not only restrains evil. It motivates us to produce excellence. Respect for God's standards not only keeps us back from doing bad things. It leads us on to produce excellence because we have respect for God's standards. As we produce works of good quality, we are free to look to God for genuine reward.

2.6 Review: Fear of the LORD

The root virtue and motivation of wisdom and the wise woman is the fear of the Lord. Those who fear the Lord:

- Reverence Him;
- Restrain themselves from evil;
- Take refuge in God;
- Rejoice in God's goodness; and
- Look to Him for reward.

3. Women of excellence: Four portraits of wisdom

Scripture gives a name to the woman who embodies wisdom. Proverbs 31:10 introduces the wise wife as "the woman of excellence." In the Hebrew the word is *chayil*,[2] and it is translated in various ways. The King James calls the *chayil* woman "the virtuous woman." Some translations call her "the woman of noble character." Chayil also communicates strength and depth of character. I like "the excellent woman" or "the woman of excellence" best.

The lifegiver aspect of woman can be pictured as a fountain or a deep well, where pure and crystal water is flowing from the love of God. The lady-of-wisdom aspect is a pillar of strength—a rock column constructed from the fear of God, set deep, and stable. This is a good picture of the *chayil* woman. The virtuous woman is exactly the opposite of anything that is flighty, silly, superficial, shallow, or naive. That is what the *chayil* woman is not. Instead, she is characterized by depth, strength, courage, nobility, discipline, and perseverance—all based in the fear of God. It is a wonderful picture, indeed.

The ideal wife of Proverbs 31, Ruth, Esther, and the wise woman of Abel—all portray wisdom in her feminine roles. Every godly woman should seek to be a portrait of wisdom. Every woman's portrait will be different, as these four diverse examples illustrate. While the root virtues are the same, the applications are different.

3.1 The Proverbs 31 wife of excellence

The Proverbs 31 woman is the sketch of an ideal wife offered to young, upper-class Israelite men of the kingdom age to help them in the wise selection of a mate. Though written for a specific place and time, this woman's description abides with timeless clarity; she has been a plumb line for God's people for centuries. The wife in Proverbs 31 is upper class. She has servants and a large household; her husband is in the ruling class of society. She is self-possessed, but not self-obsessed. Her dignity and strength are focused in serving others.

---

2. *New American Standard Exhaustive Concordance of the Bible*, **chayil**, p. 1518, entry 2428.

I do not teach this passage very often for two reasons. First, I think it has been over-done to the exclusion of what the rest of the Bible says about womanhood. Second, this woman is so powerful in her strength and diligence, she often overwhelms women instead of encouraging them, especially if she is taught in isolation from the rest of the Bible.

What about her strength and diligence? My first impression is to be tired. I am overwhelmed by her diligence and her workload. I used to read verse 15 about her rising while it is still night and verse 18 about her lamp not going out, and I concluded she never slept. I thought, "Lord, this is unbelievable. Who can consistently get up early and stay up late?" Surely most people cannot. Later I read a commentary which explained that *"her lamp not going out"* meant her home enjoyed prosperity, not that she stayed up all night.

She has untiring diligence and multiple responsibilities. She is ruling over her whole household—the servants, her children, the food, the clothing, helping her husband, doing charitable deeds, and business as well. But notice, there is a focus. Her focus is textiles. The first thing mentioned after her goodness to her husband is that she looks for wool and flax (v. 13). She stretches out her hand to the distaff (v. 19). She is at the spindle, weaving this wool and flax. She is making coverings; she is sewing (v. 22). Finally she makes linen garments and sells them (v. 24).

A woman's life goes through different seasons. Sometimes she is busier with lifegiving; other times she can be busier with industry. Nevertheless, the productive homemaker will be the predominant feminine ideal in a healthy church and culture.

Focus on a skill or an area is key to becoming the wise women we need to be. Some can do more than others. No one can do everything; everyone should do something. In some sense, homemakers must rule over all, but it is still possible and highly desirable to pick an area of specialization. For some, it might be food preparation, or even tax preparation (if you have training as an accountant), yard work, child care, teaching, home decoration, or health care. If you ever do have a cottage industry, it will grow naturally from your area of specialty.

I do not know if today's commentaries on the industry of the Proverbs 31 wife are amusing or perplexing. Some writers want to emphasize that this woman is working outside the home. They portray her selling sashes to the merchants as a major textile industry and her buying a vineyard as one of many big real estate deals. On the other hand, those who want to emphasize her domesticity downplay this and say, "This is just a little plot in the backyard."

The passage does not tell us how much volume she is doing in sashes, how big the vineyard is, or how far it is from home. We can say that it is the clear intent of the passage to present this woman as a domestic ruler. She is ruling the multi-faceted domain of the home; it is running smoothly. Her productivity is flowing beyond the walls of her home into the community in the form of both charity and capital investment. She is fulfilling the New Testament ideal of working with her own hands in order to have enough for her own and enough to share with others (Eph. 4:28; 1 Thess. 4:9-12).

This home-centered, productive, domestic ruler is a model and ideal. Where this pattern is not admired and pursued by women, and when men do not seek wives who make homemaking their central life work, that culture is in trouble. Wise women are found in other patterns of life. Some never marry; some are childless. A woman's life also goes through different seasons. Sometimes she is busier with lifegiving, and other times she can be busier with industry. Nevertheless, the productive homemaker will be the predominant feminine ideal in a healthy church and culture. Society is blessed when most women are domestic rulers, producing charity, and adding to their estates through their skill.

We should admire domestic skill. Cooking and sewing are tittered at in many circles. That shows the ignorance of those who are tittering. A friend and single attorney once told me she was determined to learn to sew. She said, "Barbara, I need to know fabrics. If I am going to decorate my house or dress wisely, I need to have this skill." She found a teacher who was a lady of wisdom in sewing and learned from her.

Notice that for all her strength, the woman in Proverbs 31 has joy. She speaks with kindness. She smiles. She is not worried about the future. There is a softness to her. It is easy to think that someone who works as diligently as this woman would be like a drill sergeant. She is not. She retains the softness of true femininity because she does all this work for love as well as for excellence.

A wise and godly people will not titter at domestic skills or domestic rulers. Some of us will never marry, many of us will never be upper class or full-time homemakers. However, many are and can be. To whatever degree we are domestic rulers (and all of us are to some degree), Proverbs 31 is an encouragement to be diligent and skillful from the inner domains outward.

3.2 Ruth: A peasant builds her house

Ruth provides a completely different example of the woman of excellence. Ruth is a foreigner, a Moabite; she is not upper class, she is a peasant. She is a widow gleaning in the fields, like a common laborer, at the poverty level. She does not have a grand husband, a big household, or lots of servants. She is on the other end of the social ladder from the Proverbs 31 woman. Yet, Ruth is a wonderful example of a wise woman who builds her house. With and through this poor woman, God built the greatest house that has ever been built—the Davidic house, the house from which Christ Himself comes. Proverbs 14:1 says, *The wise woman builds her house, but the foolish tears it down with her own hands.* How did Ruth contribute to the building of such a great house? Obviously God helped and empowered her. But what part did Ruth play? She started with the right God. She chose God to be her God. She went to His land; she took refuge in Him. Her beginning and foundation was God. Then she chose the right family. When she started, her family consisted of one bitter old woman—not a very hopeful outlook. However, Ruth was willing to start with this very humble beginning. She was loyal and took care of the family she had, Naomi.

> Ruth makes wise choices about her God, work, relationships, and marriage. Repeatedly she chooses what will glorify God and build up others. Her fame is just.

Next, she was willing to work diligently according to the Law. Working according to the laws of gleaning, Ruth availed herself of God's provision for work-fare in Israel. This meant arduous labor. She willingly did this while she accepted protection from Naomi's wise counsel and Boaz's guard.

Finally, she chose a husband not for his youth or wealth, but for the spiritual blessing he would bring her family, both living and dead. When Ruth comes to Boaz on the threshing floor he says to her in Ruth 3:10, *"May you be blessed of the LORD, my daughter. You have shown your last kindness to be better than the first by not going after young men, whether poor or rich."* What does he mean, *"your last kindness is bet-*

ter than the first?" He means she has done many kindnesses, which include coming back from Moab, gleaning in the fields, and taking care of Naomi. "But of all your kindnesses," Boaz says, "choosing me to be your husband and kinsman-redeemer is the greatest kindness." Most people presume from this passage that Boaz was considerably older than Ruth. She was not choosing one of the young men for sex appeal or flash. She chose Boaz because of his moral character and because of who he was in relation to her family. He could be the redeemer. By this match she could pull her whole family back together, re-establishing the line for her dead father-in-law, her first husband, and Naomi.

Ruth is a woman making wise choices—the choice of her God and home, the choice of loyalty and diligence, and the choice of character in marriage. Repeatedly she chooses what will glorify God and build up others. Her fame is just. *Let her works praise her in the gates* is indeed an appropriate blessing for Ruth and women like her. In Ruth 3:11, Boaz tells Ruth that she is known all over the village as a woman of excellence (this is our same word *chayil*). Three thousand years later she is known and praised not only in her village, but all over the world. Ruth was a woman of excellence who built her house and did not tear it down.

3.3 Esther: A queen pictures wisdom

Esther is not an upper-class homemaker or an alien peasant. She is a Jewish queen in the great Gentile empire of Persia. The length of Esther's story allows us to see her in many of wisdom's roles. Consider the following seven examples.

Inviting after preparation

Esther, like wisdom, invites only after preparation. In Proverbs 9, wisdom prepares her house and a great banquet. By means of careful preparation, she offers food of finest quality. Esther behaves in a similar manner. When she realizes she must go to the king and beseech him for her people, she does not rush. She fasts for three days and asks the Jews to fast with her. During this time, in all likelihood, she prayed and pondered the best way to approach the king. She must not present her petition obtrusively. That might result in a bad end for her and her petition. "No," she thought, "I need to bring him into my environment. I should prepare a banquet, arouse his curiosity, and then give him my petition." With her plan in mind, she approaches Xerxes and invites him to her banquet.

Petitioning skillfully

Wise women appeal, petition, and influence people skillfully. Wise petitioners think about whom it is they are petitioning and the best ways to persuade them. At the first banquet, Esther sensed that the time was not yet right. Perhaps Haman's pride was not yet brim full. For whatever reason, she delayed to give her petition, but invited the King and Haman for a second banquet the next day. In Proverbs 8:15, personified wisdom says, *By me kings reign, and rulers decree justice.* The great peril of anti-Semitism was hanging over the Media-Persian Empire, an evil which God has sworn to curse. Esther gives Xerxes wisdom and influences him for justice when she petitions for her life and the life of the Jews.[3]

---

3. An entire study on pondering and petitioning would be of benefit. Abigail's petition of David in 1 Samuel 25 is a masterful example of a woman wisely petitioning a man. While maintaining all her femininity, Abigail speaks to David in language that is both vivid and understandable to him, using metaphors from his own fields of endeavor. As someone has said, she talks to an outlaw as if he were a king. But of course, David was a king; a great part of Abigail's wisdom was that she knew it.

Spurning fools

Wisdom spurns fools, as Proverbs 1 makes clear. Wisdom calls to everyone, but when fools do not heed her, she spurns them. She does not help them when they run into trouble. When Haman, the wicked anti-Semite, falls on Esther's couch and starts pleading for her help at the second banquet, Esther does not help him. She, like wisdom, spurns him. She lets him go to his own destruction.

Exalting the wise

Esther, like wisdom, exalts the wise man. Mordecai is the wise man in the story. As soon as she receives Haman's house, Esther gives it to Mordecai. Wisdom turns away from fools and exalts wise people. Wise women strive to recognize fools in order to avoid them and limit their influence. At the same time, wise women use their positions of influence to exalt wise people. This is how Esther related to Mordecai, the wise man.

Hating evil and doing justice

Esther, like wisdom, hates evil and does justice. After the Jews slaughtered their enemies for a day, Esther goes back to the king and asks him for another day for the Jews to kill anti-Semites. She also asks that Haman's ten sons be executed along with him. Where is the sweet, deferential girl we saw at the beginning of the book? Who is this person who wants to multiply executions? True wisdom knows that real peace comes only with justice, the putting down and away of evil. This is as true whether your domain is the size of an empire or a living room. There will be no peace at home until the trouble-making child is disciplined, or civil tranquility until criminals are judged. Peace comes when justice is done and evil is put away.

Protecting her people

Wisdom, which is the fear of the Lord, hates evil. Esther realizes that the anti-Semites in the Persian Empire have been wounded, but not exterminated. Left alone, they would rear their ugly heads again with the Persian equivalent of pogroms and racial persecutions. So she goes back to the king and asks, in effect, that the cancer be cut out completely. The king grants her petition, and a great peace and salvation is brought to the Empire. (If Germany had had the core of Nazism cut out in the 1930s, one wonders how many lives would have been saved.) Esther, like wisdom, protects her people.

Blessing with benefits

Esther also showers her people with benefits. To this day, the Jewish people still rejoice in the Feast of Purim which she established twenty-five centuries ago. Esther is a full-orbed embodiment of archetypal wisdom and her roles. She prepares before she invites and petitions. She counsels the king, spurns the fool, exalts the wise man, brings peace through justice, and bequeaths a rich and godly heritage to her people.

True wisdom knows that real peace comes only with justice— the putting down and away of evil. This is as true whether your domain is the size of an empire or a living room.

3.4 The wise woman of Abel

In 2 Samuel 20, we find another lady of wisdom who hates evil and loves peace. King David's cousin and murderous field commander, Joab, has taken his army north to chase and execute a rebel named Sheba. Sheba takes refuge in the walled city of Abel. As the story opens, Joab is laying siege to the whole city because there is one rebel in it.

> 2 Samuel 20:15-22—*They came and besieged him in Abel Beth-maacah, and they cast up a siege ramp against the city, and it stood by the rampart; and all the people who were with Joab were wreaking destruction in order to topple the wall. 16 Then a wise woman called from the city, "Hear, hear! Please tell Joab, 'Come here that I may speak with you.'" 17 So he approached her, and the woman said, "Are you Joab?" And he answered, "I am." Then she said to him, "Listen to the words of your maidservant." And he answered, "I am listening." 18 Then she spoke, saying, "Formerly they used to say, 'They will surely ask advice at Abel,' and thus they ended the dispute.* [In other words, this town is known for its diplomats and arbitrators.] *19 I am of those who are peaceable and faithful in Israel. You are seeking to destroy a city, even a mother in Israel. Why would you swallow up the inheritance of the LORD?" 20 Joab replied, "Far be it, far be it from me that I should swallow up or destroy! 21 Such is not the case.* [This is wryly humorous in view of Joab's destructive nature.] *But a man from the hill country of Ephraim, Sheba the son of Bichri by name, has lifted up his hand against King David. Only hand him over, and I will depart from the city." And the woman said to Joab, "Behold, his head will be thrown to you over the wall." 22 Then the woman wisely came to all the people. And they cut off the head of Sheba the son of Bichri and threw it to Joab. So he blew the trumpet, and they were dispersed from the city, each to his tent. Joab also returned to the king at Jerusalem.*

The problem in this story is a rebel who needs to be judged. Joab is about to destroy a whole town in the process. But a wise woman intervenes. She submissively beseeches him and finds out about the rebel. At the critical moment, she shows her mettle. She is willing to see justice done. She does not say, "Oh, Joab, it's only one man, can't you just forgive him?" Or, "Let's negotiate a peace conference." She does not try to handle him that way. She says, "I will see that he is executed."

Wise women can often help men focus on more effective and accurate decisions in the family and society. However, these women must be willing to learn the true nature of problems and not flinch at true solutions. Consider a family example. The family is a microcosm of society wherein the husband and the father is the king. The mother and the wife is his queen and lady of wisdom. The children are the subjects, mostly little fools. Many times the father sees a problem. He comes down with the axe of justice to obliterate it. Maybe his disciplinary approach is too broad or too harsh. A wife and mother who acts like wisdom can go to the king, the husband and father, and find out how he sees things, support him and his legitimate concerns, and make suggestions on how to fine- tune justice. This way evil is dealt with in the most efficient way, and the least amount of collateral damage is done. We can and should see this dynamic all the time. This result, however, depends on women showing respect and wisdom. Some say, "This doesn't apply to me because my husband (or my boss) is too mean and foolish." Had Esther or the woman of Abel followed that reasoning, the kingdom and the city would both have been lost, for Xerxes and Joab were both mean and foolish men.

When a woman is offended by a man's excesses, she often positions herself in antagonism to him. Nothing is gained by this, except that each hardens in his or her position. Harshness from the man and permissiveness from the woman often results. God's desire is that true justice and mercy come forth from both. A woman without justice is as bad as a man without mercy. Fortunately for all, Esther and the woman of Abel pled for mercy, even as they worked for justice.

4. Summary questions

In closing these three lessons on wisdom, ask yourself the following questions for self-evaluation:

a. Are you becoming a woman of excellence?

b. Are you pursuing specific skills in order to increase productivity and enrich those about you?

c. Do you ponder in order to gain insight into God and His wisdom so that you are a treasury?

d. Is your speech wise so that you are able to invite, petition, counsel, reprove, and instruct others with maximum effectiveness?

e. Finally, do you fear the Lord? Do you have a stand-alone, inner core of strength and self-possession based on reverence for God?

•

Heavenly Father,

Help us to practice and embody wisdom,

turning away from folly.

May we fear you in reverence and joy.

In Christ's name,

Amen.

•

Personification of Wisdom—*redeemed*

I am Lady of Wisdom—*redeemed.*

I am the capacity of saved women to emulate Lady Wisdom and empower her traits with the very spirit of Christ. I motivate young Christian women to grow through Bible study, for I am their drive for insight and knowledge. I also keep them working to develop their gifts and skills, because I desire quality and excellence. Without these, how can we offer service to the Lord that is worthy of Him?

One of my greatest gifts to Christians is the rein I provide on the monster of the human tongue. Only with lifelong attention to the development of my aspect will a woman gain any righteous control over that wily beast. With great effort I can help transform James' fire into Solomon's tree of life—capable of silence, praise, petition, reproof, instruction, and healing words of comfort.

I help protect against the Evil One, false doctrines, and my counterfeit—worldly wisdom. With the Bible as my foundation and the Holy Spirit as my guide, I can often see through deceptions, manipulative offers, and impure motives. Wise men seek me, for they know that successful rulers have always depended upon my counsel. I am humble. Although my role is indispensable, I know I am not the most important aspect, and my virtues are not the most fundamental. Lucifer himself had beauty and wisdom to perfection. Yet he rebelled against God. More important than wisdom is love—love for God and love for people. I show my humble and redeemed nature by keeping love for God and for others central.

I am a handmaiden to the worship of God. The fear of God is foundational to my being, and skill in worshiping Him is one of my greatest gifts. My fear of God is not like the trembling of demons who also fear Him. Rather, my fear of God is the fear which casts out all other fears. My fear of God brings refuge, reward, and rejoicing.

The Lord summed me up best—*I am shrewd as a serpent, and innocent as a dove* (Matt. 10:16).

Bible Study of Wisdom—*redeemed*

Before beginning this study, read the entire lesson, pages 46-57.

"Many daughters have done nobly, but you excel them all." Charm is deceitful and beauty is vain, but a woman who fears the LORD, she shall be praised. Give her the product of her hands, and let her works praise her in the gates.

PROVERBS 31:29-31

The twelfth Biblical view of woman

Forsaking folly, the redeemed lady of wisdom embodies God's ideal, the woman of excellence.

The woman of excellence: Who is she?

The previous lessons present both wisdom and folly as archetypes of femininity. That is, they are original patterns or role models, one for good, the other for evil. Throughout the Bible, we see many literary parallelisms between wisdom and wise women. These parallelisms are not accidental. By virtue of God's design, all wise women embody the patterns of "lady" wisdom.

The Hebrew word *chayil* is used to describe a woman of strength, virtue, depth, and noble character. Often translated *the woman of excellence* (Ruth 3:11; Prov. 31:10), this is the term we will use most frequently for the redeemed lady-of-wisdom aspect. A woman who turns away from folly to embody wisdom for others becomes a woman of excellence. Where in the Bible can we see such women? How can we, through Christ, learn to be like them?

1. In the space beneath each reference below, write down the quality or action displayed by "lady" wisdom and by the wise woman of Proverbs 31:10-31.

"lady" wisdom	**the wise woman**
Job 28:12, 18; Prov. 2:1-5	Prov. 31:10
Prov. 8:6-9	Prov. 31:26
Prov. 9:1	Prov. 31:15, 21-24
Prov. 9:10	Prov. 31:30

Points to ponder

While most Christians are familiar with the Proverbs 31 woman, few understand why this poem forms such an appropriate conclusion to the book of Proverbs. In an artistic way, this epilogue about real women answers to the prologue's two metaphorical women—wisdom and folly (Prov. 1-9). In the prologue, young men are urged to seek and love wisdom and are urgently warned to flee folly. In the epilogue, they are exhorted to seek a wise wife. This conclusion describes a real woman who is like the archetypal "lady" wisdom in the book's introduction. Chapter 31 is a character sketch designed to help young men see past mere beauty or charm to "walking wisdom," a wife whose character reflects and even embodies "lady" wisdom. The specific details of this portrait fit an upper-class wife of Israel's kingdom period. Of course, the underlying moral principles are timeless guides for any wise woman and for any man seeking her.

The fear of the Lord

Because the fear of the Lord is the beginning of wisdom and the basis of the character of the woman of excellence, let us examine it more closely.

2. Read Psalm 34:1-14. What do those who fear the Lord do, according to this psalm? What does God do for those who fear Him?

3. How did Nehemiah's fear of the Lord affect his behavior (Neh. 5:15)?

4. If we fear the Lord, how do we use Scripture and prayer to battle sin (Ps. 19:9-14)?

5. As we grow in the fear of the Lord, how will we respond to other fears (Ex. 1:17; Dan. 3:15-18; Matt. 10:28)?

Review

The fear of the Lord is reverential respect for God and His standards based on the conscious knowledge that God is God. Those who fear the Lord:

- Reverence Him;
- Restrain themselves from sin;
- Take refuge in God;
- Rejoice in God's goodness; and
- Seek their reward from God.

Women of excellence: Three portraits of "lady" wisdom

Ruth: A peasant builds her house

Like the wise wife of Proverbs 31, Ruth is a woman of excellence. But unlike the Proverbs 31 woman who is married and well-to-do, Ruth is an impoverished widow. Nevertheless, as a true lady of wisdom, she builds her house. In fact, the house or dynasty she builds is the greatest one of all time, for it becomes the house of King David and Christ.

6. Read the book of Ruth if it is unfamiliar. How does Boaz describe Ruth's reputation in the town (Ruth 2:11-12; 3:11)?

7. What qualities of wisdom do you see in Ruth's daily life (Ruth 2:6-7, 21-23; 3:10)?

8. Ruth exhibits a day-to-day lifestyle of wisdom. Yet it was two great watershed decisions which defined her life and ministry—where to live and whom to marry. In Ruth's day, Israel and Moab were bitter enemies (Deut. 23:3-4; Judg. 3:28-30). Ruth made her new home in a country where she could have been despised as a foreigner. Why did Ruth decide to stay with Naomi and travel to this new home (Ruth 1:16-17; 2:12)? Why do you think Ruth decided to marry Boaz rather than seek a younger man?

Esther: A queen portrays "lady" wisdom

The Proverbs 31 woman is a wealthy wife. Ruth is a poor proselyte. Esther is a believing queen in a pagan harem. Yet Esther, like the other two wise women, also built her life on the fear of the Lord, and has reaped praise for her works down through the centuries.

9. Esther provides one of the most complete portraits of "lady" wisdom in Scripture. As you read the book of Esther, note how Esther emulates "lady" wisdom in the following roles and activities. Write down appropriate verse references for each action listed.

   fears the Lord

   invites only after preparation

   petitions with skill

   spurns a fool

   exalts the wise man

counsels the king

hates evil and does justice

protects her people

showers her people with benefits

The wise woman of Abel

10. How do we know that the wise woman of Abel feared the Lord and loved justice (2 Sam. 20:15-22)?

11. Which of the "inner domains which women guard and keep" do we see her protect in this passage?

Wisdom reproves fools and counsels kings (Prov. 8:14-16). As we seek to emulate wisdom, we should be careful to train and reprove those under our authority, such as our children or students. But it is not proper to reprove or train our authorities, even if they are acting foolishly. If you are married, your husband is your king and you should treat him as such (just as you are his "queen," and he should treat you as such). We are tempted often to mother and scold our men when they act foolishly; that is a wisdom impulse. However, it is not a mature wisdom impulse. A mature lady of wisdom will seek to "counsel the king" as Queen Esther did—with respect, timing, skill, and substantive content.

Christ: Our wisdom

For help answering the following questions, refer to Supplement B, pages 191-192, "How Jesus is our wisdom."

12. Explain the difference in Jesus possessing the divine attribute of wisdom and Jesus being the complete human Sage. How is this a parallel to Jesus being the all-righteous God and Jesus earning perfect human righteousness?

So teach us to number our days, that we may present to Thee a heart of wisdom.

PSALM 90:12

13. We will never share God's divine attributes nor will we attain human perfection in this life as Jesus did. However, Jesus models for us the process by which we will grow in righteousness and wisdom. List some specific ways Jesus grew in wisdom (Luke 2:40, 52; Heb. 2:10, 18; 5:7, 13-14; James 1:1-5).

14. Select the wisdom area in which you most desire to grow: Pondering for insights, increased fear of the Lord, skill in speech (inviting, petitioning, counseling, reproving, or teaching). Explain how you can marshal Bible study, prayer, and your personal relationship with Christ to aid you in this area.

A point to ponder

What is the difference between knowing the works of Rembrandt and knowing Rembrandt himself? How would knowing the works of an artist help you fellowship more deeply with the person of the artist? Conversely, how would personal fellowship with the artist give you insight into his works? How do these questions apply to knowing wisdom and knowing Jesus? Why should a person who claims to know Jesus be wise?

LESSON 17 : Lady of Wisdom – *life lessons*

Learning... to fear God and grow in skill and insight.

1. In one or two paragraphs, write how you would describe this aspect to your daughter or a friend. Feel free to incorporate other creative formats, such as a prayer, song, poem, recipe, story, skit, or even a sketch illustrating this aspect. Include all the basic truths about this aspect.

2. What part of this aspect has meant the most to your life? Why?

3. How is this aspect being lived out in your life right now?

4. Write a paragraph explaining how you are asking God to mature and perfect this aspect in your life. Be specific.

Pray specifically each day this week for God to bring circumstances and people into your life to strengthen your attitudes and actions concerning this aspect.

5. For each of the following categories, identify and describe one woman you think displays in a clear and obvious way the lady-of-wisdom aspect. Briefly explain your choice—what you see in this woman's life or character which illustrates this aspect. You may mention more than one woman, if you wish.

a. A character from the Bible

b. A woman from history (ancient to recent)

c. A fictional character in a novel, fairy tale, legend, etc.

Now may the God of peace Himself sanctify you entirely; and may your spirit and soul and body be preserved complete, without blame at the coming of our Lord Jesus Christ. Faithful is He who calls you, and He also will bring it to pass.

1 THESSALONIANS 5:23-24

d. A character in a film you have seen

Glory of Man

Woman, worship, and sexuality. *Woman is responsive, submissive, beautiful, adorned for her husband and Christ.*

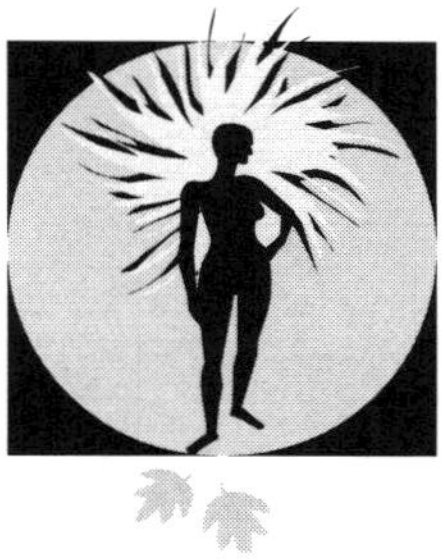

God created

woman to be

Glory of Man.

For a man ought not to have his head covered, since he is the image and glory of God; but the woman is the glory of man. For man does not originate from woman, but woman from man; for indeed man was not created for the woman's sake, but woman for the man's sake. 1 CORINTHIANS 11:7-9

Wives, be subject to your own husbands, as to the Lord. For the husband is the head of the wife, as Christ also is the head of the church, He Himself being the Savior of the body. But as the church is subject to Christ, so also the wives ought to be to their husbands in everything. Husbands, love your wives, just as Christ also loved the church and gave Himself up for her; that He might sanctify her, having cleansed her by the washing of water with the word, that He might present to Himself the church in all her glory, having no spot or wrinkle or any such thing; but that she should be holy and blameless. So husbands ought also to love their own wives as their own bodies. He who loves his own wife loves himself; for no one ever hated his own flesh, but nourishes and cherishes it, just as Christ also does the church, because we are members of His body. FOR THIS CAUSE A MAN SHALL LEAVE HIS FATHER AND MOTHER, AND SHALL CLEAVE TO HIS WIFE; AND THE TWO SHALL BECOME ONE FLESH. This mystery is great; but I am speaking with reference to Christ and the church. Nevertheless let each individual among you also love his own wife even as himself; and let the wife see to it that she respect her husband.

EPHESIANS 5:22-33

LESSON 18 : Glory of Man – *created*

1. The glories of sexuality

1.1 A description of woman

1 Corinthians 11 is about headship. It explains that God is the head of Christ, Christ is the head of man, and man is the head of woman. According to Paul, these headship truths should affect the behavior of believers in public worship. Embedded in his teaching on decorum in worship is our fifth and final definitive statement about woman from the Bible. The key verses are 7-9: *For a man ought not to have his head covered, since he is the image and glory of God; but the woman is the glory of man. 8 For man does not originate from woman, but woman from man; 9 for indeed man was not created for the woman's sake, but woman for the man's sake.*

1.2 From the man and for the man: A source of glory

We have dealt already with the issues of headship and submission in the helper-completer aspect in Genesis 2, where we saw woman created for and from the man at the beginning of creation. In Genesis 2, the key and defining word was **helper**. In 1 Corinthians 11 we have a different view. The topic is worship and the key word is **glory**, a subject we have not covered in the four previous aspects.

1.3 God's image in man and woman is the same.

Before we talk about glory, we need to review ***image***. 1 Corinthians 11:7 says *man is the image and glory of God; but the woman is the glory of man*. It does not specify in whose image woman is. Some teachers down through Church history have said that woman is in the image of man. She is an image of an image. This is wrong. Remember from our Mistress-*created* lesson that woman is the image of God just as the man is (*FAW—Vol. One*, pp. 19-22). Paul does not say woman is in the image of man. He assumes the truth of Genesis 1—that she is the image of God.

1.4 The glory in man and woman is different.

In 1 Corinthians 15:41, Paul writes: *There is one glory of the sun, and another glory of the moon, and another glory of the stars; for star differs from star in glory*. Each part of God's creation reflects a different glory. In image, man and woman are alike; in glory, they differ.

KEY Glory–*created*
person—FEMALE FIGURE ("clothed" in nakedness according to her untested, unashamed, sinless standing before God)
character—SQUARE (untested, sinless)
femininity—CIRCLE (untested, sinless)
role/work—LONG HAIR, SUNBURST (untested, sinless feminine glory)

1.5 What is glory?

Before we can understand what it means for man to be the glory of God or for woman to be the glory of man, let us define ***glory***. First, to glorify or to give glory is to give praise or honor. We might say the man glorified God by telling about Christ's great deeds, or the soldier was honored by a 21-gun salute. In this meaning of glory, something is done to give praise or honor to the one who is being glorified. This is giving glory by **doing** something.

Another way to glorify is by **being** something, showing forth praiseworthy and distinguishing characteristics. Proverbs 20:29 says, *The glory of young men is their strength, and the honor of old men is their gray hair.* This means there is something categorically praiseworthy that distinguishes young men—they are vigorous and strong. Their muscles and their strength are their glory. Old men do not have that glory. What is distinguishing and remarkable about old men is that they have longevity and wisdom based on experience. Gray hair is a symbol or evidence that highlights and shows forth the glory of old men—their years.

2. How is man the "glory of God?"

We will not be able to understand how woman is the glory of man apart from understanding how man is the glory of God. Man is the glory of God in at least three ways. Two are based on who man is. The third is based on something man does.

2.1 Men show forth God's glory in their physical bearing.

First, man's physical bearing and physique show forth evidence of strength and authority. Ultimate strength and authority belong to God alone. But God has granted to men evidences of strength and authority. Man is characterized by heavier bones, bigger muscles, a deeper voice, and chiseled features (the heavier brow and the jutting jaw). All these characteristics project an aura of power and strength.

Man's bearing is different from woman's. It is characterized by self-possession and decisiveness, bespeaking authority. It is completely different from the more graceful sway of the woman.

Man's bearing is different from woman's. It is characterized by self-possession and decisiveness, bespeaking authority. It is completely different from the more graceful sway of the woman. Proverbs 30:29-31 says: *There are three things which are stately in their march, even four which are stately when they walk: 30 the lion which is mighty among beasts and does not retreat before any, 31 the strutting rooster, the male goat also, and a king when his army is with him.* This is a proverb about the stateliness of masculine bearing—a glory which bespeaks courage and leadership.

Consistently and over the decades, men have ranked overwhelmingly as the box-office draws for movie- goers. We like to see men of manly bearing and physique in action. As much as we like to see beautiful women in the movies, they are not nearly as important to most moviegoers as manly men. However, as my husband and I were walking through a photographer's studio one day, I noticed that most of the pictures were of women. I said, "Where are some pictures of men?" My husband replied, "It is very hard to take good still pictures of men, but photographs are a great medium for capturing the beauty of women." I thought about how many magazine covers have beautiful women on them. Action and bearing one can see only through movement; beauty, on the other hand, is made for gazing upon. It makes sense—men in movies, women on covers. It's a difference in glory.

Think about the masculine voice. Think of the voices of a powerful tenor, a resonating bass, or the projection of a skillful stage actor—all different, but all communicating a strength, authority, and depth completely unlike the feminine voice. Think about the sound of a men's choir. It is a glory different from the clear, high, and pure beauty of a feminine choir. Ultimately, all power and authority reside in God. He granted to men the honor of displaying these characteristics in their physical bodies and bearing. This is the first way men are the *glory of God*.

2.2 Man's created roles show forth God's glory.

The second way men show forth the glory of God is in sharing with God His masculine roles, roles such as father, son, bridegroom, husband, warrior, king, and priest. Men take these roles by virtue of their created masculinity. God is the Father, the ultimate Father. Christ is His Son. Christ is the Bridegroom. God the Father and the Son husband Israel and the Church in covenant love. Exodus 15:3 declares that God is a Warrior. In Malachi 1:14, God insists He is a great King, worthy of honor. Hebrews 3:1 says Christ is the ultimate High Priest. These are the roles of God Himself. When men take these roles, they are a glory to God. They show what God is like in a way that women do not. When righteously performed, these roles contain a consistent pattern of activities: Men are to be initiating lovers, leaders, protectors, providers, saviors, and husbandmen.[1] The more men fulfill these activities, the more they are the glory of God, the more they show what God is like.

2.3 Man gives glory to God by leading in worship.

Finally, men are the glory of God because they are created to be the worship leaders for the human race. This is true in both the Old and the New Testaments. The patriarchs built the altars and led their families in praising God. Moses led the nation in building and dedicating the tabernacle as a place to worship God (Ex. 40). David wrote most of the Psalms, designed numerous musical instruments, organized the Levitical choirs, and danced before the Lord with all his might, thus leading the nation in worship. He also planned and prepared for the construction of the temple; Solomon, his son, built and dedicated it (1 Kin. 1-8).

The New Testament commands that men, and not women, be ordained to lead the church as elders and pastors, leading in the interpreting and defending of Scripture and in the care and discipline of the flock (1 Tim. 2:12; 3:1-7; 5:17-18; Titus 1:5-9). Men are to lead in congregational prayer (1 Tim. 2:1-8). According to 1 Corinthians 11, men are to uncover their heads in worship because Christ is directly their Head. Man and woman should be distinguished in worship because they have different heads and different glories. When women are covered in worship, two secondary glories are thus de-emphasized—the glory of man who is woman, and the glory of the woman, which is her hair.

Even in eternity, a great and blazing testimony to man's headship of God's people will shine forth in the New Jerusalem. There the names of twenty-four men will be inscribed forever, the names of the twelve patriarchs of Israel will be on the gates, and the names of the twelve apostles of Christ will be written on the foundation stones (Rev. 21:12-14). Truly, man's headship and his created role as the glory of God are not mishaps of the curse; rather, they are created from the beginning and gloriously redeemed for eternity.

2.4 Review

- Men show forth God's glory in their physical bearing of strength and authority.
- Men share the masculine roles with God (including Father, Son, Bridegroom, King, and Priest).
- Men are the glory of God because they lead the human race in worship.

1. For further development of these ideas, refer to section 4.3 in this chapter, as well as the summary of *Five Aspects of Man* in Supplement B—FAQ, pages 173-179, questions 11 and 12.

3. How is woman the glory of man?

3.1 Woman was made from and for man.

1 Corinthians 11: 7 says woman is the *glory of man*. Verses 8-9 explain why: *For man does not originate from woman, but woman from man; 9 for indeed man was not created for the woman's sake, but woman for the man's sake.* How does woman being from and for the man bring glory to him? Man is the only creature to have another creature fully in the image of God, tailor-made for him. This is a great honor and glory for man. The greatness of this truth will be highlighted if we consider God's other creatures, those both lower and higher than man—the animals and the angels.

Animals were made directly from the earth. They have mates, to be sure. There are daddy lions and mommy lions, boy ostriches and girl ostriches. But the female ostrich was not made from the side of the male ostrich, and the mommy lion was not made from the side of the daddy lion. They were all made simply and directly from the earth. None of these animals, male or female, has the image of God. They are magnificent beasts, but finally, just beasts. They are mated animals. This is a marvel, but what happens with man if far more wonderful.

Angels, unlike the animals, do bear the image of God as men do. But unlike men, they were not given mates.[2] Always referred to in the masculine and appearing as men, angels are organized in armies,[3] not families. These masculine and military creatures spend their time singing God's praises, debating, working, ruling over nature, acting as God's emissaries, and making war (the elect angels against the fallen demons). Angels are intelligent, powerful, awesome creatures; nevertheless, they were not given mates, and thus they do not receive the kind of sexual glory human men do.[4]

These things in combination—the image of God, the female coming from the male, romantic and sexual love, marriage, babies, genealogies—are a unique glory to the human race in this age. Particularly this glory belongs to man, because it is an honor for him to have someone made from him and for him. There is nothing else like this in the revealed universe except Christ and His own Bride. Man is allowed to picture Christ in having his own bride come out of his side. This is definitely a glory.

Genesis 6 gives evidence that the fallen angels were jealous of man's glorious gift. Genesis 6:2 says, *the sons of God* [always an expression for angels in the Old Testament] *saw that the daughters of men were beautiful; and they took wives for themselves, whomever they chose.* Apparently, these fallen angels were jealous that men had beautiful women to be their counterparts. The demons, perhaps angry that God had not made anything like this for them, transgressed the angel/human boundary and somehow took women for themselves. God washed away these illicit angel/human bondings and their offspring (Gen. 6:4) in the flood. It is very possible that Jude reveals the fate of these same wicked angels in 1:6 when he writes, *And angels who did not keep their own domain, but abandoned their proper abode, He has kept in eternal bonds under darkness for the judgment of the great day.*

2. In the Old Testament, angels are called the *sons of God* repeatedly and exclusively (Gen. 6:2, 4; Job 1:6; 2:1; 38:7). As His sons, they share God's image, as can be substantiated in verses such as Genesis 5:3 and Luke 20:36. In Luke 20:34-35, Jesus makes clear that angels do not marry.

3. *The Lord of Hosts* means "the Lord of armies," or as Eugene Peterson paraphrases it, "God is King of the Angel Armies." *The Message: New Testament With Psalms and Proverbs*, "NavPress, 1995."

4. For a more complete study of the nature, organization, and duties of angels, see your concordance and/or a Biblically based angelology such as G. B. Funderburk, "Angel," in *The Zondervan Pictorial Encyclopedia of the Bible*, Vol. 1, ed. by Merrill C. Tenney (Grand Rapids, MI: Zondervan Publishing House, 1975),160-166.

The fact that angels lack wives may also explain 1 Corinthians 11:10 in part: *Therefore the woman ought to have a symbol of authority on her head, because of the angels.* 1 Peter 1:12 says that the angels long to look into the redeeming grace of God in the lives of human beings. Angels are not saved by grace (Heb. 2:16); they are either elect or damned. Saving grace is something they learn about by watching us. But if we, as human beings, do not handle authority properly in the worship of God (which is something angels understand very well), then how can we teach them about gracious love (which is something they understand very little)? Perhaps this is what Paul is thinking—that our ability to worship God in proper relationship to headship, keeps us from ruining our testimony, not only among ourselves, but also before unseen, angelic observers.

In summary, woman is a great glory to man. He alone of all creatures—not the animals below, not the angels above—has a person fully in the image of God who is made from him and for him.

3.2 Woman's sexual response is a special glory to man.

We have talked about woman as man's helper, companion, and counselor. However, we have not focused on sexual and erotic love, which are a very important part of our lives. In God's plan, beauty and glory are inextricably linked with sexual love. The whole book of Song of Solomon is devoted to expressing the beauty and wonder of erotic love between a man and a woman. That book is filled with passages of the husband praising the beauty and feminine charms of his wife, and the wife praising the man for his masculine traits. Romantic love is something God intended to be a unique and crowning glory in our sexuality. Other passages on this topic: Psalm 45 (the royal wedding psalm); Ezekiel 16 (compares the love of God and Israel to a husband and wife over a lifetime); Ephesians 5 (reveals the husbandly love of Christ for His Church); and Revelation 21 (unveils the New Jerusalem in bridal glory). Sexual glory is an important gender theme, reflective of God's glory.

After making love to his bride, the bridegroom in Song of Solomon 5:1 says: *I have come into my garden, my sister, my bride; I have gathered my myrrh along with my balsam. I have eaten my honeycomb and my honey; I have drunk my wine and my milk.* Notice the bridegroom uses the most lavish metaphors imaginable to describe the sensual delights of love. He also emphasizes that all these treasures belong to him. His wife is his garden and the delights therein are his. The rest of the verse is spoken by the narrator of the song, probably God Himself, who says, *Eat, friends; drink and imbibe deeply, O lovers.* God blesses the pleasure and the joy of sexual love in marriage.

In lovemaking, the man actually enters the woman. His entering into the woman's body is likened to entering a garden or opening a spring or well (Song 4:12-16; Prov. 5:15-18). God made the woman's body and her soul to have a response to the man's entering. What is this response—indifference, yawning, mild interest? Ideally the response should register somewhere between thrill and wild ecstasy! This is the orgasmic joy and climax of the sexual response which God created the woman to have. When that response is not there, there is a sense of lost glory. There are many reasons why this response may not be there. This may not be the fault of the man or the woman. Nevertheless, if a man's wife does not respond to him, or cannot respond to him, something that was to be a unique glory to him—an affirmation of his manhood—has been lost.

Man can earn glory and affirm his manhood in only two areas. One area is the world of work or combat (whether academics, sports, war, or business), where he goes out into nature to conquer, rule, and subdue. The other is the world of relationships and love, where he wins the response of the woman. If the response of his wife is taken away, something very basic to his psychological and sexual foundation will be taken away. Many times such a man will feel that his glory is lost.

4. How woman is the glory of mankind

4.1 Woman: The glory of man the creature

Before going further, I want to shift our focus from thinking about woman as the glory of man the individual male, to thinking of woman as the glory of mankind. Is this valid to do? In the first and tightest focus, we see woman from and for man, the male. If we step back and see man as the glory of God, we can also see woman as the glory of man in the sense of mankind. Man is the glory of God the Creator; woman is the glory of the creature.

4.2 The glory of God and the glory of humanity

Remember the creation scene from Genesis 2. God takes some clay and builds the first masculine body. He puts the breath of life into the man, and he becomes a living soul. In so doing, God gives the man an aura of glory, one that bespeaks authority, strength, and power, the capacity to be a father, a son, a bridegroom, and a king. That is, He makes man the glory of God. Then God takes a portion of flesh and bone from the man and makes a second human being. He makes this body from human flesh, and puts the divine image in this human being just as He did with the first. But this time, this creature is covered with a different aura of glory. This person is not covered with the glory of God. This human, the woman, is covered with the glory of mankind, the glory of being the creature. What does this mean?

What is man, the creature, really? He is not all powerful or full of authority. The Scriptures ask what man is that God should be mindful of him? He is a vapor. His glory is but a flower. He is like the grass. Human beings are actually weak, transitory, and dependent, needing to walk by faith. When God glorified the woman, He made that delicate, transitory, needy, dependent nature beautiful and resplendent. He highlighted all the creaturely traits in her. Think about woman's physical being. Her bones are smaller and weaker. Is that a shame to her? No, delicacy is considered beautiful, because God made the relative weakness of women glorious. Most women don't mind their smaller frames, because they rightly sense that the fineness of their bones is beautiful. It is not a humiliation to be weak in this sense. Delicate features are beautiful.

Being covered and adorned is basic to woman's glory as a creature in a way it is not to man's.

Men are not built in soul or body to be responders. Customarily, they are unreadable. Yet God fashioned the entire feminine facial structure for responsiveness. He glorified the responder nature in her by giving her bigger eyes, softer facial muscles, fuller lips, and sensitive skin which displays many more shades of color. Woman's emotional range is greater than the man's. Physically and biochemically, her highs tend to be higher, her lows lower. She can change faster, and in so doing, she pictures in another way the responsive and transitory nature of the creature.

1 Corinthians 11:15 says that long hair is a glory to a woman because it was given to her for a covering. The woman's body is smaller, softer, and rounder. Her weakness calls for protection; her beauty calls for adornment. Artists invariably depict Eve with long and beautiful hair. Her hair was a glorious covering—her first adornment and her first protection. The consensus through history, down to the little boys of our modern day, is that long hair is beautiful and feminine. Women have added many other coverings for protection and adornment—veils, full dresses, cloaks, all kinds of jewels, and ornaments. Men wear clothing and some adornments, but the emphasis is not nearly so great. Being covered and adorned is basic to woman's glory as a creature in a way it is not to man's.

4.3 Woman's roles glorify the man's roles.

Finally, woman's roles are a glory to the man. Her roles are the counterparts to his. Man is father, she is mother. He is bridegroom, she is bride. He is husband, she is wife. He is king, she is queen. The feminine roles answer to, and correspond to, the masculine roles. What we do in these corresponding roles emphasizes how our glories differ. There are certain activities which are fundamental to the masculine roles. Man should be the initiating lover, leading, protecting, providing, and husbanding. What does the woman do in her roles that corresponds to the man?

Initiator and responder

Wherein man is the initiating lover, woman is a responding lover. Man pursues the woman; he makes love to her. She receives him and responds to his love. This is pictured in our bodies, in our souls, and in our spirits. Woman is adorned and glorified with beauty in order to please and receive her man.

Leader and helper

When we shift the emphasis from man as lover to man as leader, the emphasis in woman shifts from responder to follower/helper. New Testament submission emphasizes the woman's response to and support of the man's leadership. This is not about "beating her into place." Wifely submission is about supporting the husband as leader and fulfilling her role as his helper.

Husbandman and lifegiver

When woman is lifegiver, man must be her husbandman, protecting and providing. If a woman stays home to focus on giving life to others, she cannot be out in the world earning a living. She has to trust the man to be the principal breadwinner. The work of lifegiver makes the woman vulnerable; it requires dependence upon someone else to do most of the providing and protecting. Psalms 128:3 says to the man who fears the LORD: *Your wife shall be like a fruitful vine within your house, your children like olive plants around your table.* To be a fruitful vine, a wife must be willing to receive her husband's provisions, respond to his care, and embrace fruit-bearing; she must be willing to see herself as a fruitful vine. If she wants only to be like the man, by his side or leading him in the world, she will never be a beautiful garden for him *in the very heart of his house* (Ps. 128:3, NKJV), and he will never fulfill his husbandman role. Fulfilling these roles takes faith and a willingness to be dependent on the part of the woman, and diligence and service on the part of the man.

Submission to authority; trust in faithfulness

Virtues of the responder are the essence of femininity. 1 Peter 3:4 tells us that... *the imperishable quality of a gentle and quiet spirit, ... is precious in the sight of God.* What is *a gentle, quiet spirit*? The word ***gentle*** means meek, under authority; it is synonymous with submission. The word ***quiet*** means full of faith, not troubled, not upset or fearful; it is synonymous with trust. From God's viewpoint, the height of femininity—its most treasured and valuable essence—is the gentle, quiet spirit. These two qualities—submission (the opposite of a rebellious, contentious spirit) and trust (the opposite of a fearful, worried spirit)—are the height of feminine beauty.

Notice that these two virtues are creaturely qualities. They are virtues of a responder: Submission is an attitude toward the authority of God; trust is an attitude about the faithfulness of God. All people, both men and women, are creatures and all people should have submission and faith.

But because woman is the glory of the creature, these creaturely virtues are brought to a special height and beauty in her, just as courage and integrity are emphasized in the man (who is not the glory of the creature, but who is, instead, the glory of God).

Imitating Christ and the Church

If all is not yet clear on the differing glories of man and woman, Ephesians 5:22-33 clears away the fog. Husbands are to be like Christ; wives are to be like the Church. Men are to take as their role model the masculine Christ; wives are to take as their role model the feminine Church created from Christ's side, even as Eve was created from the side of Adam. Husbands are to model their love and leadership after Christ. Wives are follow the pattern of the Church's subjection in her relationship to Christ. **Christ and the Church are the role models that anchor and amplify the glories of man and woman.** To be the glory of God means that man in marriage takes Christ's roles and seeks to imitate Him. To be the glory of man means that woman takes the believer's roles toward her husband, the roles of the Church toward Christ.

5. Interdependence: The balancing truth

5.1 "However"

Thus far we have been emphasizing the differences between the sexes. While man and woman are the same in image, in glory they are different. Consider 1 Corinthians 11:11-12 for the very important balancing truth of interdependence: *However, in the Lord, neither is woman independent of man, nor is man independent of woman. 12 For as the woman originates from the man, so also the man has his birth through the woman; and all things originate from God.*

5.2 Sex classic

Paul has been talking about the basic and foundational differences between the sexes, what I call **sex classic**. Man is the leader, woman the helper. Man is strong, woman is beautiful. Man is brave, woman is merciful. Man is aggressive, woman is conciliatory. Man is logical, woman is intuitive. These basic characteristics have been observed through all time and in all cultures as typical of the sexes. But as soon as you say something is true about one sex, you sense that in a way it is also true about the other sex. Paul knows this. Paul has just been emphasizing that it is important that woman came from man, that Eve came from Adam, that Adam was the head and Eve was his helper. He has just been teaching this. But then he says, it is also true that man is from the woman. Men are born from their mothers. Therefore, there is an interdependence.

> The sexes do the same things in different ways such that they are interdependent, but not interchangeable.

5.3 Examples of sexual interdependence built upon the differences

Woman came from man. Men come from women. But notice that they do not come from each other in exactly the same way. The way that woman came from man is in the original creation. God made the first woman from the side of the first man. But the way that men come from women is that little boy babies grow in their mothers' wombs and are born. So while each comes from the other, it is not in exactly the same way. Adam did not have a womb, and he did not give birth to baby Eve. Sons do not come out of their mothers' sides. The sexes are balanced, but they are different. In the balance, there is interdependence. The sexes do the same things but in different ways such that they are interdependent, but not interchangeable. This is important. Let me give you four more examples.

Both are dependent.

Women lean on men, but men lean on women. Song of Solomon 8:5a describes a familiar picture, *Who is this coming up from the wilderness, leaning upon her beloved?* The poet sees the Shunammite leaning on the arm of her lover. This is the classic picture of a woman resting on a man's shoulder. The woman is usually smaller, shorter, and there is a time she likes to lean on her husband. But Proverbs 31:11 says the husband's heart safely trusts his wise wife. To **trust** means to depend on, to rest on with all one's weight. So here is the picture, not of the wife leaning physically or spiritually on the man, but of the man resting on the woman, depending on her. In Proverbs 31, the husband is sitting at the gate helping run the community. He is depending on his wife's virtue and strength to run his household, take care of his children, manage his wealth, and rule his servants. Proverb 12:4 says, *An excellent wife is the crown of her husband, but she who causes shame is like rottenness in his bones.* Certainly, the man is presented in a position of almost horrifying vulnerability. If his wife is not wise, his bones will rot. He is depending upon her. If she lets him down, he will suffer decay at the core of his structure.

Both glorify.

In a previous section, we learned how the woman glorifies the man with her sexual response. When she responds to her husband with desire, it glorifies him, affirming his masculinity. Yet, his desire for her is also a glory to her. Song of Solomon 7:10 records the mature statement of the Shunammite's marital security, *"I am my beloved's, and his desire is toward me."*[5] If the man desires the woman, seeks and pursues her, it is a glory to her, just as her receiving him is a glory to him. She is glorified by his pursuit; he is glorified by her response. They are mutually glorified, but not in exactly the same way.

Both protect.

Man protects woman. We all have the picture of the man going off to war to protect the nation from the enemy. If an attacker comes, we expect the man to be the first one to step forth, to beat off the criminal physically. But there are ways women protect men. In Scripture, women frequently protect men physically by hiding them in their inner domains: Rahab hides the spies (Josh 2); and David's wife helps him escape (1 Sam. 19:11-17). Spiritually, women protect men with their purity, as we have discussed already (*FAW–Vol. One*, pp. 163-166). Abigail petitions David and thus protects him from his murderous fury against Nabal (1 Sam. 25). When a woman is pure, she protects a man from his lower nature. She makes it easier for him to be a good man. An evil woman opens up a man to his own destruction.

---

5. The progression from Song 2:16 (*My beloved is mine, and I am his*) to 6:3 (*I am my beloved's, and my beloved is mine*) to 7:10 has been noted often. The bride goes from emphasizing her possession of her man, to his possession of her, to rest on his possession and his desire for her. (Refer to Susan Foh quote, *FAW–Vol. One*, p. 114.)

Both nurture.

What about nurturing? We know women are nurturers; they give life and nurture to their children and families. But the husbandman role is a nurturing role as well. Christ nurtures the Church and expects husbands to follow His lead toward their wives. God is a vinedresser—One who tends His gardens carefully (Is. 5:1-7). Part of a man's manliness is learning to care for his domain—whether it is wife, farm, or business. Men should be nurturers, but not because they morph into housewives. They should be nurturers because they fulfill their role as husbandmen in their domains—protecting, cultivating, and making productive all that is under their charge.

5.4 Review

Man and woman both glorify each other. They nurture each other. They lean on and protect one another. But they do not do so in the same ways. Those who make the interdependence of man and woman a reason for sexual interchangeability are either foolish or wicked, because the created differences are essential. Man is man. He is the leader, the husband, the father, the glory of God. Woman is the helper, the mother, the glory of man. One must never deny the truths of sexual difference in an attempt to bolster the truths of sexual mutuality. The interdependence and mutuality of man and woman are built upon their differences, all leading to the glory of God Himself. To use the interdependence of the sexes as a weapon to destroy their created differences is wicked. It not only destroys the glory of God in our sexuality, but it cuts us off from one another and from ourselves. Instead, we must handle these doctrines the same way we handle the deity and the humanity of Christ. We teach and understand both, holding them together as a non-contradictory unity.

5.5 Closing pictures

Fulfilling your glory-of-man aspect is not dependent upon being beautiful physically. Those who are unremarkable in body are nevertheless capable of apprehending the marvel of sexuality—the wonder of the glory of God in man, the beauty of the glory of man in woman. Holding these truths as precious in our souls is the foundation of a feminine confidence and beauty which will be appreciated by both God and men.

To illustrate these glory truths, consider a few meditations on ice dancers. One main reason why ice dancing is soaring in popularity is because it pictures the beauty of sexual glory. The dancers picture masculine and feminine glory coming together in interdependence and beauty. Remember, our bodies are not all that we are, and they are not the most important thing that we are. Yet our bodies are consistent with who we are; thus they can illustrate beautifully what God intends for our whole beings. In these dancers, we can see some of the beauty and the glory that God intended to be in the spirit of all of us, as we dance and skate through life together.

The first characteristic of an accomplished ice dancing or pairs skating team is that they are individually strong skaters. Skating weaknesses will be exacerbated in partnership, not covered up. It is the same in life. We must be strong individuals, whether man or woman, full of the basic virtues, if we are ever to be a glory with the opposite sex. Ice dancers sometimes skate side by side, not even touching, doing the same thing at the same time. This reflects man's and woman's commonality and their ability to do the same things.

The dramatic moves—the spirals, lifts, and throws—especially picture the glory of sexuality. In the death spiral, the man braces himself in order to hold the entire weight of the woman with her head mere inches off the ice. It requires strength and stability from him. What does it require from her? Amazing trust and courage (!) to be willing to be that vulnerable and dependent, in order to create the beautiful motion. To perform lifts, the man must work continually on strength. He must lift and hold the woman in a stable position, sometimes even at high speed. That the lifts glorify the woman by literally exalting her is plain to see. The throws require even more strength from the man and more courage from the woman. She has to be dependent in allowing the man to launch her, and yet independent in landing on her own skates with only her own balance to guide her.

Sometimes the man drops the woman. How do you think she feels? Who do you think is mad? What about the times the man does everything right but the woman falls and spoils the routine? What a picture of marriage! Sometimes the husband, who is supposed to be supporting his wife, drops her on the ice of life, as it were, and makes her very angry. Sometimes he does everything perfectly, but she is the one who falls down and ruins the whole sequence. I wonder how many pairs have walked off the ice and said, "Forget this." Pairs succeed only when both the man and the woman keep forgiving and keep trying. He has to keep working at being strong and stable. She has to keep working on trust, proper dependence, and balance, even when he throws her cockeyed. They must practice harmony until they move as one.

I know a young woman who is teaching her fiancé to dance, not only for the enjoyment of it, but for the tutorial it will be for their whole marriage. As she says, it is amazing how the techniques of ballroom dancing picture the dynamics of the man-woman relationship. Most people not only see, they feel the beauty and glory of a couple spinning around the floor in harmony—man leading, woman following, both moving as one to music that envelops them. This is the glory aspect of sexuality. This is a picture of how God intends the relationship of man and woman to be. Not marching, not dragging, not pushing or pulling; rather, moving as one to a music that comes from beyond them both.

5.6 Application questions

Here are five questions to help you evaluate your understanding of God's plan for the sexes and their individual glories:

- Do you enjoy being a woman?
- Do you like men and think they are a good idea?
- Do you see the glory of each sex as different, yet wonderful in its own way?
- Do you see the glory of each sex as completing and complementing the other, or do you think that men must be put down so women can be raised up, or vice versa?
- Finally, do you love beauty? Is it in your soul? Do you seek to give it to others?

Woman is the quintessential creature. If man is the head of the creation, woman is the crown. If he is the first person, the leader, she is the last person, the completion. In her, all the creaturely traits and roles are beautified, made resplendent, and highlighted. It is a glorious thing to be a woman. It is a glory different from the man's glory, but it is a great glory, for we all are creatures. Our privilege and calling as women is to highlight creatureliness in our beings, to model the gentle spirit, to display faith, trust, and peacefulness, thus adorning our lives with the lasting beauty that pleases God Himself.

Profile of Glory—*created*

Key Bible passages
1 Corinthians 11:3-16; Ephesians 5:22-33

Focus on God
Father, Christ as Bridegroom and King

Created basis of this aspect
As image-bearers, man and woman are the same; they are both in the image of God. As glory-bearers, they differ. Man is the glory of God who is his Head; woman is the glory of man who is her head.

Roles of this aspect
Reverer/admirer of male leader; desired and cherished lover of husband, adorned and adored as such; especially bride; dependent on father or husband for leadership, protection, and provision; pleasing and submissive responder

Related Bible passages
Fathers and husbands oversee daughters' and wives' vows (Num. 30:1-16); the royal Bridegroom and bride (Ps. 45); an excellent wife is the crown of her husband (Prov. 12:4); *"I am my beloved's, and his desire is for me"* (Song 7:10); Israel the bride and wife of God (Ezek. 16:1-63); queenly beauty (Esther); commands to revere and be subject to husbands (Eph. 5:22-33); woman the weaker vessel (1 Pet. 3:1-7); Church as bride of Christ (Rev. 19:7-9; 21:9-24)

Chief drives and motives
To find in men that which she can admire, praise, and depend upon; to find a man who commands her respect and wins her love; to please, be beautiful for, desired, and cherished by such a man

Focus and/or areas of application
The sexes as they differ; men—as leaders, providers, lovers; especially father and husband

Characteristics
Responsive, attentive, sensitive, pure, trusting, pretty, dependent, adorned, temperamental, charming, amorous, soft, delicate, glorious

Character emphasis
Purity, worship, beauty

KEY to diagram at right

SYMBOLS OF GOD

Person–HAND–God is Creator (hand creates man). He is Spirit (hand is transparent), infinite (hand fades, as into infinity), and preeminent (hand's position–above creation; hand's size–able to hold world).

Character–SQUARE–God's character is holy (square suggests the cube of the Holy of Holies) and infinite in all His attributes (square fades, as into infinity).

Masculinity–TRIANGLE–The triangle represents the original Masculine–the Trinity. God is the Initiator who descends and enters into His creation (triangle penetrates world). His masculinity is infinite (triangle fades, as into infinity).

Words
God the Father–2 PETER 1:17; EPHESIANS 1:22-23
God the Son–JOHN 17:4
God the Son speaks of God the Holy Spirit–JOHN 16:14

Roles/work–HAND, CROSS, DOVE, WORDS–God is active within His creation as Initiator, Father, Bridegroom, King, Teacher, and Comforter.

SYMBOLS OF CREATION

Femininity–CIRCLE–The circle reflects the spherical shape of the sun/moon/world/womb. Feminine in relation to God, the creation is designed to receive her masculine Creator (pale triangle at top of world). All femininity is created and therefore finite (bounded edge doesn't fade).

Mankind's dwelling–PHOTO of EARTH–The world is man's home (peaceable place full of life). The world is finite (bounded edge) and subordinate to God (position–below God; small size–fits in God's hand).

SYMBOLS OF MANKIND

Persons–SEX-DISTINCT FIGURES–God created man, male and female (sex-classic silhouettes). They are "clothed" in nakedness according to their untested, unashamed, sinless standing before God. Man is finite (bounded edges).

Character–SQUARE–Man is created in the image of God (squares smaller than but reflective of God's square). Both man and woman are created in the image of God (they don't share a square). Man's character is finite in all his attributes (bounded edges).

Masculinity–TRIANGLE–Man's masculinity reflects God's, but is finite (bounded edges).

Femininity–CIRCLE–Woman's femininity reflects creation's and is likewise finite (bounded edge).

Words–1 TIMOTHY 1:17; 1 CORINTHIANS 11:3, 7–Mankind responds to God with faith, praise, and worship. Mankind's differing glories are revealed.

Feminine role/work–Glory of Man–LONG HAIR, SUNBURST–Sharing in the creation's and the Church's femininity, woman reflects their characteristics and roles. She is not worship, but a picture of it.

Masculine role/work–Glory of God–LIGHT RAYS–Sharing in God's masculinity, man reflects God's characteristics and roles. The position of his icon–above woman–is consistent with man's position as her head; he is to lead worship (refer to *FAW–Vol. Two*, p. 179).

Glory of Man –
created

God the Father
is the Head of Christ.

"This is My beloved Son with whom I am well-pleased."

And He put all things in subjection under His feet, and gave Him as head over all things to the church, which is His body...

God the Son
is the Head of every man and of the Church.

"I glorified Thee on the earth, having accomplished the work which Thou hast given Me to do."

God the Holy Spirit
descends from the Father and from the Son.

"He shall glorify Me; for He shall take of Mine, and shall disclose it to you."

Woman glorifies God by magnifying the faith and fruitfulness of the creation, and by emulating the Church.

Man glorifies God by displaying His masculine nature and roles, and by emulating Christ's headship.

Woman is the glory of man and mankind.

She takes the creature's roles as helper, fruit-bearer, glorifier.

She glorifies her human lord and her heavenly King with submission, adornment, purity, and love.

She emulates the Church's membership, as her husband emulates Christ's headship.

Personification of Glory—*created*

I am Glory of Man—*created.*

The flower and crown of all creation, I am the quintessential creature. The glories of the creature and creation are brought to their most beautiful expression in me. Seasonal, fragile, and responsive, I can be as delicate as a tundra flower or as fiery as a volcanic explosion. My temperament and moods are legendary.

My deepest longing is to be cherished and passionately desired by a man who commands my respect and wins my love. I delight in masculine men—their objective grip on the world, their strength, courage, and bearing. I delight in being a feminine woman.

I am not ashamed of my vulnerability or my prerogatives. If there are fire and ice or secret gardens of desire, they are my domain. If passion is inflamed by restraint and satisfied with water and wine, it is because I am cherished.

I am the weaker, more delicate vessel. To live and flourish, I need man as hero and lover, one who will protect, adore, and adorn me. My beauty and response, like many luxuries, cannot bear their own weight entirely. I need support and shelter; therefore covering is a glory to me. In fact, I love to be covered—in a lovely home, in beautiful clothes, fabulous jewels, luxurious perfumes, and a God-given cloud of hair!

My father and husband provide a home for me, protect me with their names, and guard my purity. My husband's love is, by definition, jealous. I am his uniquely exclusive and glorifying possession. He does all he can to keep me for his own.

I am not worship, but I am a picture of it.

Bible Study of Glory—*created*

Before beginning this study, read the entire lesson, pages 68-82.

For a man ought not to have his head covered, since he is the image and glory of God; but the woman is the glory of man. For man does not originate from woman, but woman from man; for indeed man was not created for the woman's sake, but woman for the man's sake.

1 CORINTHIANS 3:15

The thirteenth Biblical view of woman

As creation's crown, woman honors God and man with her respect, purity, and love.

Looking at woman again, for the fifth time

Woman is described as from and for the man in Genesis 2 and 1 Corinthians 11. In Genesis 2, she is defined as man's helper; in 1 Corinthians she is called his *glory*. As the helper-completer aspect explored the world of work and fellowship, the glory aspect explores the world of love and desire. Beauty, adornment, passion, and romance are glory themes in the Bible, just as they are in our own lives. Scripture not only describes the nature of this sexual glory, but reveals the ultimate meaning behind it as well. Learning to be the glory of man righteously is basic to our femininity. More importantly, it is basic to glorifying God as our Creator and Redeemer.

The glories of sexuality

1. Fill out the following chart (according to Gen. 1:27; 1 Cor. 11:3; 15:41).

	Man	**Woman**
Who is his/her head?		
Whose image is he/she?		
Whose glory is he/she?		

2. Define **glory** according to your dictionary.

3. Consider the following two definitions of glory, and indicate whether you think definition (a) or (b) best describes the verses below:

   a. the act of honoring someone through praise, recognition, or gratitude (something one does);
   b. a characteristic that displays distinguishing or praiseworthy traits (something one is).

Prov. 17:6	1 Cor. 11:7
Prov. 20:29	1 Cor. 11:14-15
Luke 2:13-14	Heb. 1:3

4. Proverbs 30:29-31 is an interesting passage on masculine presence. When you think of glorious physical masculinity, what do you think of? Consider such things as height, physique, features, singing and speaking voice, and bearing.

5. When you think of glorious spiritual masculinity, what do you think of? Consider Ephesians 5:25-29 for husbands, Ephesians 6:4 for fathers, and Acts 20:17, 28-31 for church elders.

6. By virtue of their masculinity, men share many of God's roles with Him. In these roles they represent and reflect God. For example, men share the roles of father and son with God. What other roles do men share with God (Ex. 15:3-4; Mal. 1:14; Heb. 2:17)?

7. All through the history of the human race—from Adam to the Patriarchs, to the priests, prophets, apostles, and pastors of the New Testament age—men have led and been expected to lead the human race in worship, because Christ is their direct Head (1 Cor. 11:3-7). What eternal testimony to this truth is mentioned in Revelation 21:10-14?

Review

Men are the glory of God in at least three ways:

- Men show forth God's glory in their **physical bearing**, strength, and authority;
- Men share the **masculine roles** with God including Father, Son, Bridegroom, King, and Priest; and
- Men are the glory of God because they lead the human race in **worship**.

How is woman the glory of man?

8. Why is it a special glory to man to have woman made from him and for him? In answering this question, consider how humans differ from the animals and the angels as regards mating and marriage. As far as we know, there is only one other relationship in the universe that follows the pattern of human sexuality as outlined in Genesis 2. What is it (Eph. 5:31-32)?

9. In Song of Solomon 4:9-5:1, God reveals how He intended sexual love to be. Briefly summarize the bridegroom's feelings about his wedding night. How is this experience a glory to him?

How is woman the glory of mankind?

10. If man's masculine roles reflect God's roles, who or what do woman's feminine roles reflect (Eph. 5:24, 31, 32; Rev. 21:2, 9-11)?

11. What physical characteristics of woman especially suit her role as a picture of Christ's Church (Ps. 128:3; 1 Pet. 3:7)? What spiritual ideals of womanhood highlight her as a picture of the faithful believer (Ps. 45:10-11, 13; 1 Pet. 3:1-4; Titus 2:3-5)?

Review

At the creation, Eve was made from and for the man, to picture the Church as she relates to her husband. The man was created to picture Christ, the Head of the Church, as he relates to his wife. Woman is not just the glory of a man. She is the glory of mankind because creaturely qualities are highlighted in her as the divine qualities are highlighted in man. In woman, the weak, fragile, and transitory nature of the creature is highlighted and made resplendent in feminine beauty. Her smaller bones, larger eyes, softer voice, and capacities to nurture and bear fruit picture the dependent, responsive, and fruitbearing believer. It is woman's glory to picture the believer. Therefore, willing submission and faith (*the gentle, quiet spirit*) are the hallmarks of her spiritual beauty, because these are the quintessential virtues of the believer.

Interdependence: The balancing truth

12. Read 1 Corinthians 11:8-12. How does this passage teach the following:

    Man and woman are different.

    Man and woman are interdependent.

    Man and woman are both dependent upon God.

13. Examine the following verses to find how men and women are doing the same things for one another. Do they do the same things in the same ways? If you can, add other examples from the lesson material, or from your own experience, of man's and woman's interdependence.

Man	**Woman**
Eph. 5:28-29	Prov. 31:11, 14-15
1 Pet. 3:7	Prov. 12:4
Neh. 4:13-14	Josh. 2:1-4

Review

God has created us either male or female. These roles are interdependent, balanced, and equally valuable. Man and woman do the same things, but not in the same ways. The interdependence and mutuality of man and woman must never be used as arguments for their interchangeability. The attempt to level or destroy the created differences in man and woman and their roles destroys the very created capacities which make their unity possible. It is the complementary interlocking of man and woman in their created differences which allows us to bless one another and glorify God.

Accepting the glory God has given me

You are the glory of man because God has created you a woman—whether you are single or married, old or young, pretty or plain. Being the glory of man is not something you earn or do. Rather, it is something you accept and fulfill, much like your salvation. If you have accepted Christ as your Savior, then you are a Christian. You can walk in His ways or you can rebel against Him. You can adorn your faith or you can dishonor it. It is much the same with your femininity and your glory-of-man aspect. If you were born a woman, then you are the glory of man by definition. It is your heritage to express for evil or good.

14. Think through why you do or do not enjoy being a woman. Write a prayer thanking God for creating you to picture the believer and the Church. Ask Him to help you accept your femininity in specific areas which you may have rejected it before.

15. Men and women do almost all the same things—but they do them in different ways. Select one of the following: Nourishing, protecting, counseling, glorifying, defending. Explain how you have learned to do this in a way appropriate for a woman. Can you think of at least one new attitude or action which will help you live interdependently with men, but not as if you were interchangeable with them?

> *For God, who said, "Light shall shine out of darkness," is the One who has shone in our hearts to give the light of the knowledge of the glory of God in the face of Christ. But we have this treasure in earthen vessels, that the surpassing greatness of the power may be of God and not from ourselves.*
>
> 2 CORINTHIANS 4:6-7

LESSON 19 Glory of Man – *fallen*

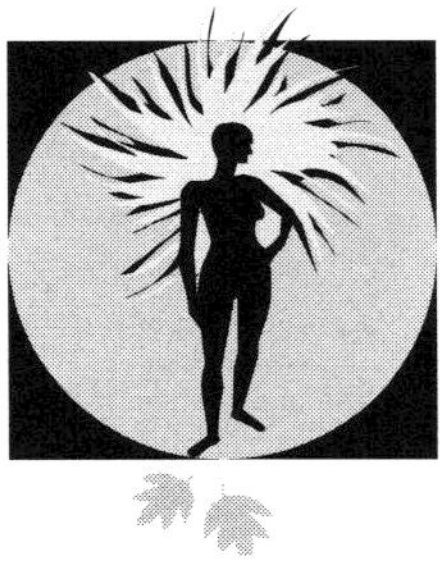

1. Characteristics of sexual glory turned to shame

1.1 Eyes that don't see

Sometimes women tell me that the glory-of-man aspect is the most difficult aspect for them to grasp. In the past I have been puzzled and even amazed by this, because the glory aspects of both man and woman are those most glamorized and commercialized in the media and the ones most often treated in the arts. From pulp romance to Shakespeare, from sitcoms to epic films, romance permeates our lightest moments and our most serious ponderings. Heroic love and erotic passion, desire and rejection, possession and jealousy, yielding and ecstasy are basic to melodrama; they are also basic to the human heart. It may surprise you to know they are basic to the Bible.

The glory of the sexes is presented concisely in 1 Corinthians 11, but the bigger theme of human sexuality is developed throughout Scripture. In all the Bible, sexuality reflects God's jealous and passionate love for His people and their fire and ice responses—the fire of zealous worship, the ice of rejection and betrayal, or the insult of apathy. These ideas permeate the Old Testament prophets, as well as the rest of the Bible. The romance of redemption is like one of those changeable pictures that you either see or you don't. When you have eyes to see it, it is very plain.

However, lack of Biblical insight is not the basic reason why some women find this aspect distant and opaque. All too often, another foundation stone is missing. A woman's glory-of-man aspect is founded upon her father's unconditional and gracious love. Long before a girl has any consciousness of her body or sexuality, she should receive from her father a masculine endowment of approval and delight. Every dad has the power to use his august role as father to communicate to his little girl, "You are beautifully feminine, adored, and cherished because you are mine." A woman's realization of her glory-of-man aspect is dependent upon the glory of the men around her and their gracious love, most especially father, brothers, and early friends who are boys. When we are able to admire the men around us, that admiration awakens our glory-of-man aspect. More importantly, when men cherish us because of who we are and not just because of how we look, our confidence and joy in being feminine is awakened and strengthened. When glorious manhood is absent, as it will be in a decadent society, the glory-of-man aspect in women does not cease to be, but it is dull and buried. Or, in the case of abuse, it is damaged and broken. Where God intended trust and delight, scorn and enmity grow.

KEY Glory–*fallen*
person–FEMALE FIGURE (unclothed–discarded fig leaves, flaunted immorality–according to her fallen-but-un-ashamed guilty standing before God)
character–DARK SQUARE (polluted with sin)
femininity–DARK CIRCLE (polluted with sin)
role/work–SHAVED HEAD, DISTORTED SUNBURST (corrupted glory/shame)

1.2 Sexual shame: The second effect of sin (Gen. 3:7)

If asked to name the opposite of love, most would say hate; some would say indifference. Most would say the opposite of courage is cowardliness. But if asked to name the opposite of glory, what would you say? Based on life and Scripture, I believe the opposite of glory is shame. Have you ever noticed a great sports star, a quarterback for instance, who is riding the crest of glory?

When he makes a few mistakes, the people who were cheering start booing and throwing trash. The hero who falls off the knife-edge of glory finds shame and humiliation on the other side. Glory is one of the hot buttons of existence, whether it is military glory, sports glory, or sexual glory. It is indeed a great high, but the opposite of the high is a correspondingly deep low. As the old TV sports slogan described, it is "the thrill of victory and the agony of defeat." We will never understand gendered existence or the Bible's use of sexuality until we understand the thrill of our sexual glory, the agony of sexual shame, and how they relate.

The very first thing that Adam and Eve did after they sinned was cover their loins. Their eyes were opened, they knew that they were naked; and so they covered themselves with fig leaves. Isn't that odd? Their disobedience was not sexual, but their general guilt led to sexual shame. Understanding the deep tie between our sexual natures and our spiritual natures is not easy, but it is very real. We will address this link more deeply later in this chapter. Suffice it to say here that no one goes too far up or down **spiritually** or **sexually** without the other being affected. Emphasizing the evil of sex, some people see the sexual nature as almost coterminous with the sin nature. There is a powerful connection. If you look at the deeds of the flesh listed in Galatians 5:19, you will see that the first three are sexual sins.

1.3 Pride, lawless violence, and self-gratification among men

After shame, the next effect of sin on sexuality is a fundamental perversion of masculinity. Men become prideful, lawlessly violent, and self-glorifying. We have to turn only one page from Adam and Eve to meet Lamech, the first polygamist of history. Genesis 4:23-24 records, *Lamech said to his wives, "Adah and Zillah, listen to my voice, you wives of Lamech, give heed to my speech, for I have killed a man for wounding me; and a boy for striking me; 24 if Cain is avenged sevenfold, then Lamech seventy-sevenfold."*

In his pride and arrogance, Lamech breaks God's model of one woman for one man. He takes two wives and demands the attention of both. For a husband to want his wife's attention is not bad, but what does this man want to tell his wives? He wants to brag and glory in his excessive violence. He has turned God's standard on its head. Instead of forgiving in multiples of seven, as Jesus will command, Lamech seeks vengeance seventy-seven fold. Lamech is an excessively violent and self-glorifying man who violates God's plan by taking two wives instead of one.

The problem of powerful men seeking to build their own glory by taking multiple women runs through Scripture. Abraham and Isaac were both plagued by the harem-building habits of their neighboring kings (Gen. 12, 20, 26). Powerful men take women for their own glory. So much so, that harem-building is almost synonymous with great kings (Esth. 2). God warns Israelite kings against it (Deut. 17:17), but to no avail. Today's headlines will reveal the same penchant for sexual conquest and violence from sinful men. All through history powerful men (whether powerful through wealth, war, sports, or politics) glorify themselves by taking more and more women. Please note: Monogamy takes great humility, especially for the powerful.

1.4 Lust: Taking all and giving nothing

The sister evil, or perhaps in this case I should say brother evil, of man's self-glorification is lust. Lust takes and gives nothing. In 2 Samuel 13, we have one of the most chilling accounts of pure lust in the Bible. Amnon, the first son of David, "loves" his half-sister, Tamar. He is determined to have relations with her, so he deceives her. She begs him not to violate her and suggests they get married; but he, being stronger than she, forces her. Verse 15 says this: *Then Amnon hated her with a very great hatred; for the hatred with which he hated her was greater than the love with which he had loved her. And Amnon said to her, "Get up, go away!"* So Amnon has Tamar thrown out and locks the door behind her. Their father, David, is angry, but does nothing. Absalom, probably Tamar's full brother, is furious. Absalom looks for an opportunity to kill Amnon, which he does two years later. Eventually, David and Absalom go to war. The Bible says Tamar was left desolate in the house of Absalom. Tamar was failed grievously by all her men. Her brother fails her; her father fails her. Absalom avenges her, but what satisfaction can there be in one brother killing your other brother, and then going to war with your father? Her desolation was great. Have you ever wondered, why the man can rape and the woman feels shame? Rape and abuse victims do feel shame and guilt. They are left desolate. Why is this?

God made the sexual glory of the human race such that the glory of man and woman are inextricably linked. The man has the power to glorify and raise up the woman beyond what she earns or deserves. The woman has the power to glorify and build up the man with her response and her praise beyond what he earns. But when love turns to lust and glory to shame, the man's power to exalt can be used to humiliate the woman, often through physical violence. The woman's power to build up the man can be used to tear him down and destroy his manhood, usually through rejection and verbal violence. This complex is one of the ugliest, most horrifying, and heart-wrenching results of fallen sexual glory. As we have a gift to glorify one another and spiral up together, so we have the power to humiliate one another and spiral down together.

1.5 Pride, excessive adornment, and frivolity among women

In Isaiah 3, we see an example of the other side of the equation—not prideful men taking women, but rather, prideful women destroying men.

> Isaiah 3:16-23—*Moreover, the* L*ORD said, "Because the daughters of Zion are proud and walk with heads held high and seductive eyes, and go along with mincing steps and tinkle the bangles on their feet, 17 therefore the Lord will afflict the scalp of the daughters of Zion with scabs, and the* L*ORD will make their foreheads bare." 18 In that day the Lord will take away the beauty of their anklets, headbands, crescent ornaments, 19 dangling earrings, bracelets, veils, 20 headdresses, ankle chains, sashes, perfume boxes, amulets, 21 finger rings, nose rings, 22 festal robes, outer tunics, cloaks, money purses, 23 hand mirrors, undergarments, turbans, and veils.*

It does not take a literary genius to figure out that Isaiah makes his list of these feminine ornaments excessively long to draw attention to the fact that these women are excessively vain. He is holding them up for derision. Isaiah continues:

> Isaiah 3:24-4:1—*Now it will come about that instead of sweet perfume there will be putrefaction; instead of a belt, a rope; instead of well-set hair, a plucked-out scalp; instead of fine clothes, a donning of sackcloth; and branding instead of beauty. 25 Your men will fall by the sword and your mighty ones in battle. 26 And her gates will lament and mourn, and deserted she will sit on the ground. 4:1 For seven women will take hold of one man in that day, saying, "We will eat our own bread and wear our own clothes, only let us be called by your name; take away our reproach!"*

Isaiah 3 is about prideful women who built their whole lives around self-glorification through adornment. This is a perversion of the glory-of-man aspect. God's judgment on them is twofold. He takes away their beauty and their men. Because they glory in being voluptuous and promiscuous, God takes away both their glamour and their lovers. He takes away their beauty through the hardships of military conquest; He takes away the men in battle. Did you ever think that how women dress and comport themselves back home could affect how men fare on the battlefield? This is an approach to military science that West Point probably has not investigated. But Isaiah makes this revelation: When women become too vain, God may kill their men in battle. Said in more familiar words, the moral fiber of any nation affects their battlefield performance. God often brings military defeat on nations as a judgment for their decadence and corruption. When either men or women become self-glorifiers, the beauty of sexual glory is destroyed for all.

When either men or women become self-glorifiers, the beauty of sexual glory is destroyed for all.

2. A case study of fallen glory: Israel, the wife of God

Ezekiel 16 is one of my favorite passages in all the Bible because it unites two of my great loves. One is the study of sexuality; the other is the study of history. In this one passage we have the entire history of Israel told in the metaphor of marriage, beginning with the Egyptian captivity all the way into the Millennial Era. We could spend hours delineating each era and noticing details of the descriptions. However, here we will summarize verses 1 -14 in order to look more closely at the progression of Israel's fallen glory in verse 15 and following.

2.1 Israel's idolatry was adultery

Ezekiel 16:1-14 describes the rise of Israel. Israel was a nobody, consisting only of a gaggle of rowdy slaves in Egypt. God speaks in verses 7-8: *"I made you numerous like plants of the field. Then you grew up, became tall and reached the age for fine ornaments; your breasts were formed and your hair had grown. Yet you were naked and bare. 8 Then I passed by you and saw you, and behold, you were at the time for love; so I spread My skirt over you and covered your nakedness. I also swore to you and entered into a covenant with you so that you became Mine," declares the Lord GOD.* This refers to the Mosaic Covenant which is likened to marriage. *Spreading My skirt over you* is an idiom for getting married. In the ancient world the marriage ceremony often included the man putting his mantle around the woman, indicating that he was taking her to himself and under his protection. In the same sense, God married Israel.

Verses 9-14 record the romantic story of a Jewish "my fair lady." God takes this nobody of a people from nowhere and makes her into a great queen.

> Ezekiel 16:9-14—*"Then I bathed you with water, washed off your blood from you and anointed you with oil. 10 I also clothed you with embroidered cloth and put sandals of porpoise skin on your feet; and I wrapped you with fine linen and covered you with silk. 11 I adorned you with ornaments, put bracelets on your hands and a necklace around your neck. 12 I also put a ring in your nostril, earrings in your ears and a beautiful crown on your head. 13 Thus you were adorned with gold and silver, and your dress was of fine linen, silk and embroidered cloth. You ate fine flour, honey and oil; so you were exceedingly beautiful and*

advanced to royalty. 14 Then your fame went forth among the nations on account of your beauty, for it was perfect because of My splendor, which I bestowed on you," declares the Lord God.[1]

This last verse describes the Davidic reign and the first twenty years of Solomon's reign, when Israel became a great kingdom and the major power of the ancient world (1010 B.C. to 950 B.C.). It was literally the kingdom of God on earth; God reigned over the world from His Holy of Holies.

Now look at the tremendous shift in verse 15. *"But you trusted in your beauty and played the harlot because of your fame, and you poured out your harlotries on every passer-by who might be willing."* Israel makes the utterly disastrous shift from trusting in the God who gave her beauty to trusting in her beauty. Israel had become great in power, in wealth, and wisdom. She shifted her focus from the Giver of the gifts to the gifts; from God to herself. The picture is of a woman who forgets the husband who has adorned her in order to worship herself. She makes her beauty her god. However, as soon as she has made her own beauty her god, she must find worshipers for her beauty. She begins to seek lovers.

Israel makes the utterly disastrous shift from trusting in the God who gave her beauty to trusting in her beauty.

Ezekiel 16:16-19—*"You took some of your clothes, made for yourself high places of various colors and played the harlot on them, which should never come about nor happen. 17 You also took your beautiful jewels made of My gold and of My silver, which I had given you, and made for yourself male images that you might play the harlot with them. 18 Then you took your embroidered cloth and covered them, and offered My oil and My incense before them. 19 Also My bread which I gave you, fine flour, oil and honey with which I fed you, you would offer before them for a soothing aroma; so it happened," declares the Lord* GOD.

The point is, late in Solomon's reign, Israel began to build idol temples all over Jerusalem, using the very wealth that God had given her to build these brothels of infidelity! Speaking as a husband to His wife Israel, God says, "You have taken the things I gave you and you have given them to other men."

In case the Biblical equation of idolatry and adultery is unfamiliar to you, let me give a few words of explanation. Israel, as God's wife, was to be loyal in her covenanted love to God. This included caring for His tabernacle (house), bearing fruit to Him, and glorifying Him with her worship and trust. When God's nation looked to another nation or the god of another nation for provision or protection, she is likened to a wife turning her back on her own husband in her own home in order to go down the street to find another man to care for her. When Israel made treaties with other nations for defense, God took this as an insult. God, as Israel's Husband, wanted to be looked to and depended upon by her for her protection and provision. **Misplaced trust** is a fruit of idolatry.

2.2 More characteristics of prideful beauty

False worship is an even more inflammatory expression of idolatry than misplaced trust. Israel's building of idol centers and adorning them with lavish jewels, statuary, and fabrics is likened to a woman taking money her husband earned to redecorate the bedroom in order to

1. Often I tell my husband to include this passage prominently in the *Five Aspects of Man*. I think all the men need to see how God treats a wife!

invite the plumber in to make love. The act of bowing down in worship is compared to the act of making love. The point of comparison is that in both cases, the wife or the nation gives herself unreservedly and with a glorifying response to her lord. Jeremiah speaks of Judah's committing adultery with stones and trees (v. 3:9). The whole book of Hosea is built upon the comparison between adultery and idolatry. Paul alludes to this comparison in 2 Corinthians 11:1-3, and John speaks of it in Revelation 17:1-5.

In addition to the insults of misplaced trust and the betrayal of false worship, Judah adds a more horrifying sin. Ezekiel 16:20-21—*"Moreover, you took your sons and daughters whom you had borne to Me and sacrificed them to idols to be devoured. Were your harlotries so small a matter? 21 You slaughtered My children and offered them up to idols by causing them to pass through the fire."* God, as Husband and Father, is beside Himself with rage, horror, and hurt. He says, in effect, it is one thing to take everything I have given you to go out and make love to other men, but how can you possibly take our children and offer them as sacrifices? **Rejected motherhood** will always be a characteristic of the glory-of-man aspect gone bad. Women who become vain and self-centered will be terrible mothers. They will both neglect and be cruel to their children. Or, as in this case with Israel, they will actually kill them. In the world today, millions of babies are killed through abortion every year; more are sacrificed through neglect. Promiscuity is the first result of turning away from God to our own glory, our own beauty. Rejecting motherhood is the second.

Ezekiel 16:22 speaks of a third characteristic: *"Besides all your abominations and harlotries you did not remember the days of your youth, when you were naked and bare and squirming in your blood."* **Ingratitude** is the third characteristic of a self-glorifying woman. She is not grateful to God for what He has done, nor does she even bring His mercies to mind. As we go through this passage, think of Israel about whom it was written, think of individual women who have followed this path, and let us be sure to examine ourselves and our nation. A very similar allegory could be written about America, her rise to greatness, and her defilement of what she has been given.

Hatred of husband and children is characteristic of the fallen glory-of-man aspect at its most decadent.

Verses 25-33 describe the **lewdness** that increasingly characterized Judah as she pursued idolatry and adultery. In spite of God's efforts to chastise her, she became increasingly coarse, hardened, obscene, and seared in conscience. Verses 28-30 focus on **insatiability,** a related trait of progressing carnality: *"Moreover, you played the harlot with the Assyrians because you were not satisfied; you played the harlot with them and still were not satisfied. 29 You also multiplied your harlotry with the land of merchants, Chaldea, yet even with this you were not satisfied. 30 How languishing is your heart," declares the Lord GOD, "while you do all these things, the actions of a bold-faced harlot."* This is the way of sin; the more one consumes, the less satisfied one is. Whether money, drugs, alcohol, food, or sex—centering on anything but God brings more craving, but less satisfaction.

Finally, look at verse 45 for a seventh characteristic of prideful beauty: *"You are the daughter of your mother, who loathed her husband and children. You are also the sister of your sisters, who loathed their husbands and children. Your mother was a Hittite and your father an Amorite."* **Hatred of husband and children** is characteristic of the fallen glory-of-man aspect at its most decadent. When a woman shifts from thankfulness to God and the men who represent Him to self-worship, she will not stop with indifference to her family. She will eventually act toward them in full-blown hatred itself.

2.3 Judgments on idolized beauty

What does God do to judge beauty that is idolized? First of all, as we read in Isaiah 3:24, God **removes the beauty**. Beautifully set hair is plucked out, sweet perfume becomes putrefaction. In Ezekiel 16:39, God says this: *"I will also give you into the hands of your lovers, and they will tear down your shrines, demolish your high places, strip you of your clothing, take away your jewels, and will leave you naked and bare."* Second, glory is turned to **shame**. The woman who flaunts herself and strips to entice will be stripped in shame. Third, lovers will be turned into God's agents of **punishment**. The nations with whom Israel fornicated will become God's agents of her punishment. They will tear her down and gawk at her shame. This is a foil and counterpoint to woman folly. Woman folly approaches the young man as a seductress. When he follows her, she turns into an executioner and takes him down to death. But here there is a reversal of this death dance. When immoral women seduce men, God often uses the very lawless men with whom they fornicated to execute His judgment on the women. This is nowhere seen more climatically than in the archetypal climax of history, when God turns the kings of the earth who have fornicated with Babylon into the agents of her destruction (Rev. 17).

A fourth judgment on idolized beauty is that the idolater is **humiliated** before the women she formerly despised. God explains in Ezekiel 16:48-52 that Sodom and Samaria will appear righteous in the judgment compared to Judah's capital. When God restores all the former and wicked kingdoms around Jerusalem in the future, she will know she has been the most wicked of them all. All basis of pride and self-exaltation will be removed. Jerusalem's place of honor in the future will be based completely upon God's grace despite her many abominations. Self-righteous church women need to take this passage to heart. If we imagine ourselves in heaven looking down our noses at all the prostitutes and worldly sinners, we may find ourselves placed lower than all the worldly sinners, with nothing whatsoever but God's covenant grace to stand upon (Ezek. 16:60-63).

2.4 Review

Fallen sexuality is characterized by shame, pride, and lust. Fallen women worship their own beauty, and indulge in excessive adornment and promiscuity. They are ungrateful, lewd, and insatiable. Rejecting motherhood, they come to hate their own husbands and children. God judges such sins by removing the beauty of such women and turning their glory into shame and humiliation.

3. The theological explanation for sexual glory turned to shame

3.1 When people refuse to glorify God

Ezekiel 16 gives us a poetic description of glory turned to shame. Now look to Romans 1 for a theological explanation. These passages are different but profoundly consistent. In Romans 1, Paul says that the creation clearly shows us the greatness of God. The only logical, spontaneous, and accurate response to the creation is to fall on our faces and worship God. To do anything else is to resist the truth.

> Romans 1:18-27—*For the wrath of God is revealed from heaven against all ungodliness and unrighteousness of men who suppress the truth in unrighteousness, 19 because that which is known about God is evident within them; for God made it evident to them. 20 For since the creation of the world His invisible attributes, His eternal power and divine nature, have been clearly seen, being understood through what has been*

made, so that they are without excuse. 21 For even though they knew God, they did not honor Him as God or give thanks, but they became futile in their speculations, and their foolish heart was darkened. 22 Professing to be wise, they became fools, 23 and exchanged the glory of the incorruptible God for an image in the form of corruptible man and of birds and four-footed animals and crawling creatures. 24 Therefore God gave them over in the lusts of their hearts to impurity, so that their bodies would be dishonored among them. 25 For they exchanged the truth of God for a lie, and worshiped and served the creature rather than the Creator, who is blessed forever. Amen. 26 For this reason God gave them over to degrading passions; for their women exchanged the natural function for that which is unnatural, 27 and in the same way also the men abandoned the natural function of the woman and burned in their desire toward one another, men with men committing indecent acts and receiving in their own persons the due penalty of their error.

To summarize this passage: When people refuse to glorify God, He gives them over to sexual immorality and perversion. Our glory is always and only a derivative reflection of God's glory. When we deny His glory, He takes away our glory, which is beautiful sexuality, and allows us to turn it to shame.

3.2 Why promiscuity, adultery, and homosexuality are wrong

Promiscuity, adultery, and homosexuality are wrong because God intended sexual relations to occur only in exclusive, life-long, covenanted, heterosexual relationships. From the beginning, God intended that erotic love picture the relationship of Christ and the Church, and also that of God and Israel. The sexual relationship should be exclusive because it is to picture one Lord and one people, so there should be only one husband and only one wife. Faithfulness till death pictures the forever-faithfulness of God. Sexual love should be covenanted in life-long marriage. Only in this context does it illustrate the covenant God has made with us and our response of faith.

Our glory is always and only a derivative reflection of God's glory. When we deny His glory, He takes away our glory, which is beautiful sexuality, and allows us to turn it to shame.

The sexual relationship should be heterosexual because it is God's created design that man, as the glory of God, take the role of husband, thus picturing God. It is God's created design that woman, as the glory of man, take the role of wife, thus picturing the Church, the responder. To reject these roles is to sin against nature itself, God's very created design.

Therefore, promiscuity is wrong because it is not exclusive, life-long, or covenanted. There is not one Lord or one Church. Adultery and divorce are wrong because they break the covenant. This is the whole premise of Ezekiel 16. Adultery pictures idolatry, turning away from the one true Lord to worship other gods, bowing down to them.

Finally, what about homosexuality? Today many support homosexual marriage. They believe moving in the direction of covenanted, exclusive, and life-long relationships will be a step in the right direction. Of course, AIDS promotes interest in exclusivity. However, with a homosexual marriage you do not have a man and a woman. Man is the glory of God, and only he is to take the husband role. Woman is the glory of man, and only she has the created gift to take the wife role.

Theologically speaking, a homosexual relationship is wrong because it makes masculine love erotic. The Trinity is the foundational model for purely masculine love. The love of the Father for the Son, for the Holy Spirit, and Their reciprocating loves are not sexual. For men to introduce the erotic into their love for other men is a blasphemous act. They are defacing the glory of God created within them as men. When masculine beings love other masculine beings erotically, they dishonor the very masculine God they were created to picture. The lesbian role is a specific picture of idolatry. Woman is created to picture the believer, the creature. When women bond sexually, they picture the creature worshiping the creature—the very definition of idolatry. By these practices, we dishonor God with our bodies, and we dishonor ourselves. Thus, we violate our consciences and do harm to our bodies physically, because these practices are against God's design.

To re-visit the issue raised earlier in this chapter about the link between the spiritual and the sexual (section 1.1), I believe the deep tie between our sexual and spiritual natures is related to the fact that our sexual nature is a **picture language of worship**, written into our very bodies. What we worship in spirit reverberates in our sexuality; what we do in our sexuality feeds back into our spirituality. Hence, Adam's general disobedience triggered a sense of sexual shame, and therefore, the need for covering.

4. Admonitions: We must humble ourselves to glorify God

If human pride has caused our sexual glory to be shamed, then it makes perfect sense that humbling ourselves to glorify God would be the path to healing. How can we do this? Let me suggest five ways we can humble ourselves as individuals, as churches, and as a nation, thereby glorifying God in our sexuality.

4.1 Cleanse our words and eyes

If, like Isaiah, we suddenly received a new vision of the holiness of God, our first reaction would no doubt be like his—we would be undone by the wickedness of our own speech and that of those around us (Is. 6:1-5). The Information Age is engulfing our world and infiltrating every corner of our lives with a great explosion of words and images. A vast amount of this discourse is silly babble; a significant portion of it is filthy, coarse, and even diabolical, arising from carnal and manipulative sources (Eph. 5:3-5). As one young woman described the twenty-first century, "We talk more and think less." The first way we humble ourselves and glorify God is to govern our eyes and to battle our untameable tongues. In this age, this includes not only what we say, but what we view, type, scan, text, upload, download, or share—that is, all our communications incoming and outgoing. To repent, we need to be cleansed, as Isaiah was, with live coals of fire from God's own altar (Is. 6:6-7). We also need to think more and talk less (James 1:19).

4.2 Trust in no man

A second way to humble ourselves is to glorify God and trust no man. As women with the glory-of-man aspect, our desire to follow and depend upon men is valid. However, a weakness lurking in the glory aspect is to idolize men, insisting that they be everything for us. As women, we must love a man for who he is, remembering that he is not God or a woman. We must never allow ourselves to worship a man or put him in the place of God. Utter dependence must rest on God alone. Jeremiah 17:5 says: *Cursed is the one who trusts in man, who depends on flesh for his* [or her] *strength and whose heart turns away from the Lord.* The final dependence and expectation for love and provision must be from God Himself. No matter how good or bad your husband, father, brothers, boss, or anyone else may be, to trust in a man as if he were God is a great sin, and God will curse it. One of the worst things you can do to a man you love is to idolize him. In so doing, you could well contribute to his downfall and judgment because God is sworn to destroy both pride and idols.

4.3 Honor marriage

In addition to guarding our tongues, we must require abstinence for singles and we must honor monogamous marriage. The world expects and urges single people to be sexually active; virgins and the abstinent are ridiculed. According to this view, all "deserve" the glory of sexual activity. The unhappily married "deserve" a divorce and "another chance at happiness." Unfortunately, this is not only the message of the world, but of most churches as well. Thus, fornication, adultery, and divorce have marginalized the very institution of marriage in most of the world. However, God's righteousness is the standard for human behavior, not human happiness or self-expression.

4.4 Be sexually content

We honor God's law by being content with our own limited portion of sexual glory. God calls us to self-discipline, even to suffer for righteousness' sake. If single, we must bear with the demands of abstinence. If married, we must bear with the "trouble in the flesh" that Paul says is part of marriage (1 Cor. 7:28), whether such trouble be personal conflicts, boredom, sexual dissatisfaction, financial problems, difficult in-laws, sickness, or unruly children. If truth be known, many more people are called to suffer for righteousness in difficult marriages than are called to dungeon and fire. God calls us to bear patiently with these troubles, working through them and bearing them by grace. True humility is required to live sexually pure for a lifetime, but God's grace and strength are sufficient. Accepting the constraints and limitations of single or married life is one of the major ways we show our humility to God.

4.5 Properly exalt the single life

Finally, we can glorify God and restore human sexuality by exalting the single life appropriately. Virgins and widows have a potential to give themselves body and soul to the Lord in a way that married people do not. We should believe this and encourage it. The world says that sexual activity is fundamental to living a good life. On the contrary, the Bible gives us three examples of celibate lives which were the greatest ever lived: Jesus, John the Baptist, and Paul. Many people are facing a single life because of the breakdown of our society. They need to be encouraged to contribute to the Kingdom, because building the Kingdom is the most important thing, not our personal sexual satisfaction.

John the Baptist is an especially interesting case because he was an ascetic and a celibate. We usually think of him out in the desert eating locusts, completely scornful of sexuality, oblivious to its beauties. However, the second title he gave to Jesus was that of Bridegroom. Clarifying again that he was not the Christ, he says in John 3:29, *"He who has the bride is the bridegroom, but the friend of the bridegroom, who stands and hears him, rejoices greatly because of the bridegroom's voice. And so this joy of mine has been made full."* John, far from earthly palaces and celebrations, saw Christ as the Bridegroom. John was willing to set aside temporal weddings and marriage in order to set his heart on the eternal glory of the Great Marriage, the ultimate wedding between Christ and His people. He fixed his heart and life on that glory. In a real sense he died defending its honor, for John died opposing the divorce and remarriage of Herod (Matt. 14:1-12). The heart of the real ascetic does not despise the beauty and glory of God's world. Real ascetics and celibates set aside the temporal shadows of this world to devote themselves completely to the beauty and glory that live beyond this world.

5. Conclusion

The way to restore beautiful human sexuality comes only by an indirect route. Only as we become people who give God the glory through the obedience of purity will the beauty and glory of human sexuality be restored. This is not a novel idea. Actually it is just as simple and profound as, *Seek ye first the kingdom of God and His righteousness and all these things shall be added unto you* (Matt. 6:33).

•

Lord,

Grant us to accept

Your cleansing forgiveness

for our shame.

Enable us to glorify You,

that we may be the glory

you created us to be.

In Christ's name,

Amen.

•

Personification of Glory—*fallen*

I am Glory of Man—*fallen*.

Beauty and sex are the foundation of my identity and my tools for manipulating others. I trust in them and rely on them to get me what I want. I am too good to work or serve; I must be pampered and indulged. If not, I will make life miserable for anyone who crosses me with my tantrums and sulks.

I am proud and hard-hearted. I use coverings to create an illusion of femininity and to hide the increasingly brutal and brazen nature which is my true character. The honor of brave men or the dependence of children mean nothing to me. I willingly throw either on the altar of my vanity.

My sexual response is debased. Early on, I tried to exchange it for love, but found that doesn't work. So now men are trophies or devices to satisfy my lusts—unless I decide to cast them aside altogether and burn for other women. With exclusivity in love long-gone, I am driven by my increasing lusts and insecurities to seduce new lovers. Yet, even as I seek to use them, they use and abuse me. When the last shreds of my beauty are gone, I am left shamed, abused, and humiliated. I am the object of pornography and its consumer.

Sometimes I throw away my feminine glory to be like a man. However, this neutered persona usually is distasteful to all. I soon take up again the coverings which provoke desire in order to retain those useful weapons in my arsenal. Whatever the persona, my heart remains predatory and cruel.

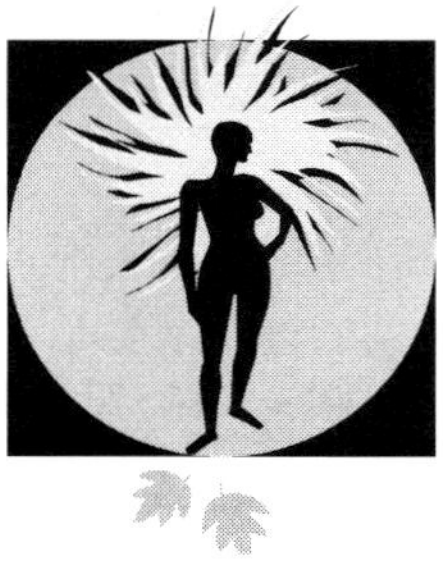

Bible Study of Glory—*fallen*

Before beginning this study, read the entire lesson, pages 88-99.

Thus you were adorned with gold and silver, and your dress was of fine linen, silk, and embroidered cloth. You ate fine flour, honey, and oil; so you were exceedingly beautiful and advanced to royalty. Then your fame went forth among the nations on acount of your beauty, for it was perfect because of My splendor which I bestowed on you," declares the Lord GOD. *"But you trusted in your beauty and played the harlot because of your fame, and you poured out your harlotries on every passer-by who might be willing."*

EZEKIEL 16:13-15

The fourteenth Biblical view of woman

Polluted by pride, idolatry, and immorality, woman's glory is turned to shame.

Characteristics of sexual glory turned to shame

No area of human life has been as glorified in poetry and song as much as romantic and sexual love. Nor has any area been as debauched and degraded by sin's pollution. After Adam's and Eve's eyes were opened to their guilt, their very first act was to cover their loins. They felt shame. Sin had broken the open fellowship and sexual purity between the first husband and wife even though their sin—eating the fruit—was not sexual. Human sexuality and spirituality are profoundly linked for good and evil.

Sex is deeply related to our sin natures; the first three sins listed in Paul's deeds of the flesh are sexual sins (Gal. 5:19-21). Sex is also related to our worship capacity. Our bodies are temples peculiarly defiled by immorality. In the woman's case, her sexual response can picture righteous worship or sinful idolatry. We can bring glory to man and God through our sexuality; or we can magnify shame through its abuse.

1. What is one way prideful men sin sexually in the Old Testament and today (Gen. 4:23-24; 12:10-15)? Why does monogamy take humility?

2. Describe the nature of Amnon's love for Tamar (2 Sam. 13:1-29). How did all of Tamar's men fail her? What did their failures produce for her?

3. Prideful men destroy and abuse women, but prideful women can also destroy men. What are the sins of the women described in Isaiah 3:16-4:1? How do these women contribute to the destruction of their men?

Case study: Fallen glory of man—Israel, the wife of God

Ezekiel 16 is a very important text for the study of sexuality, in both glory and shame. In this one chapter, the entire history of God's relationship to Jerusalem is told in the metaphor of marriage. God reveals not only the spiritual meaning of sexuality, but also His own heart and mind as the ultimate Husband.

4. What kinds of things did God do as Jerusalem's Husband (Ezek. 16:1-14, especially vv. 9-14)? What result did His husbandry have for Jerusalem?

5. List all the sins you see in Ezekiel 16:15-29, 44-45. What is the foundational sin?

6. The whole of Ezekiel 16—and many other passages, such as the book of Hosea, Jeremiah 3, and 2 Corinthians 11:1-4—rests on a comparison between adultery and idolatry. Why does adultery picture idolatry?

7. What did Jerusalem actually do which God considered adultery against Him? Who were Jerusalem's lovers?

8. In the metaphor of the passage, what judgment did God pronounce upon Jerusalem, His wife, for her immorality and sins (Ezek. 16:32-43)? Speaking non-metaphorically, what judgment happened to Jerusalem which fulfills this Ezekiel 16 judgment (refer to 2 Kin. 25:1-21)?

9. When modern women sin in the ways Jerusalem sinned in Ezekiel 16, are they ever judged in the same ways Jerusalem was judged?

Review

Fallen sexuality is characterized by shame, pride, and lust. Worshiping their own beauty, fallen women indulge in excessive adornment and promiscuity. They are ungrateful, lewd, and insatiable. Rejecting motherhood, they come to hate their own husbands and children. God judges such sins by removing the beauty of such women and turning their glory to shame and humiliation. He often uses the sinful lovers of these women as instruments of His judgment.

Keeping pure in a polluted land

10. What sort of infidelity is it that Paul fears in the Corinthian believers (2 Cor. 11:2-4)?

11. As Christian women, we need to be concerned about two kinds of adultery—spiritual adultery against Christ, and physical adultery against our husbands (or fornication, if you are single). One often leads to the other. How are you guarding yourself against wandering to other gods and to other men?

guarding against spiritual adultery

guarding against physical adultery

The theological explanation for sexual glory turned to shame

When people refuse to glorify God, He gives them over to sexual immorality and perversion. Our glory is a reflection of His glory. When we deny His glory, He takes away our glory—beautiful sexuality.

12. Homosexuality is a sin, but it can also be a judgment on other sins. Upon which sins is homosexuality a judgment (Rom. 1:18-27)?

13. Complete the following chart comparing God's plan for righteous sexuality with sinful sexual practices. (Consult this lesson's materials for help. A few sample answers are provided to get you started.)

GOD'S RIGHTEOUS MODELS FOR HUMAN SEXUALITY

Sexual practice:	Man's part, a right picture:	Woman's part, a right picture:	Overall right picture:
monogamous marriage	Christ is faithful	Church is faithful	union of Christ and Church
celibacy			

SEXUAL SINS AND WHY THEY ARE WRONG

Sexual practice:	Man's part, a wrong picture:	Woman's part, a wrong picture:	Overall wrong picture:
promiscuity			
rejection of one's mate	God as unfaithful	apostasy	alienation of God and sinner
adultery			
divorce and remarriage			
homosexuality			
lesbianism			

Or do you not know that the unrighteous shall not inherit the kingdom of God? Do not be deceived; neither fornicators, nor idolaters, nor adulterers, nor effeminate, nor homosexuals, nor thieves, nor the covetous, nor drunkards, nor revilers, nor swindlers, shall inherit the kingdom of God. And such were some of you; but you were washed, but you were sanctified, but you were justified in the name of the Lord Jesus Christ, and in the Spirit of our God.

1 CORINTHIANS 6:9-11

God intended that sexual intercourse be experienced only in exclusive, life-long, covenanted, heterosexual relationships. This is because monogamous, heterosexual marriage is to picture God's relationship to Israel and the Church. In God's design, the man is to picture God Himself—faithful, dependable, and sacrificial. A loving woman is to picture the believer and the whole Church, revering her lord and bearing fruit only to him.

A point to ponder

Exclusivity plays a part in marital love as in no other human love. Our God is a jealous God, a consuming fire who brooks no rivals (Ex. 20:4; Deut. 32:19-21; Heb. 12:28-29). Some forms of jealousy are sinful; however, the backbone of marital jealousy is the image of God in us (Prov. 6:32-35; Song 8:6-7). The husband or wife who does not care if his mate loves another probably does not love his mate.

14. How can a woman sin by putting too much trust in a man, even her father or husband (Jer. 17:5)? How might the results be the same for her as they were for Israel in Isaiah 30:1-3?

15. Like John the Baptist, we can bring glory to God by honoring His moral standards, though often it will take humility and courage to do this. Why was John the Baptist killed (Mark 6:14-29)? What did he do that caused his imprisonment and eventual death?

16. As godlessness grows in our land and moral pollution with it, keeping pure is difficult. Just as difficult is communicating proper standards of holiness to our children and grandchildren, who are growing up in this environment. Look back over this lesson and select one area of fallen sexuality (violent men, haughty women, one of the perversions). Outline in a short paragraph how you would explain this issue to a child (perhaps your own child or grandchild). Keep the language plain and clear. Don't forget that explaining what God originally intended may make more sense than rules.

LESSON 20 : Glory of Man – *redeemed*

1. Forgiveness!

1.1 David, the guilty adulterer

Since the condition of the fallen glory of man is shame, the first need of the redeemed glory of man is forgiveness. Just as there is the refreshment of God's renewal and the hope of resurrection for the weary lifegiver, there is forgiveness and covering for the shame of the sinful glory of man. Consider the words of one of the most famous adulterers of all time, King David, who suffered much and for whom many suffered. In Psalm 32:1-2, he writes, *How blessed is he whose transgression is forgiven, whose sin is covered! 2 How blessed is the man to whom the LORD does not impute iniquity, and in whose spirit there is no deceit!* Psalm 38 and 51 are the other jewels in the crown of his penitential psalms. They are wonderful statements of repentance offered and forgiveness received. When we struggle with guilt or shame in the area of sexuality, or any other area, God calls us to confess, and not only to confess, but to receive His forgiveness which He freely gives.

1.2 The sinful woman who anointed Jesus

Luke 7:35-50 provides a beautiful picture of a fallen woman who did just that. She repented and received the joyful result of forgiveness. Described simply as a *sinner* (v. 37), this woman came to Jesus as He was dining in the home of a self-righteous Pharisee. Most assume she was a prostitute or one living in sexual sin, which is what "sinful woman" usually means. The Pharisee said that if Jesus knew the kind of woman she was, He would not allow her to touch Him, implying that her very touch was polluted (v. 39).

The Pharisee, as host, did not extend to Jesus the common courtesies of the day. The woman's actions are presented in sharpest contrast. Luke 7:37-38: *And there was a woman in the city who was a sinner; and when she learned that He was reclining at the table in the Pharisee's house, she brought an alabaster vial of perfume, 38 and standing behind Him at His feet, weeping, she began to wet His feet with her tears, and kept wiping them with the hair of her head, and kissing His feet and anointing them with the perfume.*

KEY Glory–*redeemed*
person–FEMALE FIGURE (clothed in bridal dress–adorned by and for Christ, the Bridegroom–according to her forgiven, redeemed standing before God)
character–GLOWING SQUARE (redeemed from sin)
femininity–DOTTED CIRCLE (redeemed from sin)
role/work–BRIDAL VEIL, LARGER SUNBURST (redeemed feminine glory; restored headship of husband and Christ)

Christ says to the Pharisee in verses 47-50: *"For this reason I say to you, her sins, which are many, have been forgiven, for she loved much; but he who is forgiven little, loves little."48 Then He said to her, "Your sins have been forgiven." 49 Those who were reclining at the table with Him began to say to themselves, "Who is this man who even forgives sins?" 50 And He said to the woman, "Your faith has saved you; go in peace."* The woman's tears speak of her deep contrition. Because she was truly repentant, she was truly forgiven. The knowledge of her forgiveness produced her great love for Christ. He forgave her sin, received her worship, and gave her the blessing of His peace.

In Luke 7, we see this woman's fallen glory-of-man aspect transformed into a beautiful glorification of God. Often, in history and literature, we read of the good-hearted harlot, the fallen woman, who has more grace in her heart than her more self-righteous sisters. Through suffering and shame, these women learned their need for grace and turned genuinely to God.

2. Worship!

2.1 The unique opportunity

The greatest danger of the glory-of-man aspect is its perversion into the worship or idolatry of mere men, as we discussed in Glory-*fallen* (section 4.2). However, the women who walked the earth in Jesus' day had a completely unique situation. They were able to meet the only Man on earth who actually was the true Glory of God Himself. Three passages picture the power and beauty of women responding to Christ as both the Man who was God and the God who was Man. We have just looked at one such passage in Luke 7, where the sinful woman ministered to Christ physically by applying ointment to His feet, kissing His feet, and wiping them with her hair. Thus, this scene is a beautiful picture of worship. Long hair is a glory to woman (1 Cor. 11:14-15). With her actions this woman said to Christ, "My glory is your foot towel." Hers is a feminine version of what John the Baptist said when he claimed to be unworthy to untie Christ's sandals. She used her hair for Christ's foot towel and ministered to Him as a man and worshiped Him as God in ways appropriate for a woman to do. He was blessed and glorified by her actions. Luke 7 presents a repentant sinner worshiping in love. Now let us consider two more women who were allowed to use their glory-of-man aspects in the direct worship of the God-Man.

2.2 Mary of Bethany

In John 12:1-8, Mary of Bethany performed the same act as the woman of Luke 7; yet in this case, the act did not emphasize love borne of forgiveness. This time the act expressed the worship of a mature heart that understood the worth of Christ and His coming sacrifice. She understood the events of the coming Passion Week. She understood that Christ would die on the cross when the apostles did not. Bringing her alabaster vial of rare and expensive perfume, Mary brought all the aspects of her being to Christ as well:

- As Mistress, she decisively ruled over her greatest material treasure, giving it to Christ.
- As Helper, she understood His mission when others did not.
- As Lifegiver, she permeated the entire house with the fragrance of her giving.
- As a Lady of Wisdom, she sat at His feet, pondering and learning, choosing the value of Christ's presence, available for such a short time.
- As Glory of Man, she worshiped and glorified the God-Man with her perfume, her hair, and her feminine response. Like the alabaster vial, her very act represented a precious gift of worship to Christ.

Christ, as a Man, needed the help and the completion of women. Although He did not have a wife, this act of feminine glorification no doubt strengthened Him and helped Him in a way that He, as a Man, needed in order to do the things He had to do that terrible and climactic week.

2.3 The woman at the well

We have seen the woman at the well in John 4 as a lifegiver. She went to the well looking for temporal water and found instead the Fountain of Living Water. Now let us consider the John 4 passage in the light of the glory aspect. The Samaritan, who had been the wife of five husbands and had a live-in lover as well, went to the well and found the Man who is the Glory of God.

We are not told why the Samaritan had gone from man to man. Perhaps in some misguided way she was seeking God in the fallen men around her, men who were not God, but only His distorted shadows. Whether she was looking for the Glory of God in men or not, one day she went to the well, and there He was. After discussing life, they discussed worship. Christ explained to her that God looks for true worshipers, those who worship in spirit and in truth. He revealed Himself plainly as the Messiah, and she believed immediately.

Have you ever recognized something quickly because you have been looking for it for a long time? You could be looking for something trivial, like the perfect accessory to go with an outfit, or just the right wallpaper to go in your kitchen—you've looked and looked and in the process of looking, you have formed a clear idea of what you are looking for. Everything you have seen so far is not it. Then when you do see it, you know—this is it. I think this happened with the Samaritan woman. This woman knew men. She was experienced and knew the glory that was and wasn't in them. She was still looking for someone she hadn't met yet. When she did meet Him, she recognized Him very quickly.

Many times the Lord warns us to beware of appearances. Those who appear to be great sinners may be more righteous than the respectable. The Samaritan may have been more righteous than all the smug wives of her village, because she was looking for, or at least had the sense to value, the true Greatness when she found it. Outcast sinner though she was, the Samaritan's spiritual eyesight was 20/20. Meeting the Christ, she quickly understood and ran to tell those in the village that the Messiah had come.

This woman's response nurtured and encouraged Christ at a profound level. When the disciples offered Him food shortly thereafter, He refused it, saying in verse 32, *"I have food to eat that you do not know about."* Seeing God's will accomplished in the Samaritan woman's life and eventually in her village was better meat for Christ than a banquet. Like Mary of Bethany, the Samaritan began as a glorifier of Christ and became His helper and lifegiver as well.

3. Sexuality as a glory to man and woman

3.1 The greatest song of the wisest man: Song of Solomon

It has been noted that there are only a few ways to speak about physical sexuality—in the languages of the nursery, science, the gutter, or poetry. Song of Solomon is certainly an example of the last category. It is a beautiful, erotic, and poetic account of romantic and sexual love. Some people down through Church history have been quite embarrassed by this book and have not known what to do with it. It has lain buried during many generations, often covered in blankets of allegory. Is Song of Solomon something we need to hide, or is it the book which reveals, as nowhere else in Scripture, the explicit glory and beauty of sexual love? Perhaps it is best understood at face value; it is what it claims to be—a love song.[1] As a love song, it celebrates the beauty of romantic love and provides guidance about the experience of falling in love and the consummating of that love in marriage.

1. Song of Solomon is a beautiful, elaborate song, not an allegory. For clarification, read "About interpreting Song of Solomon" on the next page. For further comments on the various interpretive approaches to the Song, for a fuller bibliography, and for insights into its difficult and obscure figures of speech, refer to Jack S. Deere, "Song of Songs," in *The Bible Knowledge Commentary, Old Testament*, eds. John F. Walvoord and Roy B. Zuck (Colorado Springs, CO: Chariot Victor Publishing, 1985), 1009-1025.

ABOUT INTERPRETING SONG OF SOLOMON

The allegorical method of interpreting Song of Songs as a poem about Christ and the Church is ancient and well-respected. Those using the "normal" method of interpretation (as explained in the Introduction) will, however, first see the Song as a love poem about a shepherd/king who loves a country girl and makes her his queen.

Nevertheless, it must be remembered that Christ is the archetype (original and exemplary model) of all shepherd/kings and of all bridegrooms. His Church is the archetypal bride, specifically one loved in lowliness, and elevated to royalty by the love of her King. All true lovers love in the light of Christ and the bride Church, even as all honest knights fight for truth in the shadow of His Captaincy, even as all good teachers are patterned after Him who is the one great Word.

The Bible begins with a wedding, ends with wedding, and in the middle, greatly glorifies marriage in Song of Songs and Psalm 45. John the Baptist hails Christ, not only as the Lamb of God, but also as the Bridegroom who possesses the bride. Jesus reveals Himself as the Lord and sponsor of all marriage at His first miracle at the wedding of Cana. But Paul is the one who specifically explains that, indeed, from the sinless beginning, the marriage of man and woman is created to picture Christ and His Church (Eph. 5:22-33). Therefore, the use of the normal method of interpretation, combined with an archetypal method of application, will yield many of the same insights as the allegorical method, while retaining a more disciplined approach to the text.

The poem begins with its title in 1:1, *The Song of Songs, which is Solomon's*; this means "The Greatest Song." This song is the best of all the 1,005 songs that Solomon wrote. Isn't it amazing that the greatest song written by the wisest man in the world is a love song? This is the judgment of the Holy Spirit. The Bible places a high priority on this area of our lives. We have discussed the importance of humbling ourselves in the area of human sexuality. Sex must be kept within its boundaries and not made more than it is. However, like the fire in the hearth, when it is where it should be, it is both warm and fiery, beautiful, and profoundly satisfying.

Love, in Song of Solomon, is presented as something of a paradise regained. All nature seems to join in glorifying Solomon's love for the Shulammite and her love for him. Listen to all the nature categories included in this rather short song: Animals, plants, jewels, metals, geography, spices, and food. Under animals, he calls upon the mare, dove, gazelle, stag, turtledove, goats, fawns, lions, and leopards. Under plants, he speaks of henna, cypress, cedar, rose, lily, apple tree, flowers, vines, figs, nard, and saffron. He calls upon the sun, the moon, the stars, gold, silver, purple, bees, raisin cakes, apples, pomegranates, and wine. He weaves all of these images and all of these facets of the creation in his song, comparing his bride to this, and their enjoyment to that. If ever you have been in love, you remember that all nature does sing with you. God has not only created nature to glorify Himself, but He has given nature to us as our domain. As our entourage, it joins with us in the joy of our human and sexual love.

Second, joyful love is a mutual affair. Reading the Song through, you will note long passages where the bridegroom praises the bride and every facet of her being. Then there are passages where the bride praises the bridegroom. If the man is the custodian of the woman's glory, so woman is custodian of the man's glory. A woman who treats her husband disrespectfully or rejects him sexually, dishonors his glory and contributes to the crushing of his masculinity. In the same way, a man who does not love his wife in words and deeds of affection and passion diminishes her femininity.

Third, Solomon points out that love is a powerful force, more powerful, according to Scripture, than death, hell, fire, and flood. Chapter 8:6-7: *"For love is as strong as death, jealousy is as severe as Sheol; its flashes are flashes of fire, the very flame of the LORD. 7 Many waters cannot quench love, nor will rivers overflow it; if a man were to give all the riches of his house for love, it would be utterly despised."* Throughout history many people have been killed in lovers' quarrels or because of adultery. Stories such as that of Helen of Troy, in which nations have gone to war over one woman, are not unfamiliar. Why is love so powerful? Just as parental love pictures the compassion and forgiveness of God for His children, so erotic love pictures the jealous and passionate possessiveness God feels for His people.

3.2 The moral basis for glorious romantic love

Solomon does not merely describe and glorify sexual love in his Song; he champions its moral boundaries. The *"do not arouse or awaken my love until she pleases"* refrain of the Song is repeated three times (2:7, 3:5, 8:4). Thus he exhorts us to remember that love has its time and season, both morally and personally. The Shulammite was a virgin, a locked garden, who focused more on character development while growing up than on personal adornment. When it was her time to waken love, so it became her time for beautiful adornment.

Solomon was a gracious lover. When rejected in 5:3, he responds with sweetness and patience, not demands. The possession theme of the Song comes to its greatest maturity when the wife is secure in the knowledge that she belongs to her husband, and that he desires her. When the wife says in 7:10, *"I am my beloved's, and his desire is for me,"* she speaks not only of his sexual passion, but also of his desire to be her loving leader and head. Thus, the paradise-regained theme is sounded at an even higher level, for here the misplaced *desire* of Genesis 3:16 finds its proper home in the heart of the husband who wants to love and lead his wife.[2]

3.3 A note of exhortation

Wives, do not neglect your love life. Sometimes, in the toils of marriage, the other aspects overwhelm the glory aspect. Wear the adornments your husband gives you—the perfume, the jewelry, and clothes. If he doesn't buy these things for you, try to learn what kinds he likes and buy them for yourself. One Christmas I bought Bill what I thought was a very romantic picture of a medieval couple kissing. Along with it, I had Proverbs 30:18-19 done in calligraphy: *There are three things which are too wonderful for me, four which I do not understand: 19 The way of an eagle in the sky, the way of a serpent on a rock, the way of a ship in the middle of the sea, and the way of a man with a maid.* The way of a man with a maid is one of the wonders of the world. These pictures hung in our bedroom for many years as a tribute to our love and as a reminder that the bedroom of married people is the proper domain, the proper place, for love.

---

2. Refer to *FAW—Vol. One*, pages 113-115, section 2.2, "What man's rule is."

3.4 Glory within marriage and without

The glory of sexuality is not restricted to the married. In societies where men act nobly as gentlemen, and where women are women of excellence, there is all manner of exchange between the sexes—some fleeting, some long-term—which glorify and uplift both. To illustrate this point, and also in answer to popular demand(!), I will share an episode from my own life that has come to be known as the **"Dumpster Story."**

> Some years ago, I took a load of trash down to the dumpster in our nearby city park. For some reason, on that particular day, there was a different kind of dumpster, deeper than I had ever seen in the park before or since. It sat flat on the ground like a box car without wheels. It was about as high as my nose (I distinctly remember having to stand on my tiptoes to look down into it). I took my car keys to open the trunk, got a trash bag in each hand, then adroitly cast all three items into the cavernous and empty dumpster—two sacks of garbage and one set of car keys! Ordinarily this would represent a setback, but nothing insurmountable. A woman of reasonably sound mind and not too far into her dotage should be able to retrieve the keys. I surveyed the situation. Standing on tiptoe, I peered into the dumpster and located the keys flat on the empty bottom, about two inches from an oily puddle. I could not reach them with my arm since they were about five feet straight down. I needed either a make-shift ladder or a rod for extension. I could stand on a park bench. Well, no, they'd all been cemented to the ground because of vandalism. I could stand on the car. Well, no, I would need the keys to start the car. In its entire one-hundred-year history, I'm sure the park had never been cleaner or more free of any convertible and useful items than it was that spring morning. I would have to go to the nearby hospital and call someone. But no, surely there was an easier way out of this difficulty.
>
> I walked a few yards to the edge of the jogging track. Twenty yards away, there he was—shorts, head band, mid-forties, jogging along, fighting the paunch. When he approached, I began to explain my difficulty, trying to sound intelligent and competent, a bit self-conscious about the evidence to the contrary. He didn't appear to pay much attention to my words. He visually surveyed the situation in a way that seemed like mental short hand—woman, need, dumpster, keys, five feet down. Then he leapt into the dumpster! I am perfectly serious. One second we were standing side by side, gazing down at the keys. The next second, in one fluid motion, he vaulted into the dumpster, retrieved the keys, handed them to me, then vaulted out. Struggling to recover from surprise, I bumbled to express my thanks and amazement. He merely nodded. Before I knew it, he had jogged on down the trail. He did not seem displeased. And, I—well, I felt wonderful.
>
> Much later, I asked myself, "Barbara, what is the matter with you? You go to the park and do something stupid. Someone helps you, and then you glow for the next three hours." Another voice, representing, might we say another aspect, replied, "And what's the matter with you? Don't you think it's great to know that at mid-life, a man will still leap into the garbage for you on a moment's notice?"

In societies where men act nobly as gentlemen, and women are women of excellence, there is all manner of exchange between the sexes which glorify and uplift both.

As I'm fond of saying, we spiral down together and we spiral up together. When men and women graciously do for one another what they are gifted to do, it is not an insult or condescension—it is a glory to both.

4. Human sexuality as a glory to God

Our sexuality is created to be a glory to us; it is also a glory to God. It is glorious because God has allowed us to picture, in our very beings as men and women, God and His people, Christ and His Church. Both the Old Testament and the New Testament support this point.

4.1 The Law of Moses: A double sexual standard

Many people are offended, angered, or embarrassed by the double sexual standard of the Mosaic Law. The Law of Moses definitely contains a double standard. If a girl commits an act of promiscuity while she is in her father's house, the penalty is death by stoning. But if a young man takes an unbetrothed virgin, he is not be stoned, but must marry the girl. That is a pretty big difference! The law regarding adultery is not a two-way street either. Adultery is taking another man's wife; it is not taking another woman's husband. When a man has relations with a woman who is someone else's wife, then he has committed adultery against the husband of the woman because he has taken that man's wife. Thus, the double standard is real (Ex. 21:7-11; Deut. 21:10-17; 22:13-30; 24:1-5).

If you study the gender laws, piecing them together in search of a summary, you will arrive at something like this: Men are required to be responsible for what they do. If a man gets a virgin in trouble, he must marry her or at least pay fines if the father does not want her to marry him. If a man is polygamous, he must take care of his wives; he cannot be partial to the children of favored wives; he must fulfill the conjugal rights of all his wives. The overall thrust of the Law is to hold men accountable and responsible for their sexual actions. On the other hand, the great emphasis of the Law for women is purity. Virgins are to protect their virginity at all costs. If a girl is raped, she is not punished. But if she could cry for help and did not, she is held guilty. The emphasis for unmarried girls is pure virginity, and for wives, exclusive sexual loyalty to their husbands.

> The overall thrust of the Law is to hold men accountable and responsible for their sexual actions. The great emphasis of the Law for women is purity.

Should we be apologetic for the Law of God? Think about it. What would happen if we woke up in the morning and all the men in our country were responsible and all the women were pure? What would our society be like? If all the men were held responsible for their sexual actions and all the women were pure, we would have a fabulous foundation for a good and just society. That is exactly what God promised in the Law of Moses, a law which would make Israel a wise and understanding people.

What is God's emphasis in the Old Testament? His emphasis is monotheism. He is the Lord—there must be no other gods. Obey Him and trust Him as the only true and faithful God. This was the great lesson for the Jews. The emphasis of the sexual laws for the Jews undergirded and pictured monotheism. Men, created to be the glory of God, were commanded to be faithful fathers, husbands, priests, and kings. God wanted them to be dependable in order to picture the trustworthiness of the One True Lord. To the women, He commanded purity. Promiscuity and adultery pictured idolatry, as we have seen. Through exclusivity in sexual love, woman pictured monotheism—loyalty to one lord. As the glory of man, the women's responsibility was trust and exclusive dependence on one lord.

4.2 The New Testament Law of Christ: New emphases

The big message of the New Testament is this—Christ died for you. Be saved and grow in Him. The sexual law of the New Testament differs from that of the Old in several ways, in order to illustrate the new emphasis of salvation.

First, there is a higher standard. Polygamy and divorce were managed in the Old Testament; in the New Testament, they are forbidden (Matt. 19:3-12; Luke 16:18).

Second, there is a new emphasis on mutuality. The husband's body belongs to his wife; the wife's body belongs to her husband, according to 1 Corinthians 7:3. This not only elevates the rights of the woman, but also reflects the relationship of Christ and the Church. He has given us His body, and the Church as His body should yield her members to Christ.

Third, new virtues are emphasized for both men and women in the New Testament. In Ephesians 5, the great and central passage on Christian marriage, the emphasis for men goes beyond the Old Testament emphasis on responsibility, all the way to sacrificial love. *Husbands, love your wives just as Christ also loved the Church and gave Himself up for her* (Eph. 5:25). *Husbands, love your wives and do not be embittered against them* (Col. 3:19). Even if men have a right to be bitter, they must not give in to it. They are to humble themselves and keep loving as Jesus loves. God has done something dramatically new by coming down and dying sacrificially. So now God is expecting something dramatically new from men.

What is emphasized for women in the New Testament? The new emphasis is on the spiritual adornment of good works (1 Tim. 2:9-10; 1 Pet. 3:3-5). Women adorning themselves with good works reflect and correspond to the Church adorning herself with righteous deeds (Rev. 19:7-8). Thus, women picture the Church in her adornment, while men picture Christ in His sacrificial love. These virtues do not replace, but are rather built upon the Old Testament virtues of male responsibility and female purity. To be sure, men loved their wives in the Old Testament, and women were adorned. All these virtues (male responsibility, feminine purity, sacrificial love, adornment of good works) are enjoined upon us in both Testaments. The point here is the shift in emphasis from the Old to the New.

4.3 Modern illustrations

What do these laws have to do with the glory-of-God or the glory-of-man aspects of sexuality? Feminism's fifty/fifty sexual equality has been very hard on personal life. For a woman, part of falling in love is finding in the man some kind of hero-lover she can admire. However, if men can in no way be providers, protectors, or heros, falling in love becomes difficult, for there is very little in which to fall in love.

Movie examples

I've seen two films which deal with this problem. In both plots the women are Ph.D.s, at the top of their professions. The men are blue collar. In one, the woman doctor is married to a middle-management rough neck on an oil rig. Their marriage is on the rocks. In the other case, the woman is a doctor of seismology. Her counterpart is a fix-it man who thinks comic strips are heavy reading. With these casts, I wondered how they would generate love interests. In both cases, the stories become love stories when the men risk their lives to save the women. That does not sound too original, does it! In one, the man literally goes to the bottom of the sea to save his wife and others. He becomes a tremendous hero, rekindling his wife's love and admiration. In the other, the woman doctor of geology is saved by the blue-collar hero who rescues her from giant worms. Neither man wins the love of his woman by gaining a bigger or more prestigious Ph.D! Rather, they win their wives' love and respect by acts of courageous and sacrificial love. There is no doubt that Jesus is smarter than we are, but He has not won our love by out-thinking us. He has won our love by being our Hero, by being willing to die for us, to do for us what we cannot do for ourselves.

I do not have giant worms coming out in the front yard every day, and I haven't recently needed a hero at the bottom of the sea. Because our lives are normally humdrum, it makes it all the more important to honor and appreciate our men for the ordinary things they do for us. Give them their place as provider and protector. Maybe someday there will be bigger things to do, and we will be sorry if we have squelched and continually scorned their inclinations to be hero-lovers.

Real-life examples

Going to the bottom of the sea and killing giant worms are Hollywood-types of sacrificial love. Consider a more down-to-earth sacrificial love. One time the husband of one of my best friends told me this story. The house was full of company, which he knew was stressful for his wife. So he went into the kitchen and began to help. His new daughter-in-law came in, saw him helping, and said with a bit of a haughty tone, "Well, I am glad to see that you got the message!" In context he said her meaning was, "I'm glad you've gotten the feminist message that you are supposed to do half the housework." He answered her, "I have not gotten any messages [from the feminists]! I am doing this because Christ is my Head and He tells me to love my wife."

What is the difference between a man who is in the kitchen helping his wife because he is under the command of Christ, and the man who is in the kitchen because he thinks that he and his wife are interchangeable and equal in all responsibilities? There are several differences, but the greatest is the issue of headship. One man knows he is directly under the Headship of Christ in a way his wife is not. Christ has commanded him to care for his wife. He helps in the kitchen with a clear sense of manhood under God, directing and serving in his household as one who chooses to love. The other man does not think that Christ is any more directly his Head than his wife's; he does not think he has any more responsibility to care for her than she him. He helps in the kitchen because he's been nagged or because he has embraced the feminist/humanist agenda, which states that manhood is not significantly different from womanhood. Thus, their work must be equal, that is, by their way of thinking, the same. The problem with this is that it leaves little room for manliness or womanliness; women must jump in the dumpster for themselves, as it were. There aren't any champions, and there aren't supposed to be.

Conversely, just as God commands sacrifice from husbands, He commands reverence from wives. "Revere" is a very strong word. We must not flinch at this New Testament double standard any more than we should flinch at the double standard in the Old Testament. When we seek to show respect for our husbands, we do not do it as lesser persons; we do it because Christ has told us to glorify Him in this way. In addition, I know that respecting my husband makes it easier for him to be the man God wants him to be, and the man my children and I need him to be.

4.4 Review

First, God forgives our sexual sins. Second, sexuality is God-given, beautiful, and to be enjoyed in the proper spheres for married and unmarried. Third, human sexuality is glorious because it reflects God's love for His people. In the Old Testament, the emphasis was monotheism and turning away from idols. Therefore, men were to be responsible, and women, pure. In the New Testament, the emphasis is Christ's sacrificial love and the Church's response in reverence and good works. In addition to being responsible, Christian men are called to picture Christ with sacrificial love. Women, in addition to being pure, are to revere their husbands and adorn themselves with good works just as the Church is doing.

5. Sexuality as a glory to God, man, and woman

5.1 The unexpected and wondrous Bridegroom (Psalm 45)

Finally, human sexuality is a glory to God, to man, and woman—all at the same time. Psalm 45 is a glorious and beautiful wedding psalm celebrating a royal wedding. The Psalmist writes in verses 1-2, *My heart overflows with a good theme; I address my verses to the King; my tongue is the pen of a ready writer. 2 You are fairer than the sons of men; grace is poured upon Your lips; therefore God has blessed You forever.* This first section describes the Bridegroom. He is fairer than mere mortals and His speech is full of grace. The verbal man speaks, reads, writes, talks to women, and talks to God. This great and blessed Bridegroom is a verbal Man, a Man of the word before He is a Man of the sword. But, indeed He is also a Man of the sword.

5.2 The armament and wrath of the Prince

Consider verses 3-5: *Gird Your sword on Your thigh, O Mighty One, in Your splendor and Your majesty! 4 And in Your majesty ride on victoriously, for the cause of truth and meekness and righteousness; let Your right hand teach You awesome things. 5 Your arrows are sharp; the peoples fall under You; Your arrows are in the heart of the King's enemies.* This is what I call the armament scene.

The man who does not want to miss the armament and judgment scenes in the action movie is no less the image of God than the woman who does not want to miss the first kiss in the love story.

One of my friends wanted to talk to her boyfriend while he was watching an action movie. So she sat down and began to watch the movie. She did not see anything interesting happening. Buildings were being blown up; people were getting killed. This went on for a while. Finally she thought, well, there is not much happening in this movie—no character development, no dialogue. Therefore, I think now would be a good time to talk. So she began to talk to him. He said, "Wait! This is the most important part!" What she did not realize was that she had interrupted the great armament scene. This is how these movies go: You have to establish that the bad guys are bad. So the bad guys go around blowing up things and doing lots of wicked deeds. Then the hero gets madder and madder as he encounters more and more opposition. Finally, the armament scene comes when he gets all his gear together. He loads himself up, with all manner of ammunition, knives, daggers, handguns, heavy assault weapons, and off he goes to wreak judgment on evil. This is very satisfying to most men. Why is it satisfying to so many men and mystifying to so many women? Men are created to be saviors and warriors. They have a greater concern for truth and justice than most women. Women are generally more concerned with community and peace.

Consider the two great portraits of Christ presented in Isaiah 53 and 63. In Isaiah 53, Christ is covered with His own blood which He sheds in humility and compassion for others. In Isaiah 63:1-6, Christ is covered with the blood of His enemies as He alone treads the winepress of God's wrath, treading down in fury the nations who hate Him. When we teach only the suffering-Savior passages to the exclusion of the wrathful-Judge passages, we are not telling the truth about the Bible or about Christ. In an interesting way, we are not telling the truth about gender, either. The man who does not want to miss the armament and judgment scenes in the action movie is no less the image of God than the woman who does not want to miss the first kiss in the love story.[3] Both love and justice are basic to who God is and basic to who we are as His creatures. Remember, there finally is no mercy without justice. Men, as the glory of God, gravitate first to God's powerful leadership as Sovereign and Judge. Women, as the glory of man, gravitate first to His compassion and intimate care.

Psalm 45:3-5 is the armament scene of the Protector. He girds on His sword; He rides majestically; the enemies of the King die, because He rides for righteousness in meekness and humility. It is King Arthur's dream—not might makes right, but might for right. All the noble knights of history who have ridden and fought for truth have warred in the shadow of this one chivalrous Prince.

5.3 A greater height

It does not seem possible, but Psalm 45:6-7 take us to an even greater height in revealing the character of this Bridegroom: *Your throne, O God, is forever and ever; a scepter of uprightness is the scepter of Your kingdom. 7 You have loved righteousness and hated wickedness; therefore God, Your God, has anointed You with the oil of joy above Your fellows.* The astounding announcement of Psalm 45:6 is that this Bridegroom is God. And if we doubt, the writer of Hebrews uses these very verses in Hebrews 1:8-9 to defend the divine Sonship of Christ. This wedding psalm probably was written for the royal wedding of a Davidic prince. Yet it flashes forth to present the ultimate Bridegroom and Son of David, Christ Himself, as we see Him in Revelation 19—on His horse, with His sword, judging His enemies in the name of truth and humility.

The astounding announcement of Psalm 45:6 is that this Bridegroom is God.

5.4 The glory of His bride

In Psalm 45:8-9, we shift from the glory of the Bridegroom/King as Protector, to the glory of His court and the beauty of His bride: *All Your garments are fragrant with myrrh and aloes and cassia; out of ivory palaces stringed instruments have made You glad. 9 Kings' daughters are among Your noble ladies; at Your right hand stands the queen in gold from Ophir.* The queen is to come to her king adorned, forgetting what is past so she can be loyal to him. He will desire her. Out of this union will come sons:

> Psalm 45:10-17—*Listen, O daughter, give attention and incline your ear: Forget your people and your father's house; 11 then the King will desire your beauty. Because He is your Lord, bow down to Him. 12 The*

---

3. Women can be extremely judgmental of men's weakness for **pornography**—an excessive and sinful visual obsession with the flesh that reduces women to physical playthings. But what about the addiction of many women to tabloids and romance novels? These entertainments can be just as warped in their obsession with emotionalism as pornography is obsessed with the flesh. These "bodice rippers" degrade men by portraying them as unnaturally emotional and feminized, just as "skin flicks" degrade women by portraying them as unnatural in their physicality. Indulging in unrealistic fantasies—whether men into pornography or women into romanticism—is equally idolatrous and equally destructive of the man's ability to love a real woman or of the woman's ability to respect a real man.

daughter of Tyre will come with a gift; the rich among the people will seek your favor. 13 The King's daughter is all glorious within; her clothing is interwoven with gold. 14 She will be led to the King in embroidered work; the virgins, her companions who follow her, will be brought to You. 15 They will be led forth with gladness and rejoicing; they will enter into the King's palace. 16 In place of your fathers will be your sons; You shall make them princes in all the earth. 17 I will cause Your name to be remembered in all generations; therefore the peoples will give You thanks forever and ever.

Notice in verse 13, *The king's daughter is all glorious within*. There is some ambiguity in this verse in the original Hebrew. She is all glorious within what—her chambers, her spirit, her body, her garments? We could revisit the whole section on inner domains! Don't worry, we won't; but this verse does support the idea of the glory and femininity of inner domains.

5.5 The humble Man who comes again (Rev. 19-22)

Psalm 45 radiates with the glory that sexuality brings to men, women, and to God Himself. It is the very glory of Christ and His Church. It is the glory that touches our lives as sexual beings, and it is the glory that will one day culminate history. Indeed, *the Spirit and the bride say, "Come!"* (Rev. 22:17). The Church is eager for her Bridegroom to come back, that the consummation of all things may be hers. How fitting that the last personal metaphor of the Bible is a wedding metaphor based on a feminine response to masculine glory! It is a glory redeemed.

Personification of Glory—*redeemed*

I am Glory of Man—*redeemed.*

I picture Christ's own bride—pure, adorned with good works, the loved and cherished body of which He is Head. Picturing the believer is an honor, not an insult. I do not have to be independent and earn everything on my own. Indeed, I cannot. There is a time to lean and to receive grace from God and men as well. By taking my place in God's creation symphony, I glorify both God and men.

Masculine authority does not limit my giftedness; rather it increases the effectiveness of my labors. The interaction and teamwork of masculine men and feminine women, especially at home and in the church, get work done in the most effective and enjoyable way. I'm a *vive-la-différence* girl!

I love beauty in all its forms and seek to foster it wherever I can. I love clothes, interior decorating, flowers, crafts, and the fine arts. Beauty is a gift and ministry from me to all those whose lives I touch. However, I strive to remember that spiritual beauty is the most basic beauty. Kind deeds and a gentle, quiet, and submissive spirit are my best adornment. Well-pleasing to God above, they also soothe much strife here below.

When single, I enjoy my freedom to concentrate on the Lord as my Head and Husband. My moral purity frees me to serve God and enjoy the men who are in my life. I seek to be appropriately responsive and supportive of these men, and to follow the authorities I have, especially my father, pastor, and boss. Speaking of Dad, I was a great Daddy's girl when I was little, and now that I am grown, I appreciate him more each year.

When I marry (I love being a bride!), I am deeply loyal to my husband. I enjoy his masculinity and praise him whenever I can. The strength of his protection, the tenderness of his love, and the fire of his passion make me feel womanly, free, and safe all at the same time. I love being married. I'm free to enjoy my emotions, and sex, too! I guard against wandering eyes, but inside marriage I let myself go!

When I think of my hope in Christ, I think of Him coming on His white horse in glory, slaying His enemies with His sword. I think of the purity and beauty that will be at the great Wedding Feast when every spot and wrinkle will have been removed from my life. I especially think of getting to see Him in His greatness, power, and perfect, kingly love. I heartily agree with John who wrote, *the Spirit and the bride say, "Come."*

Bible Study of Glory—*redeemed*

Before beginning this study, read the entire lesson, pages 105-117.

> *"And I saw the holy city, new Jerusalem, coming down out of heaven from God, made ready as a bride adorned for her husband. ...And one of the seven angels who had the seven bowls full of the seven last plagues, came and spoke with me, saying, "Come here, I shall show you the bride, the wife of the Lamb." And he carried me away in the Spirit to a great and high mountain, and showed me the holy city, Jerusalem, coming down out of heaven from God, having the glory of God. Her brilliance was like a very costly stone, as a stone of crystal-clear jasper.*
>
> REVELATION 21:2, 9-11

The fifteenth Biblical view of woman

Made radiant by the light of God's glory, the redeemed glory of man is freed to fulfill her calling as a feminine worshiper in beauty and adornment.

A created longing

Beauty is basic to femininity. Vast effort and billions of dollars are spent each year by women all over the world to add, enhance, preserve, or adorn the tiniest fragments of their loveliness. Women like to adorn not only themselves, but everything they touch—their homes, tables, offices, and children. Why is this impulse so strong and universal? It is not all worldly pride. The desire for beauty and adornment is a created facet of the feminine nature. Like every other part of our created and fallen beings, the beauty that is rightfully feminine finds its redemption and ultimate expression in Christ.

Forgiveness!

Christ's death and forgiveness include the power to wash away all sexual shame and degradation. By clothing us in the beauty of His righteousness, He has restored hope and glory to human sexuality. As the redeemed glory of man, women are freed to glorify God with the beauty and brilliance of a very precious jewel.

1. The number of Christians and would-be converts who struggle with sexual guilt and shame is increasing greatly as our society turns away from the fear of the Lord. Thus, it is all the more important that we be able to explain the objective reality of forgiveness and cleansing in Christ. Review pages 105-106, Psalm 32, and 38. Outline the points you would make to assure and ground a sinner in the forgiveness of God. (This sinner might be a friend struggling with guilt, an immoral person you are evangelizing, or it might be yourself.)

2. Christ makes clear that the sinful woman of Luke 7:36-50 loved much because she had been forgiven much. Are the big sins in your past (whether sexual or not) leading you to love Christ more? What is the thought process that goes from remembering a past sin to the attitude of abundant love for Christ and a desire to serve Him lavishly? (If this thought process is not familiar to you, consider whether you have really claimed the forgiveness of Christ. Are you attempting to please Him with fig leaves and dead works?)

3. The woman at the well in John 4 had had five husbands and was living with yet another man, not her husband. Her glory-of-man aspect was definitely fallen. Yet she was quick to recognize Christ and enter into His service with joy. What truths do you think she had learned in her disreputable past that made her so open to God?

When the Samaritan woman met Christ, she found the One she was looking for—the Man she could worship and trust. The woman at the well could be any woman who has become a fallen glory of man. Whenever fallen women meet Christ, they find the one Man who is the true glory of God, worthy of faith, trust, and worship.

Sexuality as a glory to man and woman

Song of Solomon is the greatest song written by the wisest man who ever lived. A celebration of the romantic and erotic love between a man and a woman, it is the greatest of his 1,005 songs.

4. How does Song of Solomon portray romance, marriage, and sex as a glory to man and woman (refer to pp. 107-109)?

5. The helping and lifegiving aspects of homemaking frequently consume so much time and energy that many wives neglect the physical love and romance basic to the glory-of-man aspect in marriage. Why is this negligence wrong (1 Cor. 7:2-5; Heb. 13:4)? How can this sin of omission hurt others?

Human love is valuable for its own sake because God has granted us individual dignity and worth. The purity, adornment, love, and passion that the Shulammite brought to Solomon were beautiful in and of themselves, and worthy of the great artistic expression he penned. However, romantic love is not merely or simply a human experience. From the beginning and all through history, it mirrors and shadows the love affair of God and His people.

Human sexuality as a glory to God

6. Marriage law, in both the Old and New Testaments, reflects God's primary revelation about Himself. Complete the following chart with help from pages 111-114.

	Primary message in the Old Testament:	**Primary message in the New Testament:**
About God		
Summary of commands to men as sexual stewards		
Summary of commands to women as sexual stewards		

7. Psalm 45 is a Messianic Psalm, prophesying Christ and His work. Read Psalm 45:1-9, paying special attention to verse 6. Of all the glorious attributes describing Christ as Bridegroom in this passage, which two do you find most wonderful?

Adorned by and for the Bridegroom

8. We discovered in Ezekiel 16:1-14 how God adorned His wife, Israel. What is Christ doing to make His bride radiant (Eph. 5:25-27)? How and why should human husbands emulate Christ in this (Eph. 5:28-33)?

9. As a redeemed woman, how can you continue to give glory to your husband, even when he does not fulfill Ephesians 5:28-33? How does knowing Christ as the perfect God-Man and Husbandman help you in this (1 Pet. 2:21-3:2)?

10. Christ is getting His bride ready. How is she getting herself ready (Rev. 19:7-8)? What is the *fine linen, bright and clean*?

11. How does Revelation 19:8 relate to the commands in 1 Timothy 2:9-10 and 1 Peter 3:3-6 (refer to the chart in question 6)?

The lavish gift

12. Mary of Bethany is one of the few women who ever had the opportunity to express her glory-of-man aspect directly to the God-Man. How did she worship Christ in a way that was both feminine and beautiful (John 12:1-8; 1 Cor. 11:15)? What was the immediate effect of Mary's gift on her surroundings?

13. Mary poured out a lavish gift on Christ. Who objected to Mary's gift? Who benefited from Mary's gift? What were the long-term results of Mary's action (Matt. 26:10-13)?

14. How do you strike a balance between appreciation for beauty on one hand, and principles of humility and frugality on the other? In your view, when is a lavish gift appropriate?

15. Mary of Bethany, the Shulammite of Song of Solomon, and the weavers of the tabernacle (Ex. 35:25-26) provide us with a tradition of beauty. Considering their examples, how might you become more beautiful and give beauty to others in the following areas? Include elements of physical and spiritual beauty in your answers.

    a. self

    b. home

    c. church and community

The ultimate glory

16. We all know the expression "bridal glow," and have witnessed the reality of a formerly lackluster girl becoming beautifully radiant at the time of her wedding. What is your explanation for this?

17. As a believer, how are you adorning yourself for Christ's coming? What lavish gift of worship can you give Him from your life?

Give to the LORD the glory due His name; bring an offering, and come before Him. Oh, worship the LORD in the beauty of holiness!

1 CHRONICLES 16:29 [NKJV]

18. What is the ultimate beauty, glory, and adornment (Ezek. 16:14; Rev. 21:10-11)? Who will share in this glory?

Beauty is a result both of labor and a response to another. We, as women, beautify ourselves and our domains. Our drive to do so is part of our God-given feminine desire to please our Lord. The bride of Christ is making herself ready with good works. Yet, there is a final radiance which is the reflection of another. The bride of Christ will shine with radiance because her Bridegroom is like the sun. Her bridal glow will be a reflection of His greatness and glory.

LESSON 21 : Glory of Man – *life lessons*

Learning... to worship God and reflect His radiance.

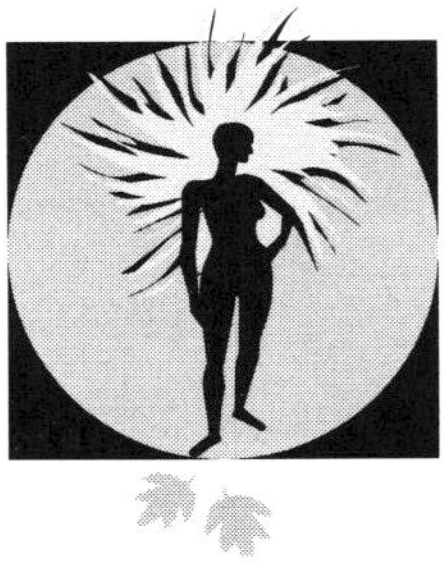

1. In one or two paragraphs, write how you would describe this aspect to your daughter or a friend. Feel free to incorporate other creative formats, such as a prayer, song, poem, recipe, story, skit, or even a sketch illustrating this aspect. Include all the basic truths about this aspect.

2. What part of this aspect has meant the most to your life? Why?

3. How is this aspect being lived out in your life right now?

4. Write a paragraph explaining how you are asking God to mature and perfect this aspect in your life. Be specific.

Pray specifically each day this week for God to bring circumstances and people into your life to strengthen your attitudes and actions concerning this aspect.

5. For each of the following categories, identify and describe one woman you think displays in a clear and obvious way the glory-of-man aspect. Briefly explain your choice—what you see in this woman's life or character which illustrates this aspect. You may mention more than one woman, if you wish.

a. A character from the Bible

b. A woman from history (ancient to recent)

c. A fictional character in a novel, fairy tale, legend, etc.

d. A character in a film you have seen

Now may the God of peace Himself sanctify you entirely; and may your spirit and soul and body be preserved complete, without blame at the coming of our Lord Jesus Christ. Faithful is He who calls you, and He also will bring it to pass.

1 THESSALONIANS 5:23-24

Summations

Five Aspects of Woman
– created
– fallen
– redeemed

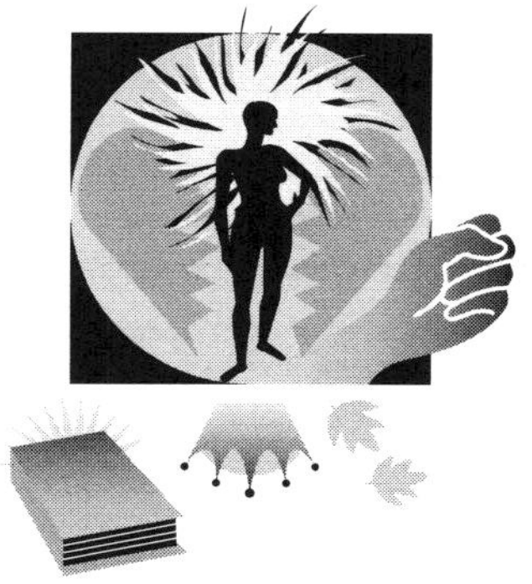

God created woman . . .

to rule her domain,

to help man,

to give life,

to serve with skill and insight,

and to glorify God.

Thy testimonies are wonderful; therefore my soul observes them. The unfolding of Thy words gives light; it gives understanding to the simple. I opened my mouth wide and panted, for I longed for Thy commandments. Turn to me and be gracious to me, after Thy manner with those who love Thy name. Establish my footsteps in Thy word, and do not let any iniquity have dominion over me. Redeem me from the oppression of man, that I may keep Thy precepts. Make Thy face shine upon Thy servant, and teach me Thy statutes. PSALM 119:129-135 *But prove yourselves doers of the word, and not merely hearers who delude themselves. For if anyone is a hearer of the word and not a doer, he is like a man who looks at his natural face in a mirror; for once he has looked at himself and gone away, he has immediately forgotten what kind of person he was. But one who looks intently at the perfect law, the law of liberty, and abides by it, not having become a forgetful hearer but an effectual doer, this man shall be blessed in what he does.* JAMES 1:22-25

LESSON 22 Summation 1 – *Foundations*

1. Seeking the whole counsel of God

If the *Five Aspects* were compared to a five-room house, what would its foundation be? The foundation of the aspects house is the whole counsel of God. I hope many find the *Aspects* helpful; much more, I hope its students grow in hunger for God's Word. My organizational schema is not as important as seeing our great need for the whole of Scripture, comparing Scripture with Scripture, to come to an understanding of the truth.

1.1 Sexuality is a major secular and sacred debate in our time.

Gender debates raged in the last half of the twentieth century and will continue to do so in the foreseeable future. One Bible verse or one set of verses will not solve the problem of gender controversy and confusion. We cannot go to Galatians 3:28, which says that in Christ *there is neither male nor female,* and say this verse has solved the whole problem—the answer is equality. Neither can we go to Ephesians 5:22, which states that wives are to *submit to their husbands,* and say that this verse settles it—the answer is female submission.

1.2 Complex issues are the substance of the faith.

The one-idea or one-verse solution is not valid and will not work with this kind of issue. Complicated issues such as sexuality are not simply side irritants to the supposedly-simple Christian faith. If you look back over the history of the faith, you will see that Christianity is built upon complicated questions. Its simple parts can be explained and believed by a child, but its rock-bottom truths are complicated ideas. Here are five examples:

- The Trinity. God is one, *and* God is three.
- God's character. God is love, He is compassionate every day; *and* God is just, He is wrathful with sin every day.
- The mechanism of history. God is sovereign, *and* men make real and responsible choices.
- Salvation. The whole issue of salvation is a subset of the mechanism of history. Salvation is by God's election, *and* whosoever will may come. God calls and draws; man believes.
- The Incarnation. Christ is God, *and* Christ is man.

> Complicated issues such as sexuality are not simply side irritants to the supposedly-simple Christian faith. If you look back over the history of the faith, you will see that Christianity is built upon complicated questions.

1.3 Complex issues require careful study.

If you take the one-verse or the one-set-of-verses approaches to any one of these issues—to the exclusion of the other truths—you will be a heretic. For example, consider the Incarnation. Orthodox Christians believe that Christ is man *and* God. Certainly the apostles came to believe this as they were with Him. However, it took 300 to 450 years before the doctrine of the Incarnation was understood, written down, and established so the Church could defend it against every basic attack. In paraphrase, the Chalcedon Creed (more accurately, the Definition of Chalcedon, 451 A.D.) states: "Christ is undiminished Deity and true humanity, united in one Person, without confusion or mixture, forever." This was written about 450 years after Christ was on the earth. Was it new truth? No, the Biblical truth is there from the moment it is penned. But God's people must dig it out, like mining gold. We must unearth the truths and come to a clear understanding of the doctrines that lie in its veins.

Almost every single word of the sentence just quoted from the Chalcedon Creed represents an intense fight, because everything imaginable was said about Christ. Some said He was all God and not man. Others said He was all man and not God. Others, that He was neither God nor man, but an angel, or a mixture of the two. Others claimed He was schizophrenic with two personalities. Thus, through these controversies, the Church, taught by the Holy Spirit, learned to rule with sound doctrine. The Church fathers honed their understanding of Scripture's teaching until they came to a full-orbed understanding of the truth of the Incarnation that believers can state, defend, and hold over time.

Though not as important as the Incarnation, sexuality is a substantive doctrine and part of the whole fabric of God's truth. As with all the complicated doctrines, we must defend against many different errors. We must look at the whole of Scripture, comparing passage to passage, to come to a full understanding of God's Word, so that we will be rooted and grounded and not subject to the winds of doctrine. You might say, "This is not really a question for me. I have a sense of what a man is and what a woman is. I intuitively have it in my bones." You may have it in your bones, but your children and your grandchildren may not. The roots of Western civilization that gave you intuitive gender sense have crumbled. We must have a clear and discussable message for the next generation if we are to explain to them who man and woman are.

2. Sources for the whole counsel of God

As stated, the foundation of the five-room aspect house is the whole counsel of God. Rising from and rooted in this foundation are four pillars, representing four different types of Biblical literature. These pillar types are definitions, laws, narratives, and archetypes (introduced in *FAW—Vol. One*, p. 8). As with the aspects themselves, these truths may be organized or named differently, but the categories are basic for all, no matter what they are called.

2.1 Definitions

The Bible gives us many definitions. *And the evening and the morning were the first day*. The fifth verse of all Scripture tells us that every day has what we would call an A.M. and a P.M. When the Bible states something categorically, it is telling us about the nature of things. For instance, God is love; sin is missing the mark; man is the image of God. When the Bible gives a clear and defining statement, we have a sure piece of knowledge about that thing, whether that thing is heaven, the devil, rivers, man, mountains, or woman.

All the aspects except lady of wisdom are built on Biblical definitions. God says in Genesis 1 that woman is the image of God; in Genesis 2, He declares that He will make her a helper to complete the man. 1 Corinthians 11:7 declares she is the glory of man. When the Bible gives a clear and definitive statement about something, then we must incorporate that knowledge into our understanding, or we will have less than a Biblical view of that thing.

Once over dinner, I began to discuss gender issues with a missionary friend. He said, "Sexuality is complicated and has so many cultural variations. We really can't talk about sexuality. We don't have anything definite to say." I responded, "Are you saying that the Church has nothing to say to a lost world about who man is, who woman is, and what sexuality is as created by God? Are you saying that we, as Christians, don't have any truth to give on how to live as sexual beings?" His answer was, "No, it's not very important to what we do."

The danger in this kind of thinking progresses like this. Someone says, "I think Genesis is myth. We don't have anything definitive to say about origins because Genesis is only moral stories." Then someone else turns to the back of the Bible and says, "Revelation is full of symbol, and no one really knows how to interpret these symbols. So we cannot say anything clear and definite about the end times." And another voice adds, "The middle of the Bible is about first-century men, like Christ and the apostles. Their teaching is culturally conditioned. We cannot apply it directly to our day. Sexuality, for example, is a cultural issue. It is so complicated and cultural that we cannot really say anything about that." Whatever you call it, this approach to the Bible is actually unbelief. When you make of no effect the claims and commands of God, you are acting in unbelief. This does not mean that we automatically understand every verse in the Bible, or that we should be arrogantly dogmatic on every point. There is a great difference between believing a passage is true and important (even without understanding it because of limited knowledge), and proclaiming a passage not relevant because it is judged to be myth, culturally determined, or indecipherable symbol.

There is a great difference between believing a passage is true, even without understanding it, and proclaiming a passage not relevant because it is judged to be myth, culturally determined, or indecipherable symbol.

We teach about sexuality because Christians do have an intelligible message about it. When God makes a definitive statement, we can understand it, and through further study we can understand it better. In 2 Corinthians 4:13, Paul quotes the psalmist, *But having the same spirit of faith, according to what is written, "I BELIEVED, THEREFORE I SPOKE,..."* Paul looks back to the psalmist and says he spoke because he believed; and, Paul spoke in the first century because he believed. In the twenty-first century we say, "It is written, we believe, therefore we speak." The written message from God is intelligible and knowable. I speak about sexuality not because I think I know it all, but because the Scriptures are clear, definitive, and intelligible. We have a clear and substantive message for ourselves and the world.

2.2 Laws

The second foundational pillar is the law. God gives us commands. The most prominent example is the Ten Commandments. He says, "Love Me. Do not murder. Adultery is wrong." In effect, "Do this; do not do that. Here is a boundary; do not step over it." Laws do not usually tell us our identity; they tell us what we should do. They mark goals and set limits for behavior.

Instruction in the law of God is very important. One is not grounded in the whole counsel of God without convictions in Biblical law and law issues such as adultery, divorce, remarriage, abortion, contraception, etc. However, *Five Aspects'* main purpose is not to tell us what to do;its first purpose is to illuminate who we are. Therefore, this study does not focus on teaching the law, but rather, assumes the law as a moral foundation and framework for understanding our sexual identity. For example, the "language of worship written in our bodies," described in Lesson 19, section 3.2, is based on the revelation that adultery, fornication, and homosexuality are wrong. Without these absolutes we could not build an understanding of archetypal patterns; yet, it is by archetypal patterns that we better understand the "why" of God's laws. All these types of revelation—definitions, laws, narratives, and archetypes—reinforce and illuminate one another, giving us a fuller picture and understanding of God, His mind, and ways.

2.3 Narratives

The third pillar is Biblical narratives, which give us examples. In 1 Corinthians 10:11, Paul clearly explains how the stories of the Bible should be used. *Now these things* [Israel's history] *happened to them as an example, and they were written for our instruction, upon whom the ends of the ages have come.* The stories are to be used to give us examples and instruction, that is, fuller insight, shades of meaning, illustrations we can remember. In 1 Peter 3:1-5, Peter gives wives general instruction, but then in verse 6, he gives Sarah as a specific example of a submissive and fearless wife; she is a specific woman from the Old Testament narrative whose story sheds more light on Peter's commands.

Narratives do not provide absolute moral standards. For example, if you turn to 2 Samuel 11 and see David commit adultery and murder, you do not say, "David was a great saint; therefore, the devotional thought for today is that adultery and murder are okay." We know that adultery and murder are wrong. We know this because the Ten Commandments, as God's law, stand in judgment over David. One cannot take narrative passages out of context and erect absolutes upon them. The commands and laws of Scripture must control how one interprets the narratives. The example of David is simple. Consider another strongly-debated narrative that is not quite so simple.

Let us compare 1 Timothy 2:12 with Acts 18. Timothy is a book written by the apostle Paul to a young preacher named Timothy, telling him how to rule in the household of God. Paul gives directives and commands about how to run the institution of the Church—what to do in worship, how to select elders and deacons, how women can serve most effectively, and so on. Acts, on the other hand, is a book of history. It tells us the exciting things that were done by the Holy Spirit and the believers in the first century.

Paul says in 1 Timothy 2:12, *I do not allow a woman to teach or exercise authority over a man.* He does not give a cultural reason for this. He does not say women must not rule and teach men because women in Corinth do not have enough education or because they had not been to seminary. This is not the reason he gives. He gives a reason based on creation: *For it was Adam who was first created, and then Eve* (1 Tim. 2:13). Paul's reason is based not on something cultural, but upon something that affects the whole human race—the created order. The final responsibility for guarding the flock and preaching the Word should be kept on the shoulders of men who were created to be the leaders of the human family.

Now, let us consider Acts 18:24-26: *Now a Jew named Apollos, an Alexandrian by birth, an eloquent man, came to Ephesus; and he was mighty in the Scriptures. 25 This man had been instructed in the way of the Lord; and being fervent in spirit, he was speaking and teaching accurately the things concerning Jesus, being acquainted only with the baptism of John; 26 and he began to speak out boldly in the synagogue. But when Priscilla and Aquila heard him, they took him aside and explained to him the way of God more accurately.* Some say that because Priscilla takes part in teaching Apollos, this story overturns 1 Timothy 2. According to this line of thought, because Priscilla took part in sharing new truth with a man in private, possibly in her own home, women should therefore be made elders in the Church. But there is a difference between a woman enjoying freedom to discuss theology with her husband and a visiting theologian in private conversation, and using that example to install women as elders of the Church. This is using narrative to overturn law.

However, the narratives do help us interpret the law. For instance, I am glad the Priscilla story is provided, because someone might take 1 Timothy 2:11, *A woman must quietly receive instruction with entire submissiveness,* and interpret it to mean a woman should never say anything at any time—not at home or at church. Priscilla gives us an example of how a first-century Christian woman behaved in the private setting, an example that is entirely in keeping with woman's humanity, her partnership in the Gospel, and her femininity as well.

2.4 Archetypes

The fourth pillar truth is archetypes. As you remember, an **archetype** is an original or exemplary pattern. In this course we have looked to the Bible for the first and pan-historic (ageless) models of masculinity and femininity. These archetypes add depth and richness to the Bible's answers about manhood, womanhood, and the meaning of sexuality. Following are the primary masculine and feminine archetypes. If we can understand why God considers these entities masculine and feminine, we will be a long way toward understanding His gender categories.

PRIMARY GENDER ARCHETYPES

Righteous masculine archetypes

- God the Father
- God the Son
- God the Holy Spirit
- Christ, the God-Man, the last Adam
- Created Adam, the first man

Righteous feminine archetypes

- wisdom, the first feminine
- Eve, the first woman
- Israel, the wife of God
- the Virgin Mary, mother of Christ
- the Church, the bride of Christ
- Jerusalem, our mother above

Evil masculine archetypes

- Satan, the father of lies
- the anti-Christ, called the man of sin
- the false prophet
- fallen Adam

Evil feminine archetypes

- woman folly
- Babylon, the mother of harlots

3. Biblical patterns of archetypal masculinity and femininity

3.1 The great interpretive passage: Ephesians 5:22-33

In my opinion, Ephesians 5:31-32 are the most important interpretative verses on gender archetypes in all of Scripture. In verse 31, Paul quotes the original marriage verse, Genesis 2:24: *For this reason a man shall leave his father and mother and shall be joined to his wife; and the two shall become one flesh.* Then in verse 32, the apostle writes this: *This mystery is great; but I am speaking with reference to Christ and the church.* Here Paul makes a startling revelation about the original pattern of marriage itself. What is this mystery? A **mystery** is something not known in the Old Testament but revealed in the New. We naturally think of Adam and Eve in the Old Testament as coming before Christ and the Church in the New Testament. But Paul says no. When God created the first man and first woman, He fashioned them with two patterns or images in His mind: The first pattern was His own image; the second pattern was Christ and His Church as one body. The first model explains our humanity, God's image, which we individually possess as men and women. The second model explains our sexuality, with the male taking Christ's part and the female taking the Church's part. Both of these things are basic to human design.

Because archetypes give us the original patterns, they, more than definitions, laws, or narratives, provide the pictures which answer the "why" behind many of God's laws. If we remember that Christ and the Church are the model for marriage, then we easily can see why promiscuity, adultery, divorce, and homosexuality are wrong. They are all wrong because they break

Biblical Patterns of Masculinity and Femininity

PATTERN	God and wisdom	Creator and creation	Adam and Eve
1. The masculine is first and alone.	God and His eternal attribute of wisdom existed before "lady" wisdom (natural law).	The Trinity was complete in eternity past, before creation (John 17:24).	Adam was created first in the world; he was established in the garden alone.
2. The feminine comes from the masculine.	God brought forth (created) wisdom before the rest of creation (Prov. 8:22-24).	Creation is from God; He made it from nothing.	Woman was made from Adam's side (Gen. 2).
3. The feminine reflects the masculine but is separate from the masculine.	Wisdom is creation principles; not the same as God or Christ.	God is not the universe; pantheism is wrong. God is to creation what an artist is to his art.	Although made for the man, woman is the full image of God apart from man (Gen. 1:27; 2:18).
4. The feminine is created for the masculine as helper, companion, fruitbearer, and glorifier.	Wisdom was God's companion at creation (Prov. 8:27-30).	The heavens are God's tent; the earth is His footstool (Is. 40:22; 66:1). Creation glorifies God by reflecting Him (Ps. 19:1-6; Rom. 1:18-20).	God gave Eve to Adam to help him and complete him (Gen. 2).
5. Masculine inititation and feminine response unify the two.	God initiated creation and wisdom responded. She delighted in what He did (Prov. 8:30-31).	God came into union with the creation through Mary. Christ is both Creator and created (John 1:14).	Sexual union is the consummating act of marriage (Gen. 2:24).
6. Union produces fruit in the image of both the providing father and nurturing mother.	God created our world with wisdom as His template (Prov. 8:27-30; Job 28:12, 23-27).	God rules the world and provides for mother nature. She produces fruits of praise, beauty, and joy (Ps. 96:1-97:6).	The union of Adam and Eve produced co-laboring and children.
7. The masculine and feminine mature as they co-labor, fellowship, and bear fruit.	Neither God nor wisdom matures. God progressively reveals Himself. Wisdom is progressively discovered by men.	God provides and the earth is satisfied (Ps. 104). Creation labors in childbirth, awaiting God's kingdom (Rom. 8:19-22).	Adam and Eve persevered through grief to bring forth Seth, the Messianic seed (Gen. 4:25-5:5).
8. Glory and dwelling are perfected in each other.	Although revealed in creation, wisdom finally dwells with God alone (Job 28:12-27).	The curse is removed. Creator and creation dwell in perfect harmony in New Heavens and New Earth (Rev. 21–22).	Adam and Eve are saints in heaven today. He is the first head of the race; she is the mother of all the living.

PATTERN	God and Israel	Christ and the Church	Men and Women
1. The masculine is first and alone.	God was the God of all nations before Israel existed (Gen. 1–11).	Christ was before the Church in His divinity and His humanity.	A man should establish something of his own identity, territory, and livelihood before seeking a wife.
2. The feminine comes from the masculine.	God created Israel supernaturally from barren people (Gen. 12–50; Ezek. 16:5-6).	The Church is built of Christ's body and blood (John 6:53-58; 19:34; 1 Cor. 11:23-30).	A man should look for a suitable wife and be willing to sacrifice for her.
3. The feminine reflects the masculine but is separate from the masculine.	Israel represents God, but is not God. She has often rebelled (Deut. 4:6-8; Is. 1:4; Rom. 9:3-5).	The mature Church reflects Christ's image (Eph. 4:12-13; Rom. 8:29). The Church remains human, is not divine.	A woman should mature in her own identity. She should not be merely a leaner.
4. The feminine is created for the masculine as helper, companion, fruitbearer, and glorifier.	Israel was created to be God's unique possession (Deut. 4:20).	A gift of the Father to the Son, the Church is Christ's body, helper, fruitbearer, and glorifier.	A woman should view marriage as a commitment to help her man in his work and person.
5. Masculine inititation and feminine response unify the two.	God gave the Law and the tabernacle. Israel built and kept the tabernacle, thus dwelling with God.	The Church is to be a pure virgin for Christ, not adulterous with the world (1 Cor. 6:17; 2 Cor. 11:2-3; James 4:4).	Marital union is enacted in sexual relations and fostered through long-term cohabitation (1 Cor. 7:1-5).
6. Union produces fruit in the image of both the providing father and nurturing mother.	God and Israel produced the Kingdom of God (1446–586 B.C.), the Bible, and Christ.	Abiding in Christ produces fruit—evangelism, good works, glory to God (John 15:1-11).	Ideally, marital union produces children, adequate wealth, Christian testimony, and service.
7. The masculine and feminine mature as they co-labor, fellowship, and bear fruit.	Israel's maturity is certain, though rebellion has necessitated a temporary divorce from God (Ezek. 16:46-63; Rom. 11:25-29).	Christ is progressively revealed and the Church is progressively perfected through the centuries (Eph. 4:11-16).	The usual path to human maturity is perseverance in married life (1 Tim. 3:2-5; 5:9-10).
8. Glory and dwelling are perfected in each other.	God will dwell in Zion and glorify her. She will dwell secure and be His glory (Is. 4:4-6; 60-66; Rev. 21:10-27).	The Church is Christ's glory; He is hers. He dwells in her; she abides in Him (Rev. 19:7-9; 21:2-3, 9-11).	Ideally, an older couple dwells in harmony and enjoys the fruit of their lifetime of labors.

the divine model. Some of you may have been reared in very moral, but pragmatic homes in which you were told what to do but were rarely given a reason why. We should obey God by faith whether we understand the "why" or not. However, understanding some of the "whys" is what gives us confidence in the goodness and the plan of God. For example, if you are taught a very satisfying explanation of origins and sexuality, you will be stronger to face such imponderables as suffering or election. God's law must interpret the archetypes, just as it does the narratives. Nevertheless, the archetypal pictures often give meaning to the laws, thus strengthening us to obey.

When God created the first man and first woman, He fashioned them with two patterns in mind: The first pattern was His own image; the second pattern was Christ and the Church. The first model explains our humanity; the second model explains our sexuality.

The need for model and meaning drives both Christians and pagans to seek archetypes for life and for sexuality. Christian archetypes controlled Western civilization for almost two thousand years. Post-moderns reject and ridicule the "old patriarchal, heroic sky God of the Bible." The Throne of law and justice, He commanded responsibility, heroism, and sacrifice. But there is no place for Him in the modern world; He must be repudiated. If modern women embrace a new femininity which repudiates picturing the Church, then modern men must have a new masculinity which repudiates picturing Christ. Some suggest a return to the old pagan gods worshiped before the Christian era, such as Poseidon and Zeus.[1] However, since the triumph of autonomy and non-rationality in the post-modern world, more often than not, no model or archetype is offered, pagan or otherwise. Men and women are just supposed to make themselves up as they go along.

Nevertheless, we all do need models as well as laws. Scripture provides both and they are far superior. They are timeless and lofty, enduring from age to age and into eternity. God's patterns and archetypes do what models should do. They provide examples vast enough to accommodate billions of unique humans, yet specific enough to give us real and individual guidance in the confusion of everyday life.

3.2 Five archetypal couples

Five great archetypal couples can be delineated in Scripture: Christ and the Church; Adam and Eve; God and wisdom; the Creator and the creation; and God and Israel. The relationships of these five couples follow a pattern which can be outlined in eight points. These points generally are reflected in the basic and wholesome life cycle of ordinary men and women. Space does not permit me to trace each of the couples in detail through each of the points; therefore, I will simply introduce the eight points with sample illustrations. (This chart appears twice: *FAW—Vol. One*, pp. 218-219; and in this chapter, pp. 136-137.)

3.3 Archetypal development: Part One

The masculine is first and alone.

Christ was before anything. He was before the whole creation. He was before the Church in His divinity; He was also before the Church in His humanity. He came to the earth and spent His whole life preparing and finally dying for His bride. The Bible also emphasizes that Adam was

1. Jungian psychologists, Robert Moore and Douglas Gillette, offer a serious humanistic model for masculinity in *King, Warrior, Magician, Lover: Rediscovering The Archetypes of the Mature Masculine* (New York: HarperSanFrancisco, A Division of HarperCollins Publishers, 1990).

created first. It was not an accident. He had to learn his need for a helper and undergo surgery to get her. Thus we see the masculine is first and alone, often preparing for the coming feminine.

The feminine comes from the masculine.

The Church has come from Christ, from both His life and from His death. It was not an accident that the Roman soldier put a spear in Christ's side such that blood and water came out. Eve literally came from the side of Adam, as the Church comes figuratively from the side of Christ.

The feminine reflects the masculine, but is separate from the masculine.

The Church is to reflect Christ. The whole Church is being built up *to the measure of the stature which belongs to the fullness of Christ* (Eph. 4:13). Christ is magnificent and majestic in His person. The Church is being built into an organic body of people suitable for Him. At maturity, she will be a match appropriate to the measure of His stature. Eve was from Adam and made reflective of him. Her first name was *woman*, meaning "out of man." Adam recognized her immediately as from him and for him, his very flesh and bones. Scripture teaches repeatedly that the creation reflects, shows forth, and displays the glory, power, and Person of God. The creation is not God, as the pantheists would have us believe, but it reflects God.

3.4 Review of part one

- The masculine is first and alone, preparing for the feminine.
- The feminine comes from the masculine.
- The feminine is reflective of the masculine, but the feminine is separate from the masculine. This is very important. The Church is not Christ. Eve was not Adam. This is the importance of holding to both Genesis 1 and Genesis 2. She was from Adam, for Adam, and reflective of Adam, yet she was an individual, separate person in the image of God all by herself. As I have already emphasized, the creation is reflective of God and for God, but it is separate from Him. If the whole universe vanished, God the Father, Son, and Holy Spirit would be perfectly complete as They were before creation.

3.5 Archetypal development: Part Two

The feminine is made for the masculine.

The feminine is for the masculine in four ways: As a helper in work, a companion in fellowship, a fruit-bearer in life, and as a glorifier in response. Consider the Church as our example. The Church is Christ's helper, laboring for Him and with Him in His fields. She is called to fellowship with Christ (1 Cor. 1:9), walking with Him in His light and even sharing in His sufferings. The Church bears fruit to Christ. Jesus says, *"If you abide in Me and I abide in you, you will bear much fruit."* Our fruit is good works and the bringing forth and nurturing of new Christians. Finally, the Church glorifies Christ with response. We are saved *to the praise of His glory*, Paul repeatedly writes (Eph. 1:6, 12, 14).

Masculine initiation and feminine response unify the two.

Masculinity and femininity are made for union. They fit together—not in an amalgamation which destroys the integrity of the individuals involved, but in a union which forms a new whole. Man and woman fit together as one new body; there are few principles of the universe more apparent than this. In marriage, this union is literally enacted in sexual intercourse. Sexual intercourse was created to be the definitive act that makes marriage different from any other relationship, its love different from any other love.

When I was a freshman in college studying the Greek tragedies, my dignified lady professor (complete with gray hair in a bun on top of her head!) made a bold statement. She said, "Now, sexual intercourse is about union." I can remember sitting there, my eyes big as saucers, thinking, "Oh my goodness! She has explained what sexual intercourse means. It means union!" I thought that was really great. As pragmatic Americans, we often run short on meaning. Sexual intercourse is very complex in its meanings; among other things, it is about initiation, response, invasion, encompassing possession, seed-planting, love, fellowship, desire, and pleasure. Its shades and interpretations are almost as complicated as sexuality itself. Nevertheless, my professor certainly had spoken a great truth because intercourse is about union. God says, The two shall be one flesh.

Spiritually, even now we have union with Christ. In 1 Corinthians 6:16-17, we find two more bombshell verses tucked away: *Or do you not know that the one who joins himself to a prostitute is one body with her? For He says, "the two shall become one flesh." 17 But the one who joins himself to the Lord is one spirit with Him.* Our human spirits can have union with Christ's spirit. This union produces fulfillment and the fruits of love, joy, peace, and good works. The union is based on masculine initiation and feminine response. God initiates toward Israel, toward the Church, and the individual members of the Church. He chooses and elects us; we respond with faith and obedience.

Consider the word **consummate**. When you say the marriage was consummated, you mean that the couple actually made love and physically fulfilled their union. When we speak of the consummation of the age, we mean the coming together of all things. We enjoy a certain kind of individual union with Christ even today as we walk in the Spirit. However, we are looking forward to that time when the Church is built to the full stature of Christ. The completed Church will be ready for what the Bible calls the *marriage supper of the Lamb*, the consummation of the ages. This is a powerful idea and speaks of the union of Christ, who has initiated, and the redeemed Church, who responds.

Union produces fruit in the image of both the providing father and nurturing mother.

This union of the masculine and feminine produces fruit in the image of both. Parents all over the world marvel and delight to see both of themselves in their children. In like manner, Christians everywhere bear fruit to Christ. This fruit bears the identifying marks of His goodness and their own unique personality and gifts. Paul's and Peter's epistles are equally the fruit of the Holy Spirit, but their writings are easily distinguishable by the marks of their own individuality as men.

Further, masculine fathers and the feminine mothers take classic roles toward the fruit of their union—their offspring. Fathers provide and mothers nurture. God has provided and protected both Israel and the Church throughout history, preserving them both from destruction. Israel followed God and bore fruit to Him, caring for His temple, writing down the Bible, and bearing His Son. In like manner, the Church has nurtured God's children, teaching, reproving, and caring for them in the world. The providing and nurturing roles of the masculine and feminine are essential and inalienable.

The masculine and feminine mature as they co-labor, fellowship, and bear fruit.

After the masculine and the feminine have borne children and other fruit, what happens? In all of the cases, time elapses. God and Israel dwelt together for hundreds of years, from 1446 B.C. to 586 B.C., before their temporary separation. The Church now has been going on with Christ for 2,000 years. Adam lived 930 years; we assume Eve was with him most of that time. Time goes by, and maturity is the result. Adam and Eve had the tragic experience of losing their first two sons. We can only imagine the heartbreak they went through together before they found their faith renewed in Seth, the promised seed. In like manner, the Church has endured these hundreds of years, learning more doctrine and wisdom through experience. Israel is now separated from God; yet, she will be brought back to God as outlined in Ezekiel 16, wiser and more humble.

Why bring up maturity? God does not mature; He progressively reveals Himself—to Israel, to the Church, to us. But we, as men and women, do mature over time. The usual path to maturity for humans is monogamous marriage. The ideal training for an elder is to be the husband of one wife and to manage his own household well. The reasoning follows that he cannot manage the church of God if he does not know how to manage his own house (1 Tim. 3:1-7). The widow to be *put on the list* (employed by the church) should have been the wife of one husband, having brought up children, having accomplished a myriad of good works (1 Tim. 5:9-10). Thus marriage is the usual path to maturity—a lifetime of living with a member of the opposite sex, bearing fruit together. Certainly people can mature in Christ as celibates, as we have discussed. They can even grow through terrible events like divorce. David, who took many wrong turns on the gender road, was a great saint. Israel failed in her marriage to God, but she will fulfill her destiny. However, theirs is a painful and sad way. The better way is the progression of character that comes through relating faithfully to one's mate over a lifetime.

Glory and dwelling are perfected in each other.

Mutual dwelling and mutual glory are the culmination of God's plan for masculinity and femininity. The masculine glories in and is glorified by his feminine counterpart and dwells in her. The feminine, on the other hand, finds her glory in her masculine lord as she abides and rests in him. I hope you immediately recognize the idea of abiding together in glory as the Christian idea of heaven—for it is. Revelation 21:3 says: *"Behold, the tabernacle of God is among men, and He will dwell among them, and they shall be His people, and God Himself will be among them."* God is **our** dwelling place in all generations; and yet the people of God are **His** dwelling place. As He dwelt among the tents of the Israelites of old, He will dwell in the New Jerusalem in the midst of His redeemed people. This is the city that Abraham was looking for, the city whose foundations were built by God, full of permanence and peace.

As it is with dwelling, so it will be with glory. In Revelation 19, Christ is presented in glory—on a white horse with many crowns. Yet in chapters 21-22, the New Jerusalem is presented as God's culminating glory. The Great City comes out of heaven, adorned as a bride for her husband. Her splendor is the glory of God. She needs neither moon nor sun, for the glory of God is her light. His glory is the praise of His people. In some marriages we do see a shadow of this final culmination. Some older couples who have walked together through the many seasons of life exude an evening glow. The decades of life have done their work. Bonded and content, such a couple presents a wedded masculinity and femininity that dwells together, glorying in each other and the fruits of a shared lifetime.

3.6 Review of the archetypal pattern

If you compare the archetypal couples, you will see these common elements:

1. The masculine is first and alone.
2. The feminine comes from the masculine.
3. The feminine reflects the masculine, but is separate from the masculine.
4. The feminine is for the masculine, as a helper, companion, fruit-bearer, and glorifier.
5. The feminine and the masculine are made for union, based upon masculine initiation and feminine response.
6. Their union produces fruit in the image of both the providing father and the nurturing mother.
7. Over time, whether centuries or decades, the masculine and the feminine mature. In the case of God, He progressively reveals Himself so that we have a fuller knowledge of Him.
8. Finally, all culminates in joy and unity, each being the dwelling place and glory of the other.

4. Conclusion

Sexuality is a complicated topic. To understand it, we need to look at the whole counsel of God, not just one passage or one set of passages. We need to get our definitions from God's definitions. We need to set our boundaries and build our convictions upon His laws. His narratives and stories should be the stuff of our meditations, providing our examples and applications. Finally, archetypes give us the universal and timeless gender models. They provide the overall patterns which give meaning and unity to the whole of God's message. As complex as it is, sexuality comes down to this: It is a glorious gift to mankind, meant to picture the love relationship between God and His people.

I am deeply satisfied with the Bible's answers as to the meaning of masculinity, femininity, and their relationship. I hope you will find this satisfaction as well in God and His whole counsel.

This also comes from the LORD of hosts, who has made His counsel wonderful and His wisdom great.

ISAIAH 28:29

Bible Study of Summation 1—*Foundations*

Before beginning this study, read the entire lesson, pages 130-142.

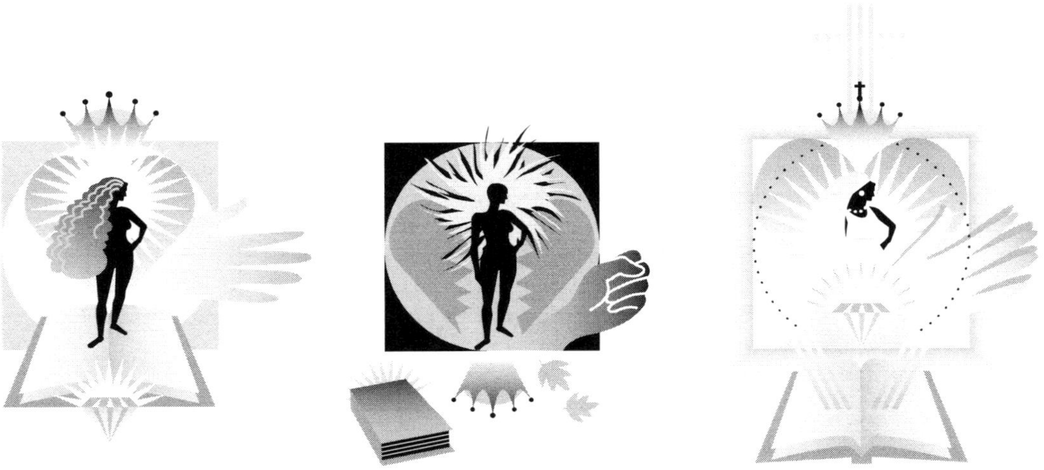

Biblical truths supporting *Five Aspects of Woman*

Based on Biblical definitions, laws, narratives, and archetypes, *Five Aspects of Woman* is founded on the whole counsel of God.

Seeking the whole counsel of God

Today in our culture, the nature of sexuality is debated, discussed, and dissected with regularity and vigor. It is difficult to read a newspaper, watch television, or walk into a bookstore without being confronted by endless controversy and confusion surrounding the topic of gender. Now that you have spent time studying the *Five Aspects of Woman's* model of womanhood, you should be more confident in your understanding and position in this great debate.

To undergird this study of womanhood, it is useful to examine the foundation upon which it is built. This study was not based upon a single verse of Scripture, nor a set of verses. Years of study were invested to examine every book of the Bible and every passage concerning sexuality in historical and theological context. In this way, I sought an understanding of God's revealed mind on sexuality and our femininity. We cannot sum up our femininity with one verse or a few verses. Instead, we must draw upon the entire Word of God to form a framework which defines and illuminates our femininity.

Sources of God's counsel

1. Four of the five aspects are based directly on Biblical definitions. Listed below are passages of Scripture which provide definitions for these four aspects. Beside each verse, write the name of the related aspect.

   Genesis 3:15-16, 20

   Genesis 1:26-27

   1 Corinthians 11:7

   Genesis 2:18-25

2. The Bible sets absolute moral standards and boundaries for us through the laws and commands of Scripture. While *Five Aspects* rarely explains Biblical law, it does assume it. Clear convictions on moral issues are essential for Christian maturity. How do the following commandments provide absolute moral guidelines for our understanding of gender?

   Exodus 20:12

   Exodus 20:14

   Leviticus 18:22

3. Biblical narratives are examples and illustrations which provide fuller understanding of God's law. *Five Aspects* uses narratives, especially in the Case Studies, to illustrate doctrinal principles. Name two women from the Case Studies in previous lessons who were most vivid to you. What Scriptural principles did you see illustrated in their lives?

4. The lady-of-wisdom aspect is based upon an archetype. An **archetype** is an original or exemplary pattern or model; a prototype. What are other Biblical archetypes of femininity?

5. Some truths not known in the Old Testament are revealed in the New. These truths are called **mysteries**. What great mystery is revealed in Ephesians 5:31-32?

6. From the gender archetypes of Ephesians 5:31-32 and 2 Corinthians 11:2-3, what new insights do you gain about marriage?

7. What else can you learn from Christ's relationship to the Church which can be applied to single life (1 Cor. 7:32-34)? In principle, to any life (2 Cor. 11:2-3)?

Biblical patterns of masculinity and femininity

By revealing the mystery of Christ and the Church, Paul has helped us understand God's pattern throughout Scripture for marriage and gender. In addition to Christ and the Church, four other pairs of masculine and feminine archetypes may be traced in Scripture: God and wisdom, God and Creation, Adam and Eve, and God and Israel.

8. Consulting the chart "Biblical Patterns of Masculinity and Femininity" (pp. 136-137), write a sentence summarizing how God is the final masculinity for each of the eight points listed below:

   a. The masculine is first and alone.

   b. The feminine comes from the masculine.

   c. The feminine reflects the masculine but is separate from the masculine.

d. The feminine is created for the masculine as helper, companion, fruitbearer, and glorifier.

e. Masculine initiation and feminine response unify the two.

f. Union produces fruit in the image of both the providing father and nurturing mother.

g. The masculine and feminine progressively reveal themselves (or mature) as they co-labor, fellowship, and bear fruit.

h. Glory and dwelling of masculine and feminine are realized and perfected in each other.

9. Read the columns down and then across on the chart "Biblical Patterns of Masculinity and Femininity." Select one part of the pattern which especially interests you. Reread that row across all the columns, reviewing how the archetypes fulfill that part of the pattern. In a few sentences, explain how your own femininity is maturing in this pattern, toward specific men or toward the Lord Himself. For example, if you chose the last segment of the pattern—glory and dwelling are perfected in each other—you could write about learning to live in harmony with your husband, or you could write about abiding in Christ.

10. At the most fundamental level, what should be the basis of our understanding of femininity (refer to John 17:17; Acts 17:11; 2 Tim. 3:16-17; 1 Pet. 4:11)?

The wonderful and remarkable thing about Scripture is that it stems from the eternal and immutable character of God. Therefore, what we learn from Him and His book regarding our sexuality, or any other topic, is not culturally based. It is dependable and not subject to change.

Now we have received, not the spirit of the world, but the Spirit who is from God, that we might know the things freely given to us by God, which things we also speak, not in words taught by human wisdom, but in those taught by the Spirit, combining spiritual thoughts with spiritual words.

1 CORINTHIANS 2:12-13

LESSON 23 : Summation 2 – *Applications*

Five Aspects is not a how-to-**be**-a-woman course; it is a how-to-**see**-a-woman course. In Matthew 6:22-23, Christ says, *"The eye is the lamp of the body; so then if your eye is clear, your whole body will be full of light. 23 But if your eye is bad, your whole body will be full of darkness. If then the light that is in you is darkness, how great is the darkness!* Christ is speaking here of our viewpoint. If you see things correctly, your whole body will be full of light; you will have understanding. But if you see things in the wrong way, then you will be in great darkness. One of the best ways to help people live better is to help them to see better—to see God for who He really is, men and women for who they were created to be, and marriage for what it is supposed to be. How we see affects who we are and what we do. This lesson on applications is quite simple. It has three points: Love God, love men, and love women.

1. Loving God

1.1 Loving God with the totality of our beings

The first and great commandment says, *You shall love the Lord your God with all your heart, and with all your soul, and with all your mind* (Matt. 22:37-38). This is the most important commandment of all commandments. After taking fifteen looks at yourself in this course, I hope you better understand your being. And with better understanding of the aspects of your being, I hope you are better able to offer your whole being to God, thus loving Him with your whole heart, soul, and mind. My categories and labels are not the important thing; what is important is getting the content of Scripture into our lives. I developed the aspects as categories to get God's Word organized and into my thinking. They are tools I use for evaluating my life before God.[1]

1.2 My own "total life" applications

How have the *Aspects* been most helpful in my own life applications? Looking back over a lifetime lived with these categories, I would answer this way. *Aspects* has helped me strive to keep the great polar virtues together in obedience, rather than allowing them to fly apart in sin. Specifically, I am referring to the **individuality** of Mistress and the **other-orientation** of Helper; the **graciousness** of Lifegiver and the **standards** of Wisdom.

Mistress of the Domain is about bearing our own burdens. Helper-Completer is about bearing the burdens of others. Galatians 6:2-3 and 4-5 bring these two ideas together. Body-life is essential to the Christian life, whether it is helping one's husband in marriage or serving others in the family, church, or community. Thus, Galatians 6:2-3 commands, *Bear one another's burdens, and thereby fulfill the law of Christ. 3 For if anyone thinks he is something when he is nothing, he deceives himself.* Without other-orientation we will fail to fulfill Christ's law. Yet, we are no good to others unless we bear our own stewardship! Thus Paul continues in verses 4-5, *But each one must examine his own work, and then he will have reason for boasting in regard to himself alone, and not in regard to another. 5 For each one will bear his own load.* We must focus on our own ruling in order to be of real help to others. Nevertheless, this self-focus must lead to other-service or it will descend into selfishness. The best dance partner is the one who follows the leader by attending to her own feet.

1. Refer to Lesson 20, page 106, section 2.2, for an example of using the aspects for a fivefold delineation of a woman's actions; in this case, Mary of Bethany and her worship.

Similarly, lifegiving and wisdom must be held together. We love through and by means of our skills. Love without skill becomes ineffectual sweetness—which is enough in a baby, but not enough in a woman. On the other hand, wisdom without love is truth without grace; it becomes cold and finally barren. It is in these fires—in the tension, stress, and battle to keep Mistress and Helper together both/and at the same time, to keep Lifegiver and Wisdom together both/and at the same time—that I have learned most of what I know about being a Christian woman.[2]

As we have said, if any model drawn from Scripture is right, then the model's main points will lead us right back to the Scripture's main points. Thus, I am very comforted and confirmed in John 1:14, *And the Word became flesh, and dwelt among us, and we saw His glory, glory as of the only begotten from the Father, full of grace and truth.* The polar virtues are brought together only in Jesus and can finally be brought together in us only by Him. When and where they are brought together, we have the true glory, and thus, our final aspect, Glory. No woman is glorious without focus on God in the obedience/reverence of the wise mistress; no woman is glorious without the service/love of the helping lifegiver.

Mistress and Helper lay down the basic principles: Individual obedience to God (the first commandment); and service to others (the second commandment). Aspects three and four repeat this melodic phrase in reverse order. Lifegiver repeats other-orientation with new emphasis on love; Wisdom repeats individual responsibility toward God with new emphasis on reverence and personal skill. So, we have this progression: Self-for-God, self-for-others, self-for-others, self-for-God, which leads to glory. When the aspects of our being are held in harmony, the glory of man in woman becomes a glory to God! Thus *Aspects* can help us love God from the totality of our beings.

1.3 Loving God, the masculine Spirit

True love focuses on the Loved. If we love God, we will love Him for who He is, not for the projection of who we think He is or should be. Increasingly people say that God is "He/She," "She," or "It." Then, as if to set everything straight, they remind us that God is transcendent Spirit. This sounds impressive because God **is** transcendent, and He **is** a Spirit. He was before all and is over all created categories. But it is not true that because God is a transcendent Spirit we should start calling Him "It," or think of Him as "The Impossibly Inscrutable One Beyond Us All."

1.4 God reveals Himself as masculine.

We should love the God of the Bible as the masculine Spirit He has revealed Himself to be. It is true that we, as finite beings, cannot fathom or fully comprehend the infinite God. The only way finite creatures know anything is through the created categories God has made and revealed. God reveals Himself as masculine in plain language through all the created categories, from Genesis to Revelation. In all His names, types, offices, and visions, God reveals Himself as "He." He is King, Judge, Shepherd, Warrior, Priest, Prophet, Husband, Father, Brother, and Bridegroom. Even the Passover lamb is specified to be a male without blemish. Jesus taught us to pray *Our Father*. In the Gospel of John alone, God is called "*the Father*" over 100 times. God is never called "the Mother." Never. He is never called "It." In John 14, 15, and 16, Jesus deliberately and repeatedly refers to the Holy Spirit as "He" rather than "It." He even "breaks the rules" of Greek grammar to do so in John

> It is not true that because God is a transcendant spirit, we should start calling Him "It."... In all His names, types, offices, and visions, God reveals Himself as "He."

2. Refer to Supplement A—FAQ, page 172, question 9, for a piece on Lifegiver and Wisdom which expands this point. The failure to keep these great and classic virtues ("aspects") together in women most often surfaces in the stereotypes of the frumpy, "just-a-housewife" who has been wife and mother, but neglected her own disciplines, and the arrogant, selfish "career woman," who is accomplished but alone. The Proverbs 31 wife forges the unity of virtues and aspects; thus, her fame is just.

16:13. From the beginning of the Bible to the end, God calls Himself a "He." He reveals Himself as transcendent, masculine Spirit. I am not speaking of exalting the natural sexual process or of imagining sex in heaven as we know it here on earth. Christ says that marriage is for this lifetime and that we will not be married in heaven. The phallic symbols and sacramental sex of the ancient world were condemned thoroughly in both Old and New Testaments.[3]

1.5 God is not a "She" or a "He/She."

However, God is masculine, not feminine. He is ultimate Masculinity as we described it in the eight-point Biblical pattern in the last lesson. He was first and alone. He is the One from whom all things came. He is the One whom all things reflect, and for whom all things were made. His whole creation is to come back to Him in fellowship, union, fruitfulness, for maturity, worship, and consummation. Union is based on His initiation. Children are cared for through His fatherly protection. These categories describe ultimate Masculinity, and they are who He is. He is the First and the Last. All lesser masculinities are derivative of Him; they are pale copies.

1.6 Masculinity is rooted in God, femininity in the creation.

God reveals Himself to be masculine, and reveals the creation to be feminine. When you look for the ultimate feminine in the Bible—the ultimate mother, or the queen of heaven—you do not find God or Jesus. You find the creation, usually the redeemed creation. In Galatians 4:26, Paul says, *the Jerusalem that is above is free, she is our mother.* In the next verse, he goes on to describe our mother Jerusalem by quoting from Isaiah 54:1, *"Shout for joy, O barren one, you who have borne no child; break forth into joyful shouting and cry aloud, you who have not travailed; for the sons of the desolate one will be more numerous than the sons of the married woman," says the LORD.* Indeed, God speaks to Jerusalem as to His wife and the mother of His children in all of Isaiah 54. In like manner, Isaiah exhorts all who love Jerusalem to respond to her motherhood as a nursing child. Isaiah 66:10-11: *"Be joyful with Jerusalem and rejoice for her, all you who love her; be exceedingly glad with her, all you who mourn over her, 11 that you may nurse and be satisfied with her comforting breasts, that you may suck and be delighted with her bountiful bosom."*

In the same line of thought, Revelation 12 describes a "queen" in heaven, a woman crowned with stars. Verses 1-2 state: *A great sign appeared in heaven: a woman clothed with the sun, and the moon under her feet, and on her head a crown of twelve stars; 2 and she was with child; and she cried out, being in labor and in pain to give birth.* The Catholic church believes this woman to be Mary. As can be seen in the rest of the chapter and from the context of the prophets, she is the nation of Israel. We will not pursue the details of these passages here.[4]

The point is, there are archetypal mothers and queens in Scripture, but they are never God. He is masculine, not feminine. He is always King; he is never Queen. He is always Father; He is never Mother. Today we know our mother as the Judeo-Christian heritage, the stream of life and truth that comes to us through the millennia of Jewish and Church history. This heritage nurtures us and provides our home civilization as a mother to her pilgrim children. One day, the mother we now know as a heritage, we will know as a real city—our true and lasting home!

---

3. The public acts of worship of many idolatrous religions were and are human sacrifice and illicit sexual intercourse. The public acts of worship for Christians are water baptism and eating—the taking of communion. For Christians, the "marriage bed" is undefiled, but private.

4. Note that Our Mother Jerusalem from above is not a person; she is a city. Just as "lady" wisdom is a body of principles and not a goddess, so our ultimate mother is a city and not a goddess. The Bible does not offer us goddesses, but it does offer us archetypal femininity. One of the great differences between Roman Catholicism and Protestantism is their understanding of Mary. Catholics see Mary as the archetypal mother, the queen of heaven. Protestants see her, or should see her, as the redeemed counterpart of Eve, the woman most blessed and who should be most honored, but who is nevertheless, a type of the mother above, not the city herself.

Israel's separation from God over these centuries is a great tragedy which has caused much suffering and confusion. However, this estrangement will come to an end. Just as Jews and Gentiles are united in the body of Christ today (Eph. 2), so God's great works in Israel and the Church will be united forever in the heavenly city. This city is one, founded on the apostles of the Church and gated by the patriarchs of Israel (Rev. 21:12-14). Biblical Christianity does give us an ultimate spiritual mother, but she is not God. She is found in Israel and the Church united, and we will be reunited with her and in her, in the Holy City of Heaven. Thus, we are not orphans in this world; we are pilgrims, but not orphans. We look forward to being with our Father in New Jerusalem, our mother forever.

1.7 Christ is the God-Man.

Some say that Jesus is claiming to be feminine when He says to Jerusalem, *"How often I wanted to gather your children together, the way a hen gathers her chicks under her wings, and you were unwilling"* (Matt. 23:37). Jesus is not telling us in this passage that He is a mother any more than He is telling us He is a female chicken! The point of the metaphor is that He would like to gather up the straying Jewish people. When God says in Isaiah 49:15, *"Can a woman forget her nursing child and have no compassion on the son of her womb? Even these may forget, but I will not forget you,"* He is not saying He is a mother. He is saying that while mothers are mindful of their children, He is even more mindful of His people. It is as if I were to say, "I am as hungry as a bear." I am not telling you I am a bear. I am telling you that my hunger is very great; it is like a bear's. However, in contrast, when God says He is our Father, He does not say, "I am like a father." The Bible claims that God is *the Father*. Hebrews 12:9 says, *Furthermore, we had earthly fathers to discipline us, and we respected them; shall we not much rather be subject to the Father of spirits, and live?* He **is** the Father of spirits, not **like** a Father of spirits.

1.8 Review

- In the Bible, God reveals Himself as only masculine.
- The feminine archetypes of the Bible are not God, but are identified with creation, primarily Israel and the Church.
- Christ is the God-Man, incarnate evermore.

Recall the quote I gave you about the nature of Christ: "He is undiminished deity and true humanity, united in one Person, without confusion or mixture, forever." Jesus is still a man. I remember discussing the humanity of Jesus with a young pilot one night after a Bible class. He said, "I thought Jesus was a man for a while, then He went back to heaven and just started being God again." Jesus never stopped being God, and since Mary's womb, He has not ceased to be man—nor will He. This is one of the most amazing claims of the Christian faith. Jesus has become the God-Man, a male of the human race, remains so now, and will remain so forever.

One of these days when I am asked to fill out a form about my religion, I plan to write, "I worship the King of the world's oldest Oriental dynasty." I wonder what the form-reader will think! Jesus is, of course, a Prince in the house of a great dynasty. God created a family—Abraham's. He created a dynasty inside that family—David's. He did this so that He could be born into that dynasty to be heir to that particular throne (the throne destined to rule the world). So while Jesus is the great God of Gods, He is also a specific Oriental king. He is heir to an Oriental throne—a real man from an actual dynasty in an historical nation of the Middle East. That is who Jesus is today—a man of the human race in His resurrected body.

2. Loving men

We have discussed the first and great commandment: To love God for the masculine God He is, with all our heart, mind, and soul, and from every aspect. The second command is like the first: Love your neighbor as yourself. Neighbors come in two varieties—men and women. First let's consider how the aspects can help us love men.

2.1 What love of men is not.

Love is not anger, scorn, resentment, fear, arrogance, covetousness, or unforgiveness. The more the sexes make war on one another in any family or nation, the more these attitudes will rise between men and women. However, we must turn away from these attitudes. Even if we feel we have a right to be mad or angry or vengeful, we must turn away from these attitudes for our own sakes.

My husband and I once watched a movie because it was highly acclaimed as an important feminist statement. It was the story of two women who leave their home, angry at men who are cast as immature, selfish, and criminal. Along the way, the women commit murder and armed robbery because of their anger and resentment, estranging themselves from civilization. With the police chasing them, they head for the border. As they travel, they commit various crimes to humiliate men, who are pictured as richly deserving this humiliation. Finally, they drive to the edge of a cliff with all the police closing in. My husband and I asked each other—how will this end? I expected the police would kill them in a most brutal way, demonstrating how oppressive men are; thus, the women would be martyrs. That's not what happened. Instead, the women join hands and drive off the cliff, committing suicide! I sat there stunned for a minute, and then I said to Bill, "I can't believe it—they told the truth." This was accurate, because embracing angry, bitter feminism is like driving off a cliff; it is suicidal, both in motive and goal.

God has created the sexes interdependent in origin, function, and destiny. Because God has created man and woman in this way, warring with the opposite sex is a complete no-win situation. Truly you cut off your nose to spite your face. If you seek to destroy or humiliate the opposite sex, then you will destroy only yourself and humiliate your own sex.

2.2 Love forgives.

Truly, all men are sinners, and some of them are vicious, mean people. They do terrible things. They wound us. This is something over which to weep. When the opposite sex goes down, we suffer great loss. This is as true for men as it is for women.

I have a friend, a tiny woman, less than five feet tall. As she lay asleep alone in her apartment one night, a man who had violated parole in the northwest, broke into her apartment, raped her, stealing her virginity. This was a tremendous evil and a great loss for her. She told me that one of the verses that helped her cope the most was Genesis 50:20 in which Joseph says to his brothers, *"You meant evil against me, but God meant it for good."* She looked to God to overcome the man's evil deeds. Another way she sought to overcome evil with good was to help the good men seeking to put the bad man away. Cooperating with the police, she testified in court against her assailant. Thus, she aided the process of justice so this man would not do this again. In these ways she sought forgiveness and rest from bitterness.

2.3 Love respects.

Years ago I presented a day seminar for a number of young single women headed for the mission field. I gave them a shortened form of the *Five Aspects*. They were not receptive. In fact, they were bordering on hostile. They did not like the ideas of masculinity and femininity I put forth. They found men to be selfish, egotistical, and incompetent; and they couldn't think of any men they admired. With this for background, it wasn't surprising to me that they thought women pastors would be a good idea. The spirit of the meeting seemed to be, "Men are losers and we do not need them anyway." After a while I said this, "If you have never met a man whom you respect, then you are greatly to be pitied. There are things about the glory of God that you will never see or learn except in and from a godly man. If it is true that you know no admirable men, then put away your arrogance and grieve." The room became very quiet. (I might note that two of those girls met young men they respected on that very mission assignment and got married. It was amazing how different their attitudes were the next time I saw them.)

If it is true that you know no admirable men, then put away your arrogance and grieve.

2.4 Love is doing to others as you would have them do to you.

How can we love men? We should love them the way we want to be loved. *Do unto others as you would have them do unto you.* My statement on how I would have men do unto me is this: I would like for all men always to show great respect for my image of God, and for me as a joint heir of Christ. I would also like for them always to be carefully observing me for any signs, no matter how faint, of feminine beauty, graciousness, charm, intelligence, loveliness, and wit, in order to appreciate and praise me for same. I would like for all men always to overlook and completely discount all my faults, failings, and bad-hair-no-make-up days. And I am not kidding!

But if I am not kidding, can I strive to do anything less for them? We need to respect men as people in the image of God, and we need to respect them as masculine people. Should I not also be diligent to look for all the signs of their masculinity—power, strength, authority, provision, love, kindness, and heroism—any time I can see it? I'm not talking about flattery or fawning. I am simply saying look for the good in men and women. We are all broken vessels, but we do not want to be just people. Men need to be loved and appreciated as manly men. I want to be appreciated and loved as a womanly woman. I am confident that in your heart of hearts, you do, too. That is the way our souls are created.

2.5 Love embraces God's creations, not the world's stereotypes.

One way we can love men is to have broad categories for masculinity. If you think the only manly man is the big football player, the war hero, or the guy who makes a lot of money, obviously you will despise many men. It is as if men would say to us, "The only woman who is womanly is the one who has a fabulous figure, a beautiful face, and perfect clothes." You know as well as I, that many of us would fail these standards. Let me give you a Scriptural example.

My father followed the Davidic model of masculinity in several ways. Like King David, he started in an agricultural setting on the farm. Next came successful war. He served in World War II for over four years; it was a defining experience for him. His was a growing experience just like David had in his wars. Next came the beginning of Israel's empire for David, and for my father's generation, the rise of America as a super power. My dad was skillful with all kinds of mechanical, agricultural, electrical, and engineering projects. He was also well-read, a man of integrity, with Victorian manners, and genuine Christian spirituality. This was the kind of masculinity he had.

My husband is very different. He is much more like Solomon, even in his historical era, because the baby-boomers originated not on the farm but amidst a wealthy, urban society. Our calling was to build a golden age on top of the empire our parents and grandparents started. My husband knows many languages. He is very articulate and writes beautifully. He has high computer literacy and learns software easily. However, I don't think he knows one end of a cow from the other. He hates yard work and has no interest in fixing the car. He loves music, architecture, and the fine arts. He served in Vietnam as a Marine cook; the cooking stuck, the firing-range culture didn't. My husband is also well-read, a man of integrity, and a genuine Christian. If I grade my husband on the Davidic model of agricultural/military man, he does not do too well. But if I grade him as a golden-age man of culture and technology, he does quite well indeed.

So, one of the ways we love is by seeing each other in God's broad categories, rather than strangling one another with wrong patterns or the narrow stereotypes of the world's fads and fashions. Take your sexual parameters from the wide and diverse portraits of Scripture. The *Aspects'* categories for both man and woman are offered to help you do just this.

3. Loving Women

3.1 Do not compare.

One of women's worst problems is comparing ourselves one with another. We compare clothes, figures, appearance, bank accounts, husbands, children, and life choices. We are always judging ourselves in light of one another. The Bible says this is wicked. Paul says in 2 Corinthians 10:12, *For we are not bold to class or compare ourselves with some of those who commend themselves; but when they measure themselves by themselves and compare themselves with themselves, they are without understanding.*

An old classmate and sister in Christ called me a while back, upbraiding me for not going to my high school reunion. At the time of this particular reunion we were broke, I was six-months pregnant with my fourth baby, and I was not interested in paying $30 to listen to '60s rock music in a dark country club while I tried to remember the names of people I didn't want to be with anyway. My former classmate and her husband both had jobs since she stopped having children after one child, having concluded that children are entirely too much work. When I hung up, I was both furious with and judgmental of her.

The verses that helped me out of that morass are in Romans 14: 4, 10, and 12: *Who are you to judge the servant of another? To his own master he stands or falls; and he will stand, for the Lord is able to make him stand....10 But you, why do you judge your brother? Or you again, why do you regard your brother with contempt? For we will all stand before the judgment seat of God.... 12 So then each one of us will give an account of himself to God.* I realized if my friend had five jobs and no babies, or five babies and no jobs, that was between her and God. After I cooled down, I also happened to remember several trials she had had in her life that I had never faced. I hope the *Five Aspects* will help you to love other women, not to judge or pigeonhole them. Seeing women in their fullness and diversity, I hope you will be freed to love other women for who they are.

3.2 Do not despise femininity.

The worst **misogynists** (women-haters) are no doubt women. Many women despise femininity.[5] They see it as something little, lowly, and stupid. Consider again three of the main reasons, covered in this study, why the feminine should be honored and not despised. First, women are created fully in the image of God. Second, they have a great glory that is different from man's—to be the crown of creation and the representative believer. Third, the Incarnation has happened. In the Incarnation, Christ shows us that taking the creature's role does not make us less than men, any more than the Son is less than the Father. Clinging to equality is not what brings glory. Christ won His glory, not by clinging to equality with the Father, but by fulfilling the role God gave Him. Women should seek glory in this same way.

Female misogynists really get themselves into a bind because in despising femininity, they despise themselves and other women as well. At the same time, they covet masculinity. Coveting masculinity, they envy men and compete with them, rather than complementing them. Further, they resent God because He is the One who made them feminine, and He is the ultimate Masculine behind all the little masculinities with whom they are competing.

It is my hope that this course communicates a love for both men and masculinity, and women and femininity, because they go together. It is not true that the greater masculinity is, the less femininity is, or vice versa. Sexuality is not a zero-sum game. We spiral up together, and we spiral down together. One of the nicest things anyone ever said about me after listening to some of my messages came from a man who said, "She has so much respect for men, and she has so much respect for herself as a woman." This is true. I love being a woman. I think men are wonderful. And I think the beauty of how we are supposed to fit together is truly one of God's wonders.

3.3 See whole women.

One day at the local library, I noticed the head librarian firmly admonishing some people who had abused library privileges. She was very firm with them, insisting that they were not to break the rules. Noting her as a reprover, I decided to observe her to see if she was a full model of feminine wisdom, or whether she simply liked to correct people. I discovered that she is quite complete as a lady of wisdom. Observing her over the months, I saw that she dealt with the patrons, the employees, the users, and the abusers all in different ways appropriate to each situation. So I see her as a feminine figure reigning over her outpost of civilization, using various skills in a rainbow of relationships. If a sexy figure or a fluttering personality were my criteria for femininity, this librarian would not be judged very feminine. However, with God's patterns in mind, she comes through loud and clear as a lady of wisdom reigning in her domain. Just as we must learn not to judge men in narrow, worldly stereotypes, we must also learn not to truncate women.

---

5. Betty Friedan, the "mother of American feminism," says that she was driven "to tangle with the tortuous questions...of the women's movement" because of "the simple driving need to *feel good* about being a woman" [emphasis original]. Betty Friedan, *The Second Stage* (New York: Summit Books, 1981), 60.

3.4 Application in a nutshell

- Love God. Give Him the totality of your being, every aspect. Love Him for the masculine God He is.
- Love men. Forgive them their sins. Find all that is admirable in their masculinity, just as you desire them to find all that is admirable in your femininity.
- Love women. Learn the value of femininity. Do not compare among yourselves. See women in the beauty of their created diversity.

If you do these things, you will be obeying the first commandment—to love God—and the second—to love one another. Perhaps this is something of a "how-to" course after all.

4. Spiraling up together

4.1 Raise the roof!

Another way we can love both men and women is by raising the roof of our overall sexual environment. When we walk into a cathedral, our eyes automatically go up. Our whole viewpoint is lifted because the pillars rise, the arches soar, and the beautiful stained glass windows draw our eyes upward. The majestic ceiling lifts our whole beings. When we turn away from the majesty of God, the environment closes in and the ceiling comes down, down, down, until we are living in hovels where the banal, silly, and vile are the habit of the day. What we must do as Christians is get that ceiling back up there where it belongs with God's great archetypes.

Our little lives should be seen back-lit by the great lives of the Father, the Son, His Church, and the saints. When their images are emblazoned in the back of our minds and on the top of our consciousness, then our tiny lives will be touched by rays of grandeur. Ordinary men and ordinary women will take on a different significance. Ordinary men are "lords," as the Scripture says. Ordinary homes are the dwellings where queens and princesses rule. Meals shared reflect communion itself. The embrace of lovers anticipates the meeting of all things—when nature will rejoice in the union of masculinity and femininity—foreshadowing the consummation of all.

4.2 Remember that star differs from star in glory.

I guess if I were to boil down forty years of gender study, and ask myself what important idea I have learned, I would say this. Masculinity is glorious; it is an eternal glory, a glory the Triune God shared with men and angels. Femininity is a different glory, not eternal, but created. Yet, it is a glory so great that God created the universe that it might exist, and He died that He might possess it for His own. This, I think, is sufficient glory.

5. Created, fallen, and redeemed: A reprise

5.1 Created: Man and woman in counterpoint

Webster's first defines **counterpoint** as "one or more independent melodies added above or below a given melody." The second definition of counterpoint is "the combination of two or more independent melodies into a single harmonic texture in which each retains its linear character." What a beautiful and accurate description of human sexuality as God created it! Adam stood in the garden as an independent melody, clear and strong. But his melody, as great as it was, lacked dimension. It was a melody alone. Then God composed another independent melody with its own linear character. This second melody was written in counterpoint to the first. When God brought the second melody to combine with the first, the garden was filled with a harmony more beautiful and full than either melody alone. Then the Composer was content that His work was finished and *very good*.

5.2 Fallen: Counterpoint to cacophony

Because the sexes were created in complementary counterpoint, their warfare, once begun, is unending and cruel. The very symmetry of their natures makes possible a new counterblow for every wound inflicted. If husband shows wife disrespect, she can refuse him the inner domains; if she rejects him, he can go to another woman; if he goes to another woman, she can welcome another man; if she welcomes another man, he can humiliate her; if he humiliates her, she can take away his children; ad nauseam. Fallen sexuality is a frenzied fit which spirals downward into death. In the power struggle between fallen masculinity and femininity, lust answers lust, pride challenges pride, materialism is answered by covetousness, seduction by abuse, and finally, death by death.

5.3 Redeemed: Cacophony to consummation

Redeemed and eternal marriage, as seen in Revelation, is a great dance which spirals upward. Masculinity and femininity answer one another in a counterpoint that is both beautiful and corresponding—alike but different, two yet one, other yet same. Christ gives His life for us that we might give ours for Him. We prepare a dwelling for Him that He might abide with us. He prepares a city for us that we might dwell with Him. We praise His glory that we might share it. He works that we might rest. We work that we might rest in Him. He died that we might live, and we die to self that we might live in Him. In the fulfillment and culmination of wedded love, there is constant call and answer, giving and receiving, building and entering, leading and following. In building the true oneness, each becomes more completely himself. We dwell secure in love, yet become ever more free. The melody lines are distinct, but the harmony is one.

Mistress of the Domain
In the image of God, woman has authority from God, responsibility in the world, and accountability to God.

Helper-Completer
Created from the man and for the man, woman completes man in his person and work.

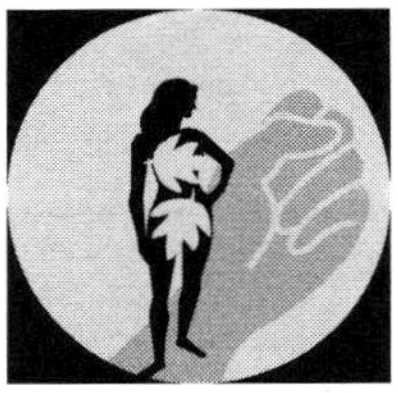

Lifegiver
In partnership with God, woman is the means to physical and spiritual life.

Lady of Wisdom
Fearing God, woman—like wisdom—reproves, counsels, teaches, and sponsors others.

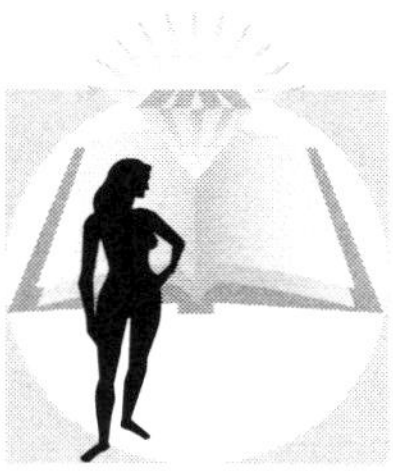
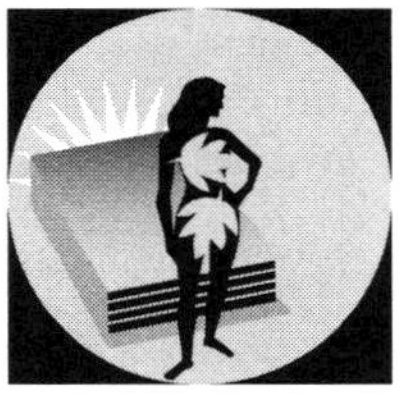

Glory of Man
Responding to authority in purity, woman glorifies God and fulfills her role as the glory of man.

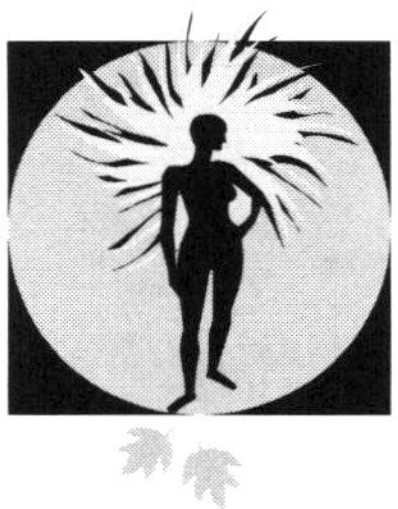

Bible Study of Summation 2—*Applications*

Before beginning this study, read the entire lesson, pages 147-158.

And He said to him, "'You shall love the Lord your God with all your heart, and with all your soul, and with all your mind.' This is the great and foremost commandment. The second is like it, 'You shall love your neighbor as yourself.'"

Matthew 22:37-39

Applying the *Five Aspects*

Principles taught in the *Five Aspects* can help you to love God more completely, and men and women more specifically.

The *Five Aspects*: A way of seeing

In Matthew 6:22-23a, Jesus tells us, *"The lamp of the body is the eye; if therefore your eye is clear, your whole body will be full of light. But if your eye is bad, your whole body will be full of darkness."* Jesus is talking about our viewpoint. If we see God as He really is, and ourselves as we really are, we will be full of light and able to walk in it. But if we see wrongly or not at all, what hope is there for our walk?

Five Aspects of Woman gives you a view of God, the universe, man, and woman based on the whole counsel of God. During this course you have caught new glimpses of God and His truth. This second Summation lesson should help you apply these new insights in the most basic and important ways—loving God and loving others.

Loving God

1. According to Matthew 22:37, how should we love God?

____

2. During this course, you have studied 15 views of yourself as a woman. God wants you to love Him with the totality of your complex being. Under each aspect, write at least one way in which you want to love God more completely by fulfilling your potential in that aspect. The accompanying passages may help your thinking.

Mistress of the Domain (1 John 2:15-17; 5:2-3)

____

____

Helper-Completer (Ps. 4:5; Matt. 25:31-40)

____

____

Lifegiver (John 4:13-14; Phil. 2:1-13)

Lady of Wisdom (Col. 2:1-3; Heb. 10:23-25)

Glory of Man (Gen. 2:22-25; Col. 3:12-15)

3. Another way we can love God more completely is to appreciate Him more fully for who He is. In previous lessons, we explained that God is the true and final Father, Son, Bridegroom, Husband, King, and Warrior. Human men glorify God by sharing these roles with Him, but in reality, they are pale, fallen, and incomplete shadows of the greatness of God Himself. Men often fail us in these roles; God never does. Select one of the following titles of God, and write a prayer of thanks and praise to God for being this great masculine Leader in your life:
   a. The Everlasting Father, The Abba (Daddy) of Believers (Rom. 8:12-17);
   b. First Born Son of the Father who is King, Priest, and Judge (Ps. 110);
   c. Brother to all believers (Heb. 2:10-18);
   d. Royal Bridegroom (Ps. 45);
   e. King of Kings and Lord of Lords (Ps. 2; Rev. 19:11-16); and
   f. The Husbandman of believers (Is. 5:1-4; John 15:1-8).

Loving men

The second great commandment is to *love your neighbor as yourself.* Our neighbors come in two varieties—men and women. We can love men by accepting them, forgiving them, and supporting them.

4. "Love men for who they are; remember they are not God or women." This is a helpful exhortation to remember. Have you gained insight about the masculine nature (perhaps in the helper-completer or glory-of-man lessons) which helps you better understand a man in your life? If so, please explain.

5. Fear, worry, bitterness, and rebellion are sins which often beset women as they serve beside and under the authority of imperfect or absent men. Select one of these sins and write a short paragraph explaining how the following two truths can give you strength to love and forgive the men in your life:

   a. Christ is the Head of this man. If this man needs correcting, Christ is the One to do it.
   b. God is my ultimate Father, Husband, and Pastor. Where men are absent or fail, God stands behind them caring for me. He never fails.

6. A young woman once expressed the following opinion of King David, "Oh, he was a terrible man. He committed adultery and murder." Was her statement true? Was it complete? (Refer to 1 Sam. 16–1 Kin. 2; especially note 1 Sam. 16:7-12; 1 Kin. 11:4; Acts 13:22.)

7. David was one of the greatest believers who ever lived, the most complete Christ-type of Scripture, the very son-king of YHWH (2 Sam. 7). He also was a murderer and an adulterer. The woman mentioned in question 6 could not forgive David his faults long enough to see his greatness. How could you help this young woman gain God's perspective on David? Outline the points you would make in a conversation with her.

8. It is doubtful any of us knows a man who is so spectacular a saint and sinner as King David. However, it is very possible we know men who are saints, but we think of them only as sinners. We cannot get past their faults long enough to appreciate their good and manly qualities. Read 1 John 2:9-12. Why is it necessary to forgive men their fallenness? What is the effect on our lives if we do not?

9. Think of a man in your family or church whom you tend to judge harshly. Write yourself an exhortation based on the following verses which will help you forgive and accept this man (Matt. 18:21-22; Rom. 14:4,10-12).

Loving women

Women compare themselves. They constantly judge themselves in comparison to other women—looks, clothes, husbands, education, houses, children, life choices. If we are to love other women, we must not measure ourselves against them. We must judge ourselves as mistresses of our own domains, by the law of God, and by the measure of the grace which God has given us (2 Cor. 10:12-13,18).

10. In what areas are you most tempted to compare yourself to other women?

11. We don't know what Euodia and Syntyche disagreed about (Phil. 4:2-3). Perhaps one home-schooled and the other didn't, or one worked outside the home and the other didn't, or one kept a very clean house and the other a messy house, or one used friendship evangelism and the other handed out tracts. Write out one principle you have learned from experience and Scripture which helps you live in peace with your sisters in Christ, especially when you disagree, or are tempted to compare yourself with them.

12. *Five Aspects* can help us look for the unique and feminine nature in every woman. Or it can be just another tool for categorizing women and grading them up or down on our personal score pad. Using *Five Aspects* concepts, write three questions which will help you understand and look for the best in other women. (For example, "What unusual things has God put in this woman's domain?" "What special skills does this woman have?" "How do I see this single woman giving life?")

a.

b.

c.

13. Write the names of three close friends. How can you use your wisdom, attributes, and skills to bless them specifically?

a.

b.

c.

For we are His workmanship, created in Christ Jesus for good works, which God prepared beforehand, that we should walk in them.

EPHESIANS 2:10

A *Five Aspects* Prayer

14. Conclude your *Five Aspects* study by meditating on the following prayer. Consider each title of God as it relates to you and the aspects of your feminine being. Add specific praises, thanksgivings, or petitions under each section as a pledge of your commitment to apply what you have seen and learned in this course.

Dear God,

Thank You for being my Creator, Sovereign, and Judge. Help me to be responsible and faithful as the mistress of the domain You have given to me.

Thank You that You are my ultimate Head, and that You have prepared good works for me to do. Enable me to be a helper, serving others with loyalty.

Thank You for being my Fountain of Life, my True Vine, and Husbandman. Help me to give life to others with love.

Thank You that You are the awesome God, Master of all mysteries. Help me to be a lady of wisdom, fearing You and rejoicing greatly in Your works.

Thank You for being my Father and for Christ, who is the Bridegroom and King. Help me to be a glory to man through purity, beauty, and reverence.

In Christ's name I pray,
Amen.

The LORD bless you, and keep you; the LORD make His face shine on you, and be gracious to you; the LORD lift up His countenance on you, and give you peace.

Bless the LORD, O my soul; and all that is within me, bless His holy name.

Supplements

SUPPLEMENT A : Frequently Asked Questions

Lady of Wisdom

In this section, I provide concise answers to common questions about wisdom. For more thorough explanations about wisdom, refer to Supplement B.

1. Nowhere in the Biblical text is wisdom explicitly called "lady." Why should we call wisdom "lady?" Are you doing this just because the word is grammatically feminine in Hebrew?

The word for wisdom in Hebrew (*chokmah*) is feminine, but the "lady wisdom" title is not based on the grammatical gender of the word. The "lady" wisdom construct of Proverbs 1-9 is based on Solomon's extended personification of wisdom as seen in her speeches (chapters 1, 8, 9), in her roles as hostess, lover, wife, and archetypal mother (Prov. 3:18; 4:6-8; 8:32), and in her obvious contrast to "woman" folly, who is also clearly feminine.

The term "lady wisdom" is not original with ICGS. "Lady wisdom" and "dame wisdom" are used for wisdom by many writers and commentators who write on the book of Proverbs, including: D. Brent Sandy (editor) and Ronald L. Giese, Jr. (editor), *Cracking Old Testament Codes: A Guide to Interpreting Old Testament Literary Forms* (Broadman & Holman Publishers, 1995); William Sanford Lasor, David Allan Hubbard, Frederic William Bush, *Old Testament Survey: The Message, Form, and Background of the Old Testament*, (Wm. B. Eerdmans Publishing Co.,1996); Eugene H. Peterson, *The Message: New Testament with Psalms and Proverbs*, (NavPress, 1995). That wisdom is personified as a woman is not a debate in scholarly literature. The debate surrounds who this woman is, not whether she is in the text.

Trinity, Incarnation, rapture, and millennium are words which do not appear in Scripture. However, each of these words names an idea that is in Scripture. When evaluating a doctrine, we must ask if the content of the teaching matches the truth of Scripture, not whether every word used to name a Biblical idea is found in Scripture. We believe that calling the personified character in Proverbs "lady" wisdom highlights and summarizes Solomon's intent and is faithful to the truth of the text.

2. Only Father, Son, and Holy Spirit were there when They created the universe out of nothing. How can you say "lady" wisdom was the helper of God at creation?

The central point must be repeated. In the context of Proverbs 1-9, a personification of principles is in view, not a person. Wisdom is an impersonal tool of God, personified in Proverbs 8 much as **blueprint** is personified in this sentence: The cherished blueprint was the carpenter's constant companion and helped him at every point in the building of his dream house.

The entity in Proverbs 8 is not Christ nor an attribute of God, since this entity has a beginning and is feminine. Neither Christ nor the divine attributes have a beginning in eternity past. Nowhere else in the Bible is Christ or God addressed as feminine. Also note that the emphasis of Proverbs 8:22-31 is not on wisdom as an active worker or helper. The master workman mentioned in verse 30 is best translated as referring to God, not to wisdom.

3. Why don't you agree with Bible teachers who say wisdom in Proverbs 1-9 is Christ? How do you account for 1 Corinthians 1:24, which says that Christ is our wisdom?

There are at least three reasons for not interpreting the wisdom of Proverbs 1-9 as Christ:

a. In verse 22, the verb translated *brought forth* or *possessed* is best translated *created*. Verses 24 and 25 say wisdom was *brought forth* and *given birth* before the material creation. Before the creation, Christ was eternal with God. He has no beginning before creation. He is the firstborn of all creation in the sense of preeminence, not in the sense of chronology. The created part of His nature came into being 2,000 years ago inside history, not before it.

b. Christ never fulfills feminine roles or offices such as sister, mother, bride, wife, or queen. The burden of proof is on those who equate Christ and the feminine wisdom of Proverbs to account for this anomaly.

c. Paul's statement in 1 Corinthians 1:24, 30—Christ is our wisdom—is the strongest, most frequent support for interpreting "lady" wisdom to be Christ. However, in light of the first two points, this is not an inviting interpretation. Plus, in context, Paul is not speaking of Solomonic or Hebraic wisdom; he is contending with the Corinthians who would pollute or replace the Gospel of Jesus Christ with Greek philosophy. It is in this context that he writes Christ is our wisdom, meaning, Christ is for us what the Greeks seek in what they call wisdom. Our wisdom, says Paul, is Christ, not the Greek philosophy by which the Corinthians were enticed.

4. Doesn't Paul devalue wisdom for Christians in 1 Corinthians 1?

The Bible repeatedly speaks of two different kinds of wisdom—*worldly wisdom* and *wisdom from above*. The first kind—worldly wisdom—is condemned and held to be ultimately ineffectual (Col. 2:23; James 3:14-16). The verse Paul quotes (1 Cor. 1:19) about God destroying the wisdom of the wise comes from Isaiah 29:14. In that context, the Jews are wickedly and foolishly seeking to take counsel against the Lord and take refuge in an idolatrous support—Egypt (Is. 30:1-3). There is no counsel against the Lord, and there is no other salvation but what God provides. The wisdom that seeks to devise such plans or means of salvation will be cast down utterly. It is another version of this worldly wisdom in Corinth that Paul is attacking in 1 Corinthians 1-2. However, godly wisdom is lauded, as can be seen in the very same passage (1 Cor. 2:6-11).

Other passages on the importance of wisdom for Christians:
a. Deacons were to have it (Acts 6:3).
b. Stephen refuted unbelief with it (Acts 6:8-10).
c. Paul prayed for believers to have it (Eph. 1:17-18; Col. 1:9).
d. Paul taught it (Col. 1:28).
e. It was to be used in society (Col. 4:5).
f. Biblical wisdom leads to salvation (2 Tim. 3:15).
g. Believers are to pray for wisdom (James 1:5).
h. Moral living is the root and fruit of wisdom (James 3:13, 17-18).

5. If wisdom is feminine, does this mean women are inherently more wise than men?

Let me answer this question with another question: Since the Church is feminine, does that mean women are more Christian than men? No, it means that women pattern their lives toward their husbands the way the Church patterns her life toward Christ—with responsiveness, helpfulness, submissiveness, fruit-bearing, glorification, etc. Women should pattern their teaching, reproving, and their style of hospitality after "lady" wisdom. Men should pattern their wisdom after Christ the Sage. As Joseph (of Gen. 37-50) and Jesus before them, they should aim their masculine pursuit of the feminine at wisdom and wise women, not folly and foolish women. Neither man nor woman is inherently wiser than the other; but the pattern and purpose of their wisdom is inherently different (refer to question 6).

6. Does wisdom look different in a man from in a woman?

In many ways, wisdom will look the same in a man and a woman—careful speech, prudent financial policies, moral purity, etc. But in general, man pursues wisdom to possess it, in order to rule with it. Woman grows in wisdom to embody it, in order to fulfill all her feminine aspects. Solomon prayed for wisdom in the first place not out of curiosity, but in order to rule God's people well. The wise women of the Bible use their wisdom to give counsel, petition, and teach. The Proverbs 31 woman has gentle teaching on her tongue while she wisely manages the household. Her husband sits in the gates, ruling in the community. King Lemuel's mother taught him, presumably as a boy; King Lemuel was the one held responsible for accomplishing justice. As a man, he remembered his mother's teaching (Prov. 31:1-9). (Refer to pp. 4-17 contrasting the "public wisdom" of men and the "private wisdom" of women in the community life of Ruth's Bethlehem.)

7. If "woman" folly comes to men primarily as an adulteress, how does "woman" folly come to women?

This is a good question to provoke a survey of evil archetypes. First, for review, refer to "Primary Gender Archetypes" (p. 135). The classic enemies of the Christian are the world, the flesh, and the devil. The world is feminine, the flesh is whatever the gender of the person is, and the devil is masculine. The evil feminine archetype (whether you call her "woman" folly, the world system, or Babylon the Harlot) is an impersonal cursed system with a passive, sensuous appeal based on love of temporal things (Gen. 19:24-26; Rev. 17-18). The evil masculine archetype is the devil who is aggressive—seeking whom he may devour, throwing fiery darts.

Folly comes to a woman as worldliness, seeking to seduce her and force her into its mold with flattery and sensuous appeals to pride and security. (This is much the same way worldliness would appeal to a man, except with a man, there might be more emphasis on power and less on security.) If a sexual temptation for the woman involved a man, the man would be playing the satanic role of tempter in the woman's life, although the affair overall might be viewed as a fling with folly and worldliness.

The masculine devil works together with the world system just as continuously as God works through His Church. This is yet another of Satan's evil counterfeits of God's work, much like the evil trinity in the book of Revelation—Satan, the anti-Christ, and the false prophet.

8. Is it right or wrong for a Christian to speak of "Mother Earth"?

The earth is the dust from which our Father God created us; it nurtures us, and it is our home. The earth also teaches us about God through "general revelation" (Rom. 1-2; Ps. 19). Civilizations all over the world have seen and understood this truth. That some have gone into the error of goddess-worship does not negate the validity of the earth's femininity, as can be seen in Psalm 139:13, 15, where David compares his mother's womb to the earth itself. It is noteworthy that the earth was the only mother Adam had. For all these reasons, the earth is a mother to us, and there is nothing wrong with speaking of her as such, as long as we are careful not to embrace or communicate an idolatrous concept.

9. Balancing the self-sacrificing, gracious love of lifegiver with the demanding, high standards of wisdom is difficult. Can you provide any more guidance on how this looks in practice?

The following is my best, short effort to answer this question.

The Good Mother: Lifegiver and Lady of Wisdom

Every mother and teacher of children needs the qualities of Lifegiver **and** Lady of Wisdom coursing continually through her veins.

Lifegiver welcomes, gives, and forgives in imitation of the everlasting mercies of God.
Lady of Wisdom reproves, admonishes, and judges severely, without appeal, in reflection of His justice.

Lifegiver wins love by loving first.
Lady of Wisdom earns respect by never forsaking her standards.

Lifegiver gives suck at her warm and gracious breasts.
Lady of Wisdom sets the banquet of life before you and requires you to be worthy of it.

Lifegiver gives existence.
Lady of Wisdom brings civilization.

Lifegiver introduces you to peas and peaches.
Lady of Wisdom shows you which fork to use.

Lifegiver sings you lullabies.
Lady of Wisdom keeps you practicing your piano.

Lifegiver soothes your wounds.
Lady of Wisdom administers not a few of them.

Lifegiver meets drool and dirty diapers with coos and soothing words, counting it her sacred privilege to serve you in your helplessness.
Lady of Wisdom won't tolerate tardiness, dangling participles, or slouching shoulders, counting it her duty to whip you into shape for the rigors of life.

Lifegiver receives you back from the pigpen of life.
Lady of Wisdom's standards condemned you all the while you were there.

Every woman must be both. Lifegiver without Lady of Wisdom is a servile puff-ball, not worthy of respect. Lady of Wisdom without Lifegiver is a cold, hard jewel—all her notes are perfect but she has missed life's song. The good mother and the good woman will be both, *"full of grace and truth."*

Glory of Man

10. Isn't it more lowly for a woman to picture the creation than for a man to picture the Creator?

If Christ, who is very God of very God, did not disdain to take the creature's part at the Incarnation and fulfill all the creature's duties (trust, obedience, lifegiving, submissiveness, worship, etc.) and suffer all the creature's limitations (weakness, pain, fatigue), then why should we as women—who **are** creatures—disdain to take that part? The more so, because we know that the more humble our walk in this life, the greater our exaltation in the next (Phil. 2:1-11).

Man can picture God more fully in his roles than woman can. But he can also picture Satan more fully than woman can. Unto whom much is given, much is required. There are no gender constraints, however, on reflecting the character of God in Christ-likeness through the fruits of the Spirit; this latter is the measure of godliness.

Five Aspects of Man

11. By far, the most frequently asked question is, "Are there Biblical aspects of manhood? If so, what are they?"

Five Aspects of Man is a parallel study of manhood and masculinity by my husband, William E. Mouser. Bill is a graduate of Dallas Theological Seminary, a pastor, a published author in the field of wisdom literature, and the director of ICGS. In response to the urging of Christian brothers and convinced that aspects of manhood are revealed in Scripture, Bill first wrote *Five Aspects of Man* in 1992. *Five Aspects of Masculinity for Young Men* followed in 2003.

The five aspects of man are built upon the same core passages as the five aspects of woman, and are named:

Lord of the Earth
Husbandman
Savior
Sage
Glory of God.

Pages 175-179 provide icons and summary material on the five aspects of man, which will give you an overview of this complementary study of masculinity. For more information on *Five Aspects of Man*, contact:

ICGS
PO Box 702
Waxahachie, TX 75168
www.fiveaspects.com.

The Larger Gender Picture

12. Why does sexuality matter anyway? Can't we all just be Christians and not worry about it, especially if it is just a metaphor?

Sexuality is a metaphor, but it is a metaphor which has a reality written into our very beings. Other metaphors of God and His creation, or of Christ and His Church, you may get by without—vines and branches, cornerstones and building blocks, shepherds and sheep. But, we **are** men and women, sons and daughters, husbands and wives, fathers and mothers. To cast these realities aside is to rebel against God and discard something of our very selves (1 Cor. 6:12-20).

Furthermore, our created sexuality is a shadow of the true and final gender world. As members of Christ's Church, we will not marry in heaven, but the True Marriage will go on forever. The True Husband will be a Husband forever. The bride of Christ, of which Eve was a shadow, will go on being feminine forever. Parts of the shadows will fade away, but only to make room for the fullness of the realities. Therefore gender categories are of constitutional importance in this life and are fundamental to the joy of the next.

For further thoughts on why sexuality matters, refer to Supplement B, page 206, section 2.3D "Conclusion: More than complementarians."

The icons on page 181 provide a summary view of the aspects of masculinity and femininity as taught in *Five Aspects of Man* and *Five Aspects of Woman*.

Passages	Aspect of manhood	Aspect of womanhood
Genesis 1	Lord of the Earth	Mistress of the Domain
Genesis 2	Husbandman	Helper-Completer
Genesis 3	Savior	Lifegiver
Proverbs 1-9	Sage	Lady of Wisdom
1 Corinthians 11, Ephesians 5	Glory of God	Glory of Man

LORD OF THE EARTH

Created in God's image and as His viceroy, man's headship rules the earth.

created

Man is created in the image of God to rule and subdue the earth for God. Bearing God's image, yet partaking of the earth in his body, man is uniquely equipped to superintend nature and rule it for God's glory. Lower than the angels, yet crowned with glory and majesty, man was made by God to rule over all the works of His hands (Ps. 8).

person—MALE FIGURE
("clothed" in nakedness according to his untested, unashamed, sinless standing before God)

character—SQUARE
(untested, sinless)

masculinity—TRIANGLE
(untested, sinless)

role/work—CROWN, SCEPTER
(chief ruling authority is untested, sinless)

fallen

When the first lord of the earth was tempted by evil, he made a catastrophic choice, resulting in the curse of death on all creation. Crippled by the fall, all subsequent lords of the earth abuse or abandon their mandate from God to rule. Abusing their delegated lordship, they become cruel and oppressive tyrants. Abandoning it, they are weak, passive, lukewarm stewards who bury their talents like cowards.

person—MALE FIGURE
(clothed in a fig leaf according to his fallen, ashamed, guilty standing before God)

character—DARK SQUARE
(fallen, polluted with sin)

masculinity—DARK TRIANGLE
(fallen, polluted with sin)

role/work—CROWN UPSIDE-DOWN, SCEPTER BROKEN
(abdicated/abused authority)

redeemed

Through man's headship, the race and the creation have been damned in Adam and saved in Christ. The last Adam, Christ, came reversing the work of the first Adam. *In Adam all die, even so, in Christ, shall al be made alive* (1 Cor. 15:22). God humbles the fallen lord of the earth by judging him and his realm. He graciously forgives the contrite man, and strengthens his faith through repeated testing, so that the redeemed steward rules his world for God.

person—MALE FIGURE
(clothed in a white robe–Christ's righteousness–according to his forgiven, redeemed standing before God)

character—GLOWING SQUARE
(redeemed from sin)

masculinity—DOTTED TRIANGLE
(redeemed from sin)

role/work—CROWN AND SCEPTER ADORNED WITH CROSS, JEWELS
(redeemed authority, headship)

HUSBANDMAN

Created to cultivate things and people, man makes his realm productive, fulfilling its potential.

created

Man is created to cultivate the persons and things within his realm, so they fulfill their full capacity for fruitfulness. By leading, providing, and protecting, men husband the earth, plants, animals, businesses, teams, governments, nations, and most importantly, their wives. The shepherd and vinekeeper are two of Scripture's most important physical examples of husbandry, both physically and spiritually.

person—MALE FIGURE
("clothed" in nakedness according to his untested, unashamed, sinless standing before God)

character—SQUARE
(untested, sinless)

masculinity—TRIANGLE
(untested, sinless)

role/work—HOE
(all tools used to cultivate and husband the earth)

fallen

The sinful husbandman abuses and abandons his duties as cultivater of the people and things in his realm. Originally made for his help and completion, his wife is now cursed with her own propensity to resist his leadership, thus making his husbandry all the more thorny. As the fallen woman seeks to dominate the fallen man, he capitulates to her, flees from her, or abuses her.

person—MALE FIGURE
(clothed in a fig leaf according to his fallen, ashamed, guilty standing before God)

character—DARK SQUARE
(fallen, polluted with sin)

masculinity—DARK TRIANGLE
(fallen, polluted with sin)

role/work
NO HOE
(abdicated/abused mandate to care for realm)
THORNS/THISTLES
(fruitlessness of man's labor and realm)

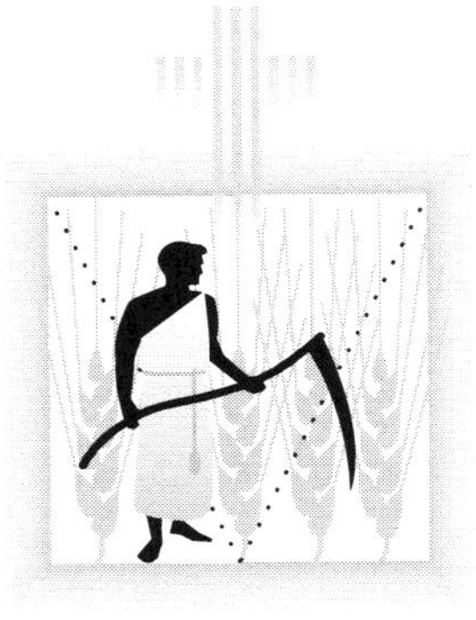

redeemed

Being a husband to a woman in marriage is the highest husbandry a man can undertake. In this office he mirrors Christ's covenant relationship with the Church. God trains redeemed husbandmen to imitate Christ's gracious cleansing and leading of His Church. Aware of his own weakness, the redeemed husband humbly leads and teaches those under his care so that they become his crown and joy before the Lord.

person—MALE FIGURE
(clothed in a white robe—Christ's righteousness—according to his forgiven, redeemed standing before God)

character—GLOWING SQUARE
(redeemed from sin)

masculinity—DOTTED TRIANGLE
(redeemed from sin)

role/work
SCYTHE
(all tools used to harvest fruitful realm)
WHEAT
(ordered, tended, fruitful realm)

SAVIOR

Trusting in God, man wars against evil to save others at personal risk to himself.

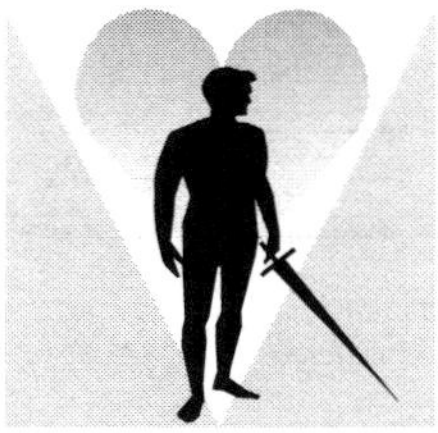

created

Man is created to war sacrificially against evil and injustice until they are vanquished. Epitomized in the God-Man Jesus Christ and His work on the cross, this aspect shines forth in all heroes, champions, warriors, rescuers, and liberators. Saviors battle physical dangers, intellectual lies, every sort of injustice, and spiritual forces of darkness at personal cost to themselves for the sake of others who are loved.

person—MALE FIGURE
("clothed" in nakedness according to his untested, unashamed, sinless standing before God)

character—SQUARE
(untested, sinless)

masculinity—TRIANGLE
(untested, sinless)

role/work
HEART
(love is primary motivation)
SWORD
(tool to judge evil and protect the beloved)

fallen

Because of his moral corruption, the fallen savior wages war against what is good rather than oppose what is evil. He battles for personal gain, rather than at personal cost, until he destroys himself, instead of rescuing others. Abusing warrior zeal, fallen saviors ravage and rape the very lands and women they were created to save. Abandoning warrior zeal, cowardly men judge no injustice worth opposing and no love worth saving.

person—MALE FIGURE
(clothed in a fig leaf according to his fallen, ashamed, guilty standing before God)

character—DARK SQUARE
(fallen, polluted with sin)

masculinity—DARK TRIANGLE
(fallen, polluted with sin)

role/work
SERPENT PIERCING HEART
(hate/indifference toward those whom he should protect)
NO SWORD
(abdicated responsibility to judge evil)
SERPENT
(the ancient enemy of mankind)

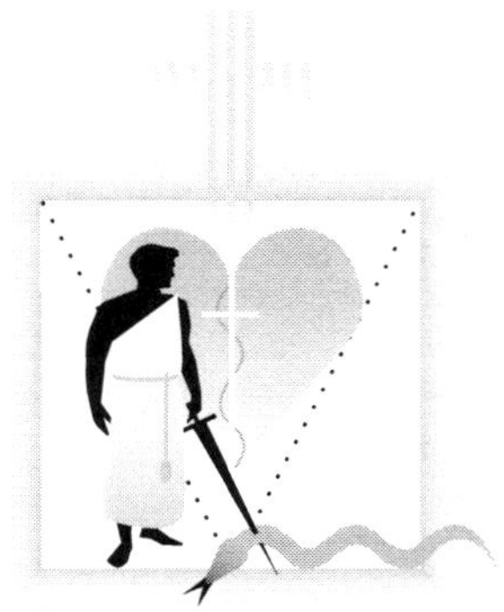

redeemed

Under the Savior Christ, the Captain of all the saints, the redeemed savior is fitted for the most ancient battle of all. He faces evil on every hand—within his own soul, in this fallen world, and against demonic oppression. Fitted in God's armor, armed with His Word, he battles with courage and prayer. Pastors and elders particularly are called to be saviors as they refute error and protect their flocks from "wolves" who attack God's people.

person—MALE FIGURE
(clothed in a white robe—Christ's righteousness—according to his forgiven, redeemed standing before God)

character—GLOWING SQUARE
(redeemed from sin)

masculinity—DOTTED TRIANGLE
(redeemed from sin)

role/work
MENDED HEART
(love healed/redeemed by Christ)
SWORD KILLING SERPENT
(sacrificial love's victory over evil)

SAGE

Disciplined by wisdom, man becomes a player-coach in life and work.

created

Wisdom, Solomon said, is like a woman who first comes to men as a disciplinarian (a mother figure). If a man responds to her reproofs, she softens to a patroness. The man who would be wise courts and pursues wisdom as he would a lover, in order to win her and make her his own. For the mature wise man, the sage, wisdom is like a wife—helping, counseling and glorifying him in his life and work.

person—MALE FIGURE
("clothed" in nakedness according to his untested, unashamed, sinless standing before God)

character—SQUARE
(untested, sinless)

masculinity—TRIANGLE
(untested, sinless)

role/work
JEWEL
(prize of wisdom)
PICK AXE
(tool to mine/pursue wisdom)
OPEN BOOK
(learning)

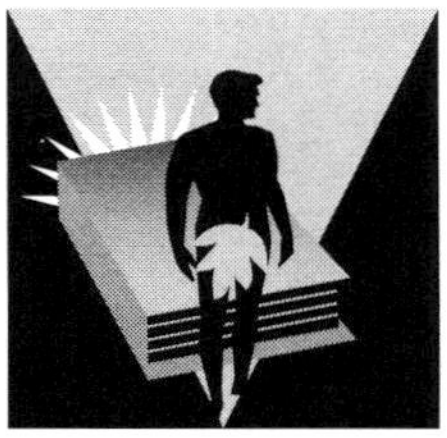

fallen

The fallen sage is a true fool. Every man is born a fool; foolishness is bound up in his heart. Rejecting discipline and instruction, the simpleton becomes a hardened fool, delighting only in his own opinions. He is a danger and harm to those around him until he destroys himself by his own folly.

person—MALE FIGURE
(clothed in a fig leaf according to his fallen, ashamed, guilty standing before God)

character—DARK SQUARE
(fallen, polluted with sin)

masculinity—DARK TRIANGLE
(fallen, polluted with sin)

role/work
HIDDEN JEWEL
(unlearned wisdom)
NO PICK AXE
(rejection of wisdom)
CLOSED BOOK
(rejection of God/Truth)

redeemed

Only the redeemed sage has access to the *"wisdom from above,"* given in Scripture and ascertained by the illumination of the Spirit of Christ. Thus enlighted, saved men grow in spiritual wisdom, enabled to deploy their knowledge of the world for God's glory. (David used his skill as a musician to glorify God in song; Paul used his knowledge of Rome to evangelize the world.) Mature in wisdom, sages are players in life who train younger men to do work that lasts forever.

person—MALE FIGURE
(clothed in a white robe–Christ's righteousness–according to his forgiven, redeemed standing before God)

character—GLOWING SQUARE
(redeemed from sin)

masculinity—DOTTED TRIANGLE
(redeemed from sin)

role/work
JEWEL, BOOK IN HAND
(acquired wisdom)
OPEN, GLOWING BOOK
(learning with mind of Christ)

GLORY OF GOD

Sharing in God's masculinity, man reflects God's characteristics and roles.

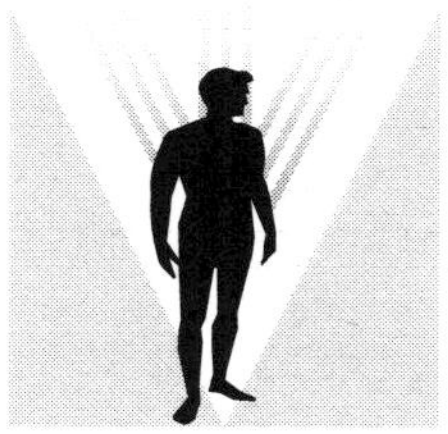

created

Man is created to display something of God's glory in his bearing, roles, and activities. As fathers, sons, husbands, brothers, kings, priests, and warriors, men reflect God who is the Ultimate Masculine. Made for a masculine God, he revels in fellowship with God and godly men. Sharing masculinity with God, he relates to nature, women, and other men in ways characteristic of God's power, righteousness, grace, and love.

person–MALE FIGURE
("clothed" in nakedness according to his untested, unashamed, sinless standing before God)

character–SQUARE
(untested, sinless)

masculinity–TRIANGLE
(untested, sinless)

role/work–LIGHT RAYS form triangle
(masculine glory reflects God's glory)

fallen

When a man rejects his masculine roles, he abandons the glory of his manhood. Bad sons rebel against their fathers; bad husbands divorce their wives; bad fathers neglect their children. In each case such a man blasphemes the character of God in a unique and special way. Instead of faithfully picturing the roles and activities of God, he pictures Satan. Abusing his masculinity, a man inflates his ego with pride, and feeds his sexual greed.

person–MALE FIGURE
(unclothed–having discarded fig leaf and flaunting immorality–according to his fallen-but-unashamed guilty standing before God)

character–DARK SQUARE
(fallen, polluted with sin)

masculinity–DARK TRIANGLE
(fallen, polluted with sin)

role/work
SERPENTINE LIGHT RAYS
(corrupted glory, reflects Satan's shame)
LONG HAIR
(corrupted glory/shame)
SERPENT
(the ancient enemy of mankind)

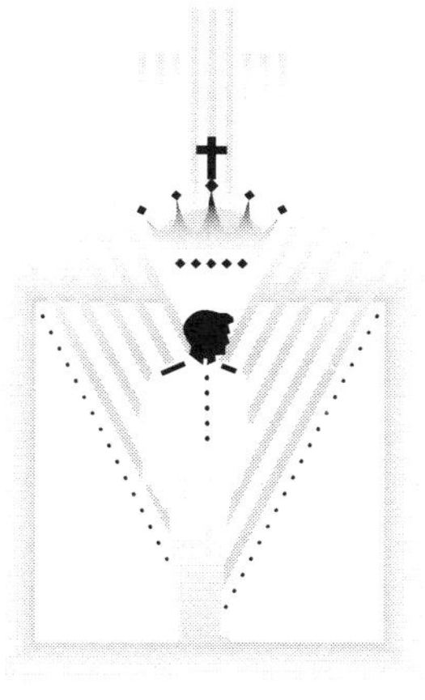

redeemed

As God sanctifies His sons, He restores their ability to mirror Him in His roles and activities. Redeemed men love women with sacrifice and chivalry; they love men for the glory of God they display in a special fellowship and brotherhood. Above all, they love Jesus Christ as their own Head and the Head of all men.

person–MALE FIGURE
(clothed in a military uniform–Savior's righteousness–according to his forgiven, redeemed standing before God)

character–GLOWING SQUARE
(redeemed from sin)

masculinity–DOTTED TRIANGLE
(redeemed from sin)

role/work
AMPLIFIED LIGHT RAYS form triangle
(redeemed masculine glory)
CROWN
(redeemed masculine glory, reflective of Christ, the King)

There are three things which are
too wonderful for me, four which
I do not understand:
the way of an eagle in the sky,
the way of a serpent on a rock,
the way of a ship
in the middle of the sea,
and the way of a man with a maid.

PROVERBS 30:18-19

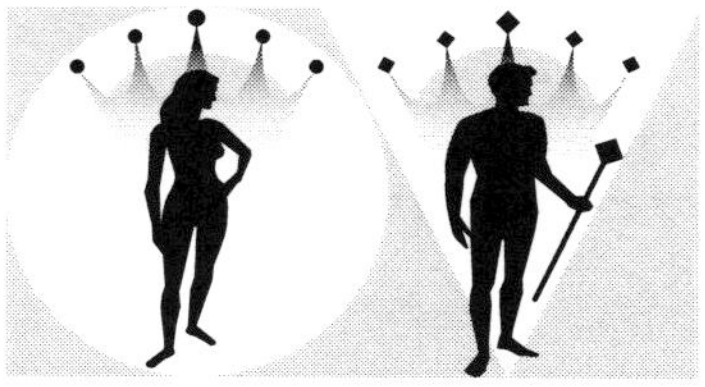

Mistress of the Domain — Lord of the Earth

Helper-Completer — Husbandman

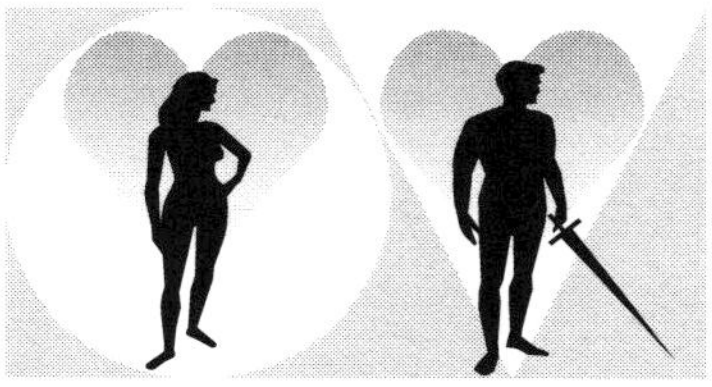

Lifegiver — Savior

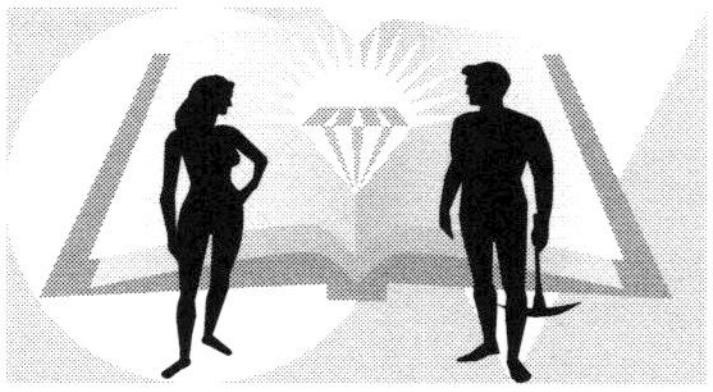

Lady of Wisdom — Sage

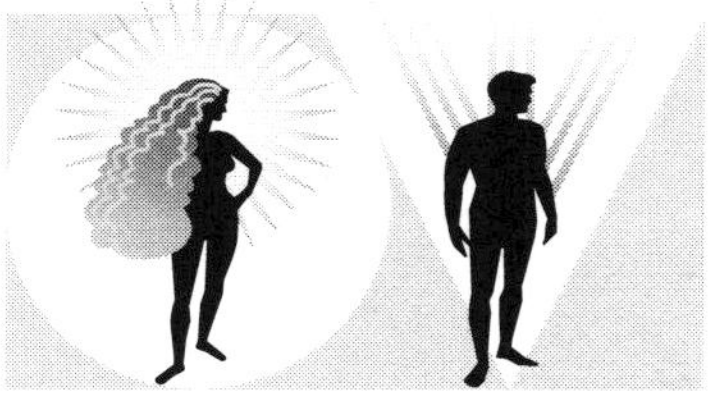

Glory of Man — Glory of God

SUPPLEMENT B **Biblical Wisdom–A Background Study**

This supplement offers a theology of wisdom from the whole Bible and is designed for those who seek a theological grasp of the *Five Aspects of Woman* course and the lady-of-wisdom aspect in particular. Since the initial foundation for wisdom has been laid already in Lesson 14, we begin in section 1 with the figure of Proverbs 8, since the identity of this figure is pivotal to the whole topic. Section 2 brings together an overview of wisdom through the Bible. This supplement is a companion to the video "Background in Wisdom," available through ICGS.

1. UNDERSTANDING PROVERBS 8

1.1 Misunderstandings and disagreements about wisdom

1.1A MISTAKEN IDENTITIES

In the Bible, mighty events and history turn on mistaken identity. Abraham masked the identity of his wife, Sarah, to avoid a perceived threat to himself. Jacob impersonated his brother, Esau, to steal Esau's blessing from their father. Later, Jacob was himself deceived when his uncle slipped his older daughter, Leah, into the wedding tent instead of the lovely Rachel, whom Jacob sought. Esther veiled her identity as a Jewess until the moment was ripe to reveal it. Jesus veiled His own identity to those of His own nation who had not ears to hear or eyes to see.

All these cases of mistaken identity are resolved in the pages of Scripture itself. But one of the greatest heroines of antiquity continues to be confused with identities never intended for her. Solomon introduced "lady" wisdom to illuminate his readers, not to confuse them. Yet, with the passage of time, the confusion surrounding "lady" wisdom's identity has grown to bizarre proportions. Is she God's feminine side? Is she a goddess? Is she an Old Testament (OT) **adumbration** (faint shadow or resemblance) of Jesus Christ? Is she a pre-incarnate manifestation of Messiah?

Disagreements in the family a long time ago

Early Christians were quick to see in Proverbs 8 what **seemed** to be an OT version of John 1 and Colossians 1, revealing another person with God at creation. When they added Paul's flat statements (1 Cor. 1:24, 30; Col. 2:3) that Jesus is our wisdom, the theological fi t seemed rock solid. So the early Christians proclaimed the figure of Proverbs 8 to be Jesus. Unfortunately for those holding this viewpoint, the exegetical and hermeneutical ground under their theological rock was not so solid. The exegetical evidence strongly suggests that the Proverbs 8 figure has a beginning. This played very well into the hands of the Arians, who, at that time, taught that Christ was not God, but rather, the first creature God created. Proverbs 8 became one of their favorite passages to prove this point, because orthodox Christians had already endorsed this figure as Christ. The Arians went the rest of the way and argued for His creaturely beginning at the dawn of time.

Leaving the family a long time ago

After many hard years of persecution from the Arians, orthodox Christians regained control of the Church and established once and for all at the Council of Chalcedon (451 A.D.) that belief in the full, eternal, and uncreated deity of Christ was essential to the faith. To this day, orthodox Christians rightly consider the modern Arians (Jehovah's Witnesses) to be heretics[1] outside the true faith. It is interesting to note that Jehovah's Witnesses are still using Proverbs 8 to teach that Jesus is the first creature. Thus, the Council of Chalcedon established that Christians would believe in the full deity and full humanity of Christ. Proverbs 8 should not be used to teach that Christ was a creature before His birth in Bethlehem. The Council did not explain or take a position on the feminine gender of the Proverbs 8 figure. Through the centuries, the majority

1. **Heretic** – One who denies all or part of the ecumenical creeds (Apostles,' Nicene, Chalcedon) which affirm the virgin birth, the deity of Christ, the Trinity, the bodily resurrection, the Second Coming, and other elementary Christian doctrine.

of Christians have interpreted the Proverbs 8 figure as the uncreated Christ. This has been the majority view, but not the monolithic view. Various interpreters always have held some version of a personification view, believing it is more true to the text.

Disagreements within the family still

ICGS takes the minority view on Proverbs 8. Section 1 of this supplement will explain why we believe it is better to interpret the figure of Proverbs 8 as a personification rather than as Jesus. Section 2 will set Proverbs 8 in a larger theological framework, establishing that the personification interpretation in no way diminishes Christ's glory or preeminence. As you take the *Five Aspects of Woman* course or share it with others, please be aware that these differences of interpretation surround this passage. It is not heretical to teach that the figure in Proverbs 8 is Christ, as long as you do not make Him merely a creature. It is not wrong to teach that Proverbs 8 is a personification. These are disagreements within the family and should be discussed with all charity. If a person takes the *Aspects* Course, studies this supplement, and still holds the view that Proverbs 8 is Christ (provided that Christ is uncreated and masculine), his view would be noble and traditional, and should be honored as such. Perhaps that person will come to understand that the personification view is on solid ground textually and can be held by those who love and honor Christ no less than he.

Leaving the family again?

The study of wisdom is even more complicated today because of feminism's new Sophia-worship. This time it is not the Arians who claim Jesus is created; it is the feminists who claim Jesus is feminine or replace Him with a goddess. This time the exegetical data favors the unorthodox more than the first time. The only way to get rid of the evidence that the Proverbs 8 figure is feminine is simply to disregard it, and that's what most of the godly have done all these centuries. Many accept the personification in chapters 1-7 and 9 as feminine; but in Proverbs 8, the femininity of the figure is ignored in order to make it Christ. This has not presented a problem in the past because gender was not a central debate. Today it is. Our present day feminist heretics have "left the family" by teaching the femininity of God and/or Sophia-worship from this very same text. Disagreeing inside the family about how to interpret a passage is vastly different from searching for a goddess. The Arians proclaimed a created Christ who was not God, and thus left the family of faith. If feminists seek a goddess—not Father, Son, and Holy Spirit—they will depart as well.

1.1B LAYING OUT THE COMPLICATIONS

Three main candidates for the figure of Proverbs 8

Thus, the passage which is the basis for the fourth aspect in the *Aspects* Course is doubly, even triply ensnared. First, most Christians come to the study of the gender themes of Proverbs with little or no background in the actual structure and message of the book. Learning about personification and archetypes will be a challenge in itself. Second, if believers do have an opinion about Proverbs 1-9, it is usually that the figure in chapter 8 is Christ. Third, the heresies of the Sophia-worshipers are understandably making everyone nervous about the passage, especially if "unfamiliar" ideas are introduced—such as an archetypal first feminine.

We will consider three basic answers for the identity of the Proverbs 8 figure: Jesus; a Hebrew goddess; or a personification of wisdom principles. We will not deal separately with the hypostasis view[2] and other inconsistent presentations[3] because they do not attempt to deal with Proverbs as a whole and are answered/can be answered as variations of the three main views.

How to decide

Proverbs 8:22-36 is a difficult text. Scholars have struggled and disagreed about it for centuries. The interpretation of any text boils down to three important questions: What do the words of the text **say**? What does the passage **mean**? How do they **fit** with everything else we know? These three questions are the starting points for the great disciplines of exegesis, hermeneutics, and theology, respectively. These ideas are so important, a review of their definitions is in order.

- **Exegesis**—The discipline which answers the question, "What does the text say?" through the study of its vocabulary, idiom, and grammar.

- **Hermeneutics**—The discipline which answers the question, "What does the text mean?" concerned with context, authorial intent, and other methods and principles of textual interpretation.

- **Theology**—Literally, "the study of God," answers the question, "How does this text fit with everything else known from Scripture?" Usually organized for consistency and often called systematic theology; concerned with fitting ideas into overall frameworks and encompassing systems.

Why this study is worth the effort

Grasping the lady-of-wisdom aspect takes work. The background material offered in this supplement is even more challenging than the course itself. However, the benefits of mastering this material are multiple and have been, in many cases, life-altering. Let me suggest five such benefits. This study can:

- Instruct you in patterns of femininity, freeing you to know yourself and God better;
- Protect you from dangerous error promulgated by feminists and goddess worshipers;
- Glorify Christ, as you see Him ever greater and more accurately;
- Alert you to the importance of God's masculinity and the need for careful interpretation of gender passages; and
- Encourage in you a calm confidence about your own views and a loving patience with others through a better grasp of history and interpretive schools of thought.

---

2. The hypostasis view is ensnared in confusion from the outset because of the vagueness of the term **hypostasis**—it can mean almost anything. Cleon Rogers writes: "Hypostasis is somewhere on a continuum between independent deity (Mesharu and Kittu in Mesopotamia) and a poetic personification. At times a distinction between the two is difficult." Cleon Rogers, "An Exegetical and Theological Study of Proverbs 8," (doctoral dissertation, Dallas Theological Seminary, 1991), 224. Even if a hypostasis describes God's attribute of wisdom found in Proverbs 8, the issues are exactly the same as with the Jesus-view on the two main points. By definition, God's attributes cannot be created because they are fundamental to His being. If He is developing or giving birth to attributes, then He is not immutable, and orthodox Christians are the ones with the wrong encompassing frame. Second, if God has feminine attributes, then there is a feminine side of God, and He is androgynous, as the feminists claim. The wisdom figure cannot be an attribute of God in one verse and a created thing in the next.

3. Examples could be given of reputable Bible scholars and teachers blatantly contradicting or illogically tripping in their explanations of Proverbs 8. For example, in one sentence a writer may state that wisdom is created and in the next sentence state that it is God's attribute. These authors are seemingly unaware that by definition God's attributes cannot be created. Or, one holding the Jesus-view skillfully deals with the gender themes in chapters 1-7 and 9, but utterly discounts them in Proverbs 8.

1.2 The figure in Proverbs 8 and interpretive issues

1.2A EXEGESIS AND DISPUTED WORDS

In the Hebrew of Proverbs 8:22-30, at least four key words have a range of meanings. How one translates these words affects the overall sense. But the overall sense affects the choices translators make. So, before trying to put the whole together, it is good to ask, what are the probable and possible meanings of these words?

- ***Qanah*** (8:22) has range of meaning: "Create, acquire, get, possess."
- ***Olam*** (8:23) usually means "from everlasting;" sometimes means "a long time" (Is. 42:14; 46:9; 57:11; 64:5; Jer. 2:20), "from ancient times" (Josh. 24:2; 1 Sam. 27:8; others), and "of old" (Is. 63:9, 11, 16; 64:4).
- ***Chil*** (8:24-25) means "brought forth, given birth." This is not contested significantly. Similar passages include Job 15:7—*were you brought forth before the hills?*, and Ps. 51:5—*I was brought forth in iniquity.*
- ***Amon*** (8:30) is translated "nursling" or "master-workman." If translated "nursling," it refers to wisdom, carrying on the "birth" theme. According to this view, wisdom was with God at the time of creation—she was young and frolicking like a child. However, *amon* has the wrong grammatical gender in Hebrew to refer to the word "wisdom" (amon is grammatically masculine while "wisdom" is grammatically feminine). Thus, many read *amon* as "Master-workman" and believe it refers to God.

According to exegesis, it is best to interpret the feminine figure in Proverbs 8 as a created entity, because none of the disputed words requires eternity in the divine sense (without beginning or end). *Chil* ("brought forth") is used twice, and seems to require the idea of a beginning. *Qanah* ("create, possess") is very compatible with this birth imagery. *Olam* ("from everlasting") must be interpreted in context to determine whether it actually means "forever" or "long ago." The points made about *amon* are interesting, but finally, not relevant to the issue as to whether wisdom is eternal or has a beginning.

1.2B HERMENEUTICS AND AUTHORIAL INTENT

Proper interpretation is a matter of understanding the author's intent in the text, not what the text "means to me." The context of a passage is fundamental to understanding the authorial intent. Thus, we will consider two concentric circles of context for Proverbs 8:22-31—its place in the prologue of chapters 1-9 and its relation to the whole book.[4]

Context of Proverbs prologue

The feminine wisdom figure of chapter 8 also appears in chapters 1, 3, 4, and 9. Any good interpretation of chapter 8 will consider these passages as well. Also, wisdom is repeatedly compared and contrasted with another feminine figure in chapters 1-9. This dual presentation climaxes in chapter 9, where wisdom's invitation and feast are contrasted to folly's. In order to handle the whole prologue with integrity, one must interpret the Proverbs 8 figure in a way consistent with all the other "lady" wisdom passages and in proper contrast to the "woman" folly passages.

4. The larger circles of context—other OT Wisdom Literature, the rest of the OT, and the NT—will be addressed in section 2 of this supplement.

Context of the whole book of Proverbs

To understand femininity and womanhood in the whole book of Proverbs, we need to ask, how do the feminine figures of Proverbs 1-9 relate to the women of the couplets and the two women of the epilogue in chapter 31? That is, how do the wise/foolish wives (Prov. 12:4; 14:1) and the king's mother and the virtuous wife of the epilogue (Prov. 31) relate to the wisdom and folly figures of Proverbs 1-9? Answer: The women of the couplets and the epilogue display the feminine patterns of "lady" wisdom and "woman" folly. Indeed they embody these patterns.

Therefore, according to standard hermeneutics, the personification view is on very strong ground. This view of chapter 8 fits with the other passages (chapters 1-7, 9), the couplets, and the epilogue, while the Christ-view seems to hang contextually in space. Feminists deal with the gender motifs of the whole book of Proverbs much more completely than the masculine Christ-view does, but their theological conclusion is to make God and Christ feminine, or to find an emerging goddess!

Crucial hermeneutical issues as interpreted by various viewpoints

Feminine figure in Prov. 1-9 is:	Divine-Christ view	Arian/JW view	Personification view	Feminist view
person or non-person	person	person	non-person	person or blurred
created or uncreated	uncreated	created	created	uncreated or blurred
gender relevant or irrelevant	gender irrelevant	gender irrelevant	femininity relevant	femininity relevant

1.2C THEOLOGY AND ENCOMPASSING FRAMEWORKS

Orthodoxy: A test for consistency

We bring our frameworks—our presuppositions and all ideas interpreted by them—with us as we approach any data. Any serious Bible student will want to bring his understanding of each passage into harmony with all other passages he knows. However, for one to choose interpretations only because they fit preconceived ideas is sloppy at best and dishonest at worst. Some hold their frameworks consciously and logically; others hold theirs subconsciously and illogically. To be honest, one must seek to understand each text "normally" in its own context before seeking to integrate it into his overall framework.

Reliable frameworks have a corrective power. If you are reading a lost letter from George Washington, and you understand George to say that he is a secret agent of the Crown, most likely the letter is bogus or you have misunderstood the letter. The eternal deity of Christ is not something orthodox Christians debate. It is part of the encompassing theological framework they bring to all their interpretations. So if you interpret a passage to say Christ was created (somewhere other than in Mary's womb), your interpretation is heretical, or you have misunderstood the passage. It has been determined already that Proverbs 8 will not be used by the orthodox to teach that Christ is a creature. We have yet to see whether the Church will allow them to teach that He is feminine.

Human perception: A confirming evidence

Another witness that can be subpoenaed to the interpreters' court is the human soul, individually and collectively. Does an interpretation ring true in general? Does it fit life as we know it? I am not talking about truth by committee or opinion poll. Rather, I am urging that an interpretation that does not fit the template of the human soul and that does not match life as generally experienced needs to be reviewed. The vast majority of women who have been taught the archetypes of "lady" wisdom and "woman" folly understand them immediately. They may not understand all the interpretive issues, but most women understand these two characters very quickly. Furthermore, a smaller, but significant group identifies immediately with these archetypal patterns and finds in them an explanation for parts of their own femininity which have hitherto been frustrated and frustrating. If this were not so, then we should question if "lady" wisdom and "woman" folly are archetypes of femininity. Why? If we are teaching something basic and created in the feminine heart, as we claim to be teaching in the *Aspects*, then the testimony of women's hearts will confirm it. If the same aspect seems strange or hard repeatedly, then it very well may not be a created aspect. Each of the aspects has seemed hard for someone somewhere. But all five aspects have been received and confirmed in heart and life by many women, including the wisdom aspect. The approval of women is certainly not the basis for the "lady" wisdom archetype—see arguments above! Nevertheless, women's approval is a voice of testimony confirming this interpretation.

1.3 Will the real "lady" wisdom please stand up?

1.3A THE POPULAR ANSWER: THE PROVERBS 8 FIGURE IS JESUS.

The strongest ground for the Jesus-view is that Proverbs 8 reminds us of John 1:1-5 and Colossians 1:15-17, where Christ is revealed as the Person who was with God before and during creation. Add Paul's flat statements that Jesus is our wisdom (1 Cor. 1:24, 30; Col. 2:3), and the theological case for the Jesus-view seems insurmountable. However, the Jesus-view is wrought with exegetical and hermeneutical problems. The text presents this figure as **created**—a point the Arians and Jehovah's Witnesses use to teach the heresy that Christ was the first creature from eternity past, rather than eternal God. The text presents this figure as **feminine**—a point feminists press to teach the femininity and/or androgyny of God, and even the existence of a goddess.[5] Finally, this figure is **ungracious**, a characteristic not consistent with Jesus.

1.3B THE NEW ANSWER: THE PROVERBS 8 FIGURE IS A GODDESS.

To understand the feminists' goddess-view, we must recall their humanistic presuppositions and liberal principles of Bible interpretation. According to feminist thought, truth is not **objective**, a matter of what is; rather, it is **subjective**, a matter of how the human mind conceives of what is. They believe the Bible is not objectively inerrant, but is, rather, an errant, evolving record of human understanding.

---

5. Indeed, the gender of this figure is significant to the text and not incidental because the believer is presented as masculine and is urged to pursue this figure in a "romantic" manner, a thought inconsistent with the rest of the Bible. Elsewhere in the Bible, where romantic, gendered language is used, God is always Bridegroom and Husband, never bride or wife. The burden of proof for this anomaly is on those who would present Christ as a "pursued" feminine. At the same time, interpreting "lady" wisdom as Christ leaves no plausible explanation for the identity of the folly figure in chapter 9 – is she the devil in feminine garb?

According to feminists,[6] the monotheistic, patriarchal Jews felt the need after the Exile and in the Diaspora (ca. B.C. 400) to develop a new response to the world; thus, the "emerging of Sophia."[7] Those who believe in the emerging goddess, Sophia, put much emphasis on the Apocryphal books, especially Wisdom, Ecclesiasticus, and Baruch, in which wisdom is personified even more extensively than in Proverbs. According to adherents of this view, Jesus was knowingly this goddess' representative. They claim this was understood by first-century Christians, was clearly written in the imagery of the Gospels, and is stated in Paul. However, Sophia's/Jesus' full recognition and acceptance were cut short by the oppression of the patriarchal Church fathers, who put too much emphasis on the Creator/creation distinction, and who believed in "power over" rather than "shared power." Many feminists who hold the goddess-view do not consider it compatible with the Jesus-view.

1.3C THE CONSISTENT ANSWER: THE PROVERBS 8 FIGURE IS A PERSONIFICATION.

As concluded exegetically, it is best to interpret the feminine figure in Proverbs 8 as a created entity. According to hermeneutics, interpreting the wisdom figure as a personification of creation principles fits well with Solomon's immediate context and the entire book. Just where the Jesus-view is weak, having no explanation for Jesus' femininity or the identity of "woman" folly, the personification view is quite strong. The principles of wisdom and folly are personified as women because wisdom and folly share patterns and roles with real women—they have femininity in common. Furthermore, the personification of wisdom and folly in the introduction beautifully fits the rest of Proverbs. The middle section follows with its specific couplets about women, and the epilogue features the real mother and idealized wife, all of whom follow the pattern of either wisdom or folly, introduced in chapters 1-9. For those who believe in the masculinity of God, the personification view stands on rock solid ground theologically. There is no escaping that Proverbs 8 presents a first feminine. Is this to be ignored? Made into a goddess? How is it to be interpreted in the light of the rest of Scripture? The only other "first feminine" in all the Bible before Eve is referred to in Ephesians 5:31-32, where Paul teaches that God fashioned Eve after the idea of the Church. Wisdom, as revealed in Proverbs 8, existed before the material universe and is a pattern for it. This concept parallels the Ephesians 5 teaching, that the Church was the pre-existing idea/pattern for Eve and all subsequent brides. In both instances, femininity is rooted in creation, whether temporal natural or eternally redeemed. Thus the personification view is more consistent exegetically, hermeneutically, and theologically than any other view. Far from dishonoring Christ, it honors Him more accurately to say He is prefigured by "lady" wisdom, than to equate Him with "her." Thus, it is the conclusion of this section that the wisdom figure of Proverbs 1-9 is a personification of wisdom, not an actual person or being. The wisdom thus personified is God's created plan for the universe. With and by this body of creation principles, God created from the beginning and sustains His universe. Feminine in its roles toward God and man, this "first feminine" is archetypal in that it provides original patterns and examples for women in their natures and behavior. In submission to these wisdom principles, people live and prosper in the world.

1.3D PREVIEW: A BIBLICAL THEOLOGY OF WISDOM

Having established an initial grasp of the nature of wisdom in Lesson 14, and having defended the personification view of the wisdom figure in Proverbs 1-9, we are ready to clarify the relationship of Jesus to OT wisdom, and to answer how Jesus is our wisdom, as is clearly stated in the NT.

6. Susan Cady, Marian Ronan, and Hal Taussig, *Sophia* (Harper & Row, San Francisco, 1986). The version of the goddess view provided here is not a comprehensive treatment of feminists' positions, but is supplied as a faithful representation of their thought, for which they themselves make no claim to consistency (refer to pp. 204-205, "Non-rationality").

7. This idea is a contradiction for them, because the introduction to the book of Proverbs was written by Solomon in B.C. 970-930 (Prov. 1:1). In other words, it predates the emergence of Sophia, and therefore contradicts the previous point. However, liberal Bible interpreters typically reject any of the Bible's claims about its authorship (e.g., Moses did not write the Law of Moses, Isaiah did not write Isaiah, Daniel did not write Daniel).

2. A BIBLICAL THEOLOGY OF WISDOM

2.1 How Jesus is prefigured in OT wisdom

Simply stated, our position is that the feminine wisdom figure of Proverbs is not to be equated with the Person of Christ, but rather, is to be seen as prefiguring Him. Countless ideas, objects, and people in the OT remind us of Jesus because the OT was written to prefigure Him and His work (Luke 24:44)! For example, the Law, the tabernacle, all its furniture, the sacrifices, Joseph, David, Esther, the cord of Rahab—all remind us of Jesus because they foreshadow Him. Some of these entities are things, some are ideas, some are men, and some are women. They all prefigure Christ. However, to say something **prefigures** Christ is quite different from saying it **is** Christ. For example, most Bible-believers would say that the Captain of the Lord's host in Joshua 5 **is** the pre-incarnate Christ. However, we would not say that the Law **is** Christ; rather, we would say that He perfectly fulfilled the Law and was foreshadowed by it. Christ's relationship with OT wisdom parallels His relationship with the OT law and can be charted as follows.

2.1A COMPARING LAW AND WISDOM IN RELATIONSHIP TO CHRIST

LAW	WISDOM
1. The Law is a body of commands coming from God and especially from His eternal attributes of righteousness and justice.	1. Wisdom is a body of principles created by God from His eternal attribute of wisdom.
2. The Law was given to man by special revelation through Moses.	2. Wisdom is given to man through general revelation. A significant portion of this insight was compiled under the authority of the Holy Spirit and concentrated in the Wisdom Literature of Scripture.
3. The Law prefigures and foreshadows Christ in countless ways.	3. Wisdom principles and personified wisdom prefigure and foreshadow Christ.
4. Christ perfectly obeyed the Law as a man, earning true human righteousness for the first time in history.	4. Christ learned obedience and wisdom in His humanity, becoming the first complete Sage.
5. Christ fulfilled the Law completely in that He is the Figure which it prefigures. He is the Lamb of God prefigured in every sacrifice commanded in the Law. He is the tabernacle and the glory of it.	5. Christ fulfills in eternal dimensions what wisdom can offer only in temporal ways. Wisdom prepares a feast and offers the good life. Christ offers Himself as the feast and gives eternal life.
6. Christ is our righteousness because he has earned perfect human righteousness, overcoming the world, the flesh, and the devil.	6. Christ established God's salvation wisdom by overcoming the prideful, demonic wisdom of this world through His work on the cross.
7. Christ is our righteousness in that He is God and possesses the eternal attribute of righteousness which created the Law in the first place.	7. Christ is our wisdom in that He is God and possesses the eternal attribute of wisdom which created the principles of wisdom in the first place.
8. The Law is a thing that can be personified. Paul says it is like a school master which brings us to Christ (Gal. 3:24).	8. Wisdom is a thing or idea and can be personified. Solomon says it is like a great lady who calls and trains us for the fullness of life.
9. Therefore Christ is greater than the Law of Moses: a. He is a Person and not a codex of commands. b. He is the source of the Law. c. He is the fulfillment of its meaning. d. He is our access to its merit and to fellowship with its Giver.	9. Therefore Christ is our wisdom as Paul writes, but not "lady" wisdom as Solomon writes. Jesus is greater than the figure of Proverbs: a. Jesus is a Person and not a body of principles. b. He is the divine source of wisdom. c. He is the embodiment of all its tenets and the eternal fulfillment of all its temporal claims. d. He is our access to eternal wisdom through fellowship with the Person who is all-wise temporally and eternally.

2.1B HOW JESUS IS OUR WISDOM.

The New Testament (NT) clearly states that Jesus is our wisdom: *But to those who are the called, both Jews and Greeks, Christ the power of God and the wisdom of God* (1 Cor. 1:24). *But by His doing you are in Christ Jesus, who became to us wisdom from God, and righteousness and sanctification, and redemption* (1 Cor. 1:30). *God's mystery, that is, Christ Himself, in whom are hidden all the treasures of wisdom and knowledge* (Col. 2:2b-3). What do these passages mean? How do they relate to the wisdom of Proverbs and the feminine figure of Proverbs 8? There are four ways in which Jesus is our NT wisdom, and we shall look at each.

Jesus is the all-wise God.

Jesus, as undiminished deity, shares all the attributes of God. After writing about God's plan for history and salvation, Paul exclaims: *Oh, the depth of the riches both of the wisdom and knowledge of God! How unsearchable are His judgments and unfathomable His ways! For WHO HAS KNOWN THE MIND OF THE LORD, OR WHO BECAME HIS COUNSELOR* (Rom. 11:33-34)? In 1 Corinthians, Paul quotes the very same OT verse (Is. 40:13) as he does in Romans 11:34, but in 1 Corinthians, he answers the question: *For WHO HAS KNOWN THE MIND OF THE LORD, THAT HE SHOULD INSTRUCT HIM? But we have the mind of Christ* (1 Cor. 2:16). Clearly Paul is teaching that the mind of Christ is the same as the mind of the Lord! Jesus, as God, shares completely in the riches and unsearchable wisdom of God.

Jesus is the complete/perfect human sage.

Jesus learned wisdom as a man does, except He learned it perfectly. For thirty years, He submitted Himself to His parents, family, work, and small town life, doing no miracles. Only Luke allows us to glimpse Jesus' life between two and 12 years of age: *And the Child continued to grow and become strong, increasing in wisdom; and the grace of God was upon him* (Luke 2:40). Writing about Jesus' life after His youthful visit to the Temple, Luke writes: *And Jesus kept increasing in wisdom and stature, and in favor with God and men* (Luke 2:52). Although the emphasis in Hebrews 2 and 5 is on Jesus as our high priest, the pattern of attaining wisdom through enduring tests applies to Jesus' perfection as the human sage as well. As the ultimate prophet, high priest, and Davidic king, Jesus prophesied, interceded, and judged. His vivid nature analogies, teaching on the two paths of life (broad and narrow), and especially His parables mark him as wise man, the sage greater than Solomon (Luke 11:31). Also noteworthy is Jesus' claim that He and John the Baptist were both wise in their method of ministry, although they differed completely in style (Matt. 11:19; Luke 7:35). Notice that Jesus does not claim to be wisdom in these two renderings, but states that He and John, or at least their works, are "children" of wisdom.

Jesus is the wisdom of salvation's plan.

Christ crucified is the hidden wisdom which God planned before time—the Lamb slain from before the foundation of the world (1 Pet. 1:18-20). By completely fulfilling God's "*foolish*" plan for salvation through weakness and death, Jesus defeated the Devil and his worldly wisdom based on pride and power. 1 Corinthians 1:18-2:16 is the most important passage on Christ as our salvation wisdom.

Jesus is the Spirit and mind behind God's wisdom.

Christ is the Person behind the wisdom principles, and we have fellowship with that Person. In Him we have more than creation or salvation principles, we have fellowship with the mind and the Spirit of the Person of God who is all-wise (1 Cor. 2:8-16). Believers acquire spiritual wisdom through the gracious ministry of the Spirit of Christ.

2.2 Laying out a history of wisdom

2.2A GOD, THE ALL-WISE PLANNER AND ARTIST

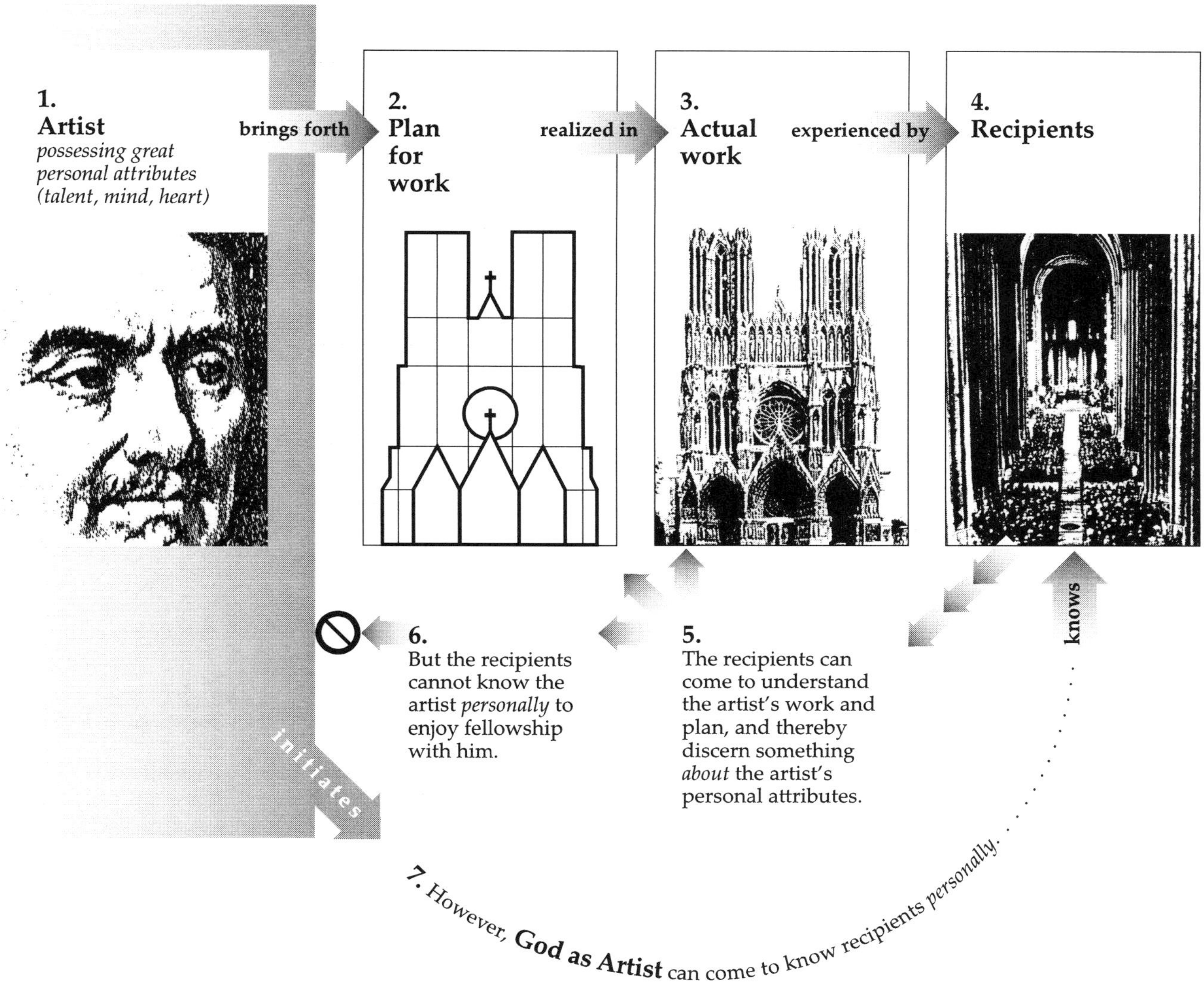

Study the diagram above with the aid of these expanded captions, coordinated by number with the diagram.

1. Great art first originates in the heart, mind, soul, and vision of an artist.
2. The artist then brings forth his artistic vision as a plan—this may be a blueprint, a sketch on a napkin, notes jotted on a page, or a melody hummed in the shower.
3. Next, the artistic plan is transfomed into the actual work of art—a building is constructed from the blueprint, a painting is rendered from the sketch, an orchestra plays the notes on the page.
4. Finally, others receive the artist's work. These recipients experience the art—they go inside the building, see the painting, or hear the symphony.
5. The perceptive among the recipients come to know and understand the art and the plan behind it, as they study its construction and interact with its sights, sounds, and textures.
6. However, it is not possible to know an artist **personally** by merely studying his works. It is possible to know something **about** the artist, but it is not possible to know **him**.
7. In like manner, remember that God is The Great Artist. He has produced His great works in nature that we may receive them and experience many things from His mind and heart. However, we cannot **know** God through His works in nature; we can only know **about** Him. However, He has come to us in the Scriptures, in Christ, and in the Person of the Holy Spirit, that we might know Him **personally**. Knowing His works increases our capacity to understand and worship Him when we do come to know Him personally.

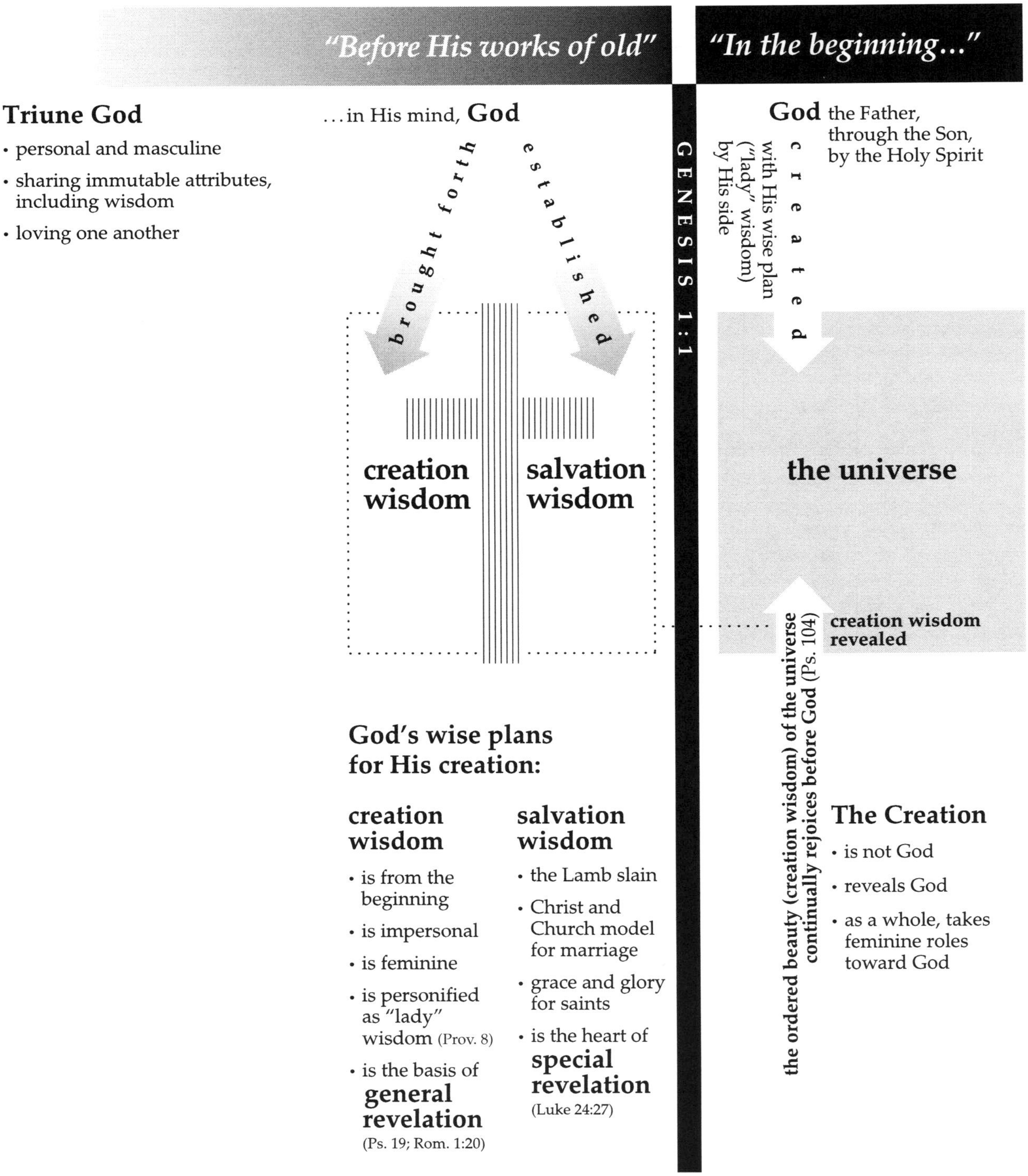
"Before His works of old"
"In the beginning..."
Triune God
• personal and masculine
• sharing immutable attributes, including wisdom
• loving one another
...in His mind, God
brought forth
established
creation wisdom
salvation wisdom
GENESIS 1:1
God the Father, through the Son, by the Holy Spirit
created
with His wise plan ("lady" wisdom) by His side
the universe
creation wisdom revealed
the ordered beauty (creation wisdom) of the universe continually rejoices before God (Ps. 104)
God's wise plans for His creation:
creation wisdom
• is from the beginning
• is impersonal
• is feminine
• is personified as "lady" wisdom (Prov. 8)
• is the basis of general revelation (Ps. 19; Rom. 1:20)
salvation wisdom
• the Lamb slain
• Christ and Church model for marriage
• grace and glory for saints
• is the heart of special revelation (Luke 24:27)
The Creation
• is not God
• reveals God
• as a whole, takes feminine roles toward God

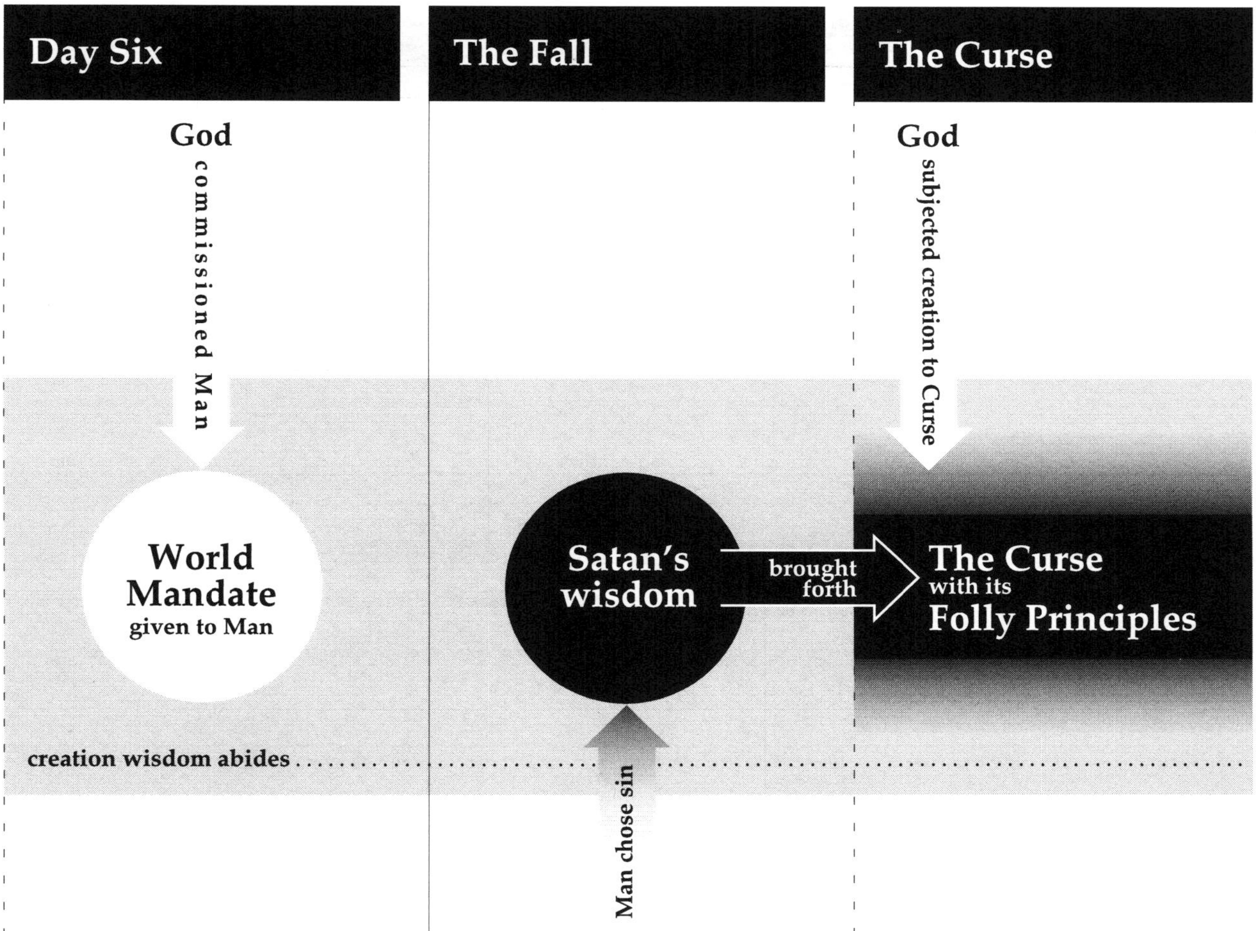

World Mandate

- Gen. 1:26-28
- to rule and subdue requires knowing the creation and its principles (creation wisdom)

Sin

- Gen. 3:1-6
- knowledge and life in rebellion against God

Curse/folly principles

- Gen. 3:15-19
- Prov. 9:13-18 ("woman" folly)
- deceit, pride, death, self-destruction

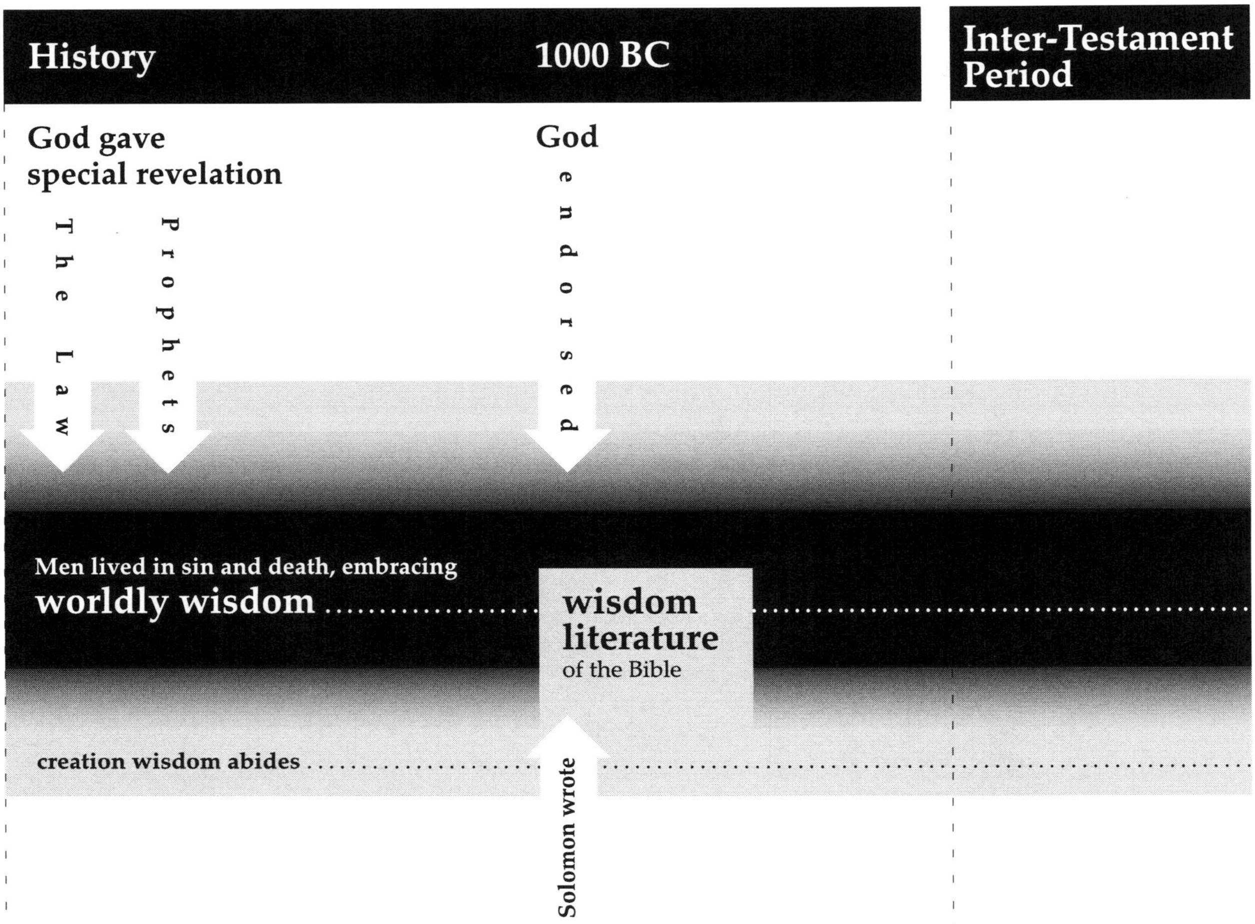

Though fallen, men:

- grew in **creation wisdom**
- by studying **general revelation**
- understood through **common grace** (Is. 28:23-29)
- and thereby increased their rule of the earth

Report from under the sun:

- update on World Mandate
- led by world's wisest man

- personified wisdom emphasized in Apocrypha
- wisdom identified with the Law
- both over-exalted

Christ Came

Christ, in His humanity, perfectly learned creation wisdom (Luke 2:40, 52)

God enacted salvation wisdom
The foolishness of the cross (1 Cor. 1-3):
- power through weakness
- glory through shame
- life through death

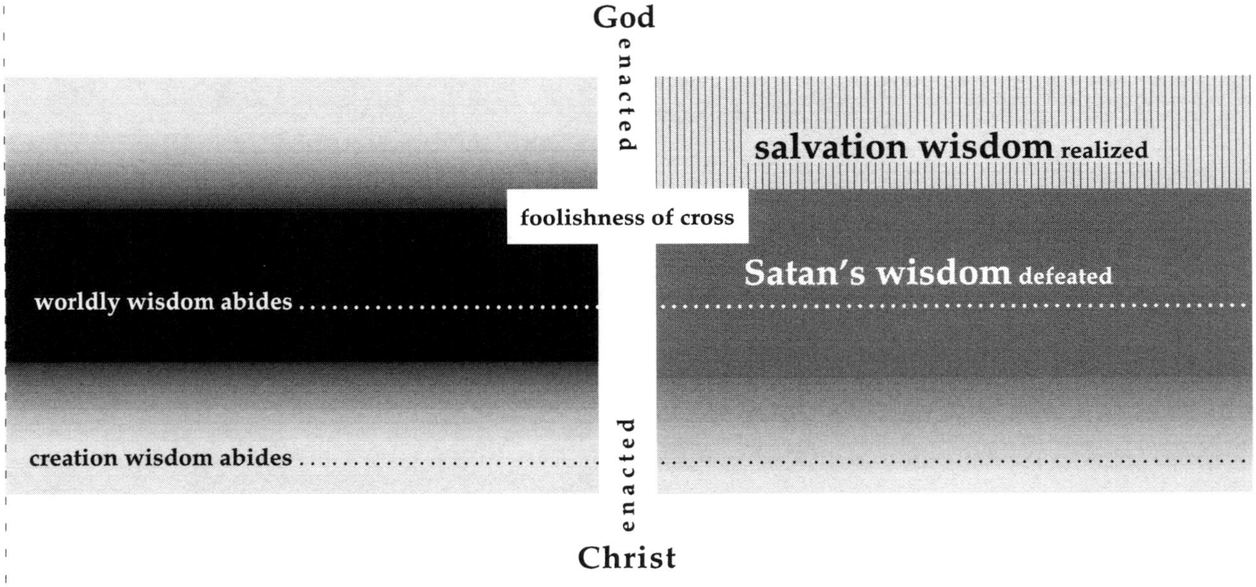

Though fallen, men are offered **salvation wisdom**:
- the heart of **special revelation** (Luke 24:27)
- understood through **saving grace**

Church Age

God revealed salvation wisdom
(established before the foundation of the world):

- the Lamb slain (1 Pet. 1:19-20)
- Christ and Church are model for marriage (Eph. 5:31-33)
- grace and glory planned for saints (Eph. 1)

Pentecost

salvation wisdom revealed

worldly wisdom abides ....

creation wisdom abides ....

Normal Christian life should be lived (1 Cor. 1-3; Eph. 1, 5-6; Col. 1, 3; James):
- in fellowship with and dependence upon the **Spirit and Mind of Christ**
- in the harmony of **creation wisdom** and **salvation wisdom**
- on guard against the pollution and deceit of **worldly wisdom**

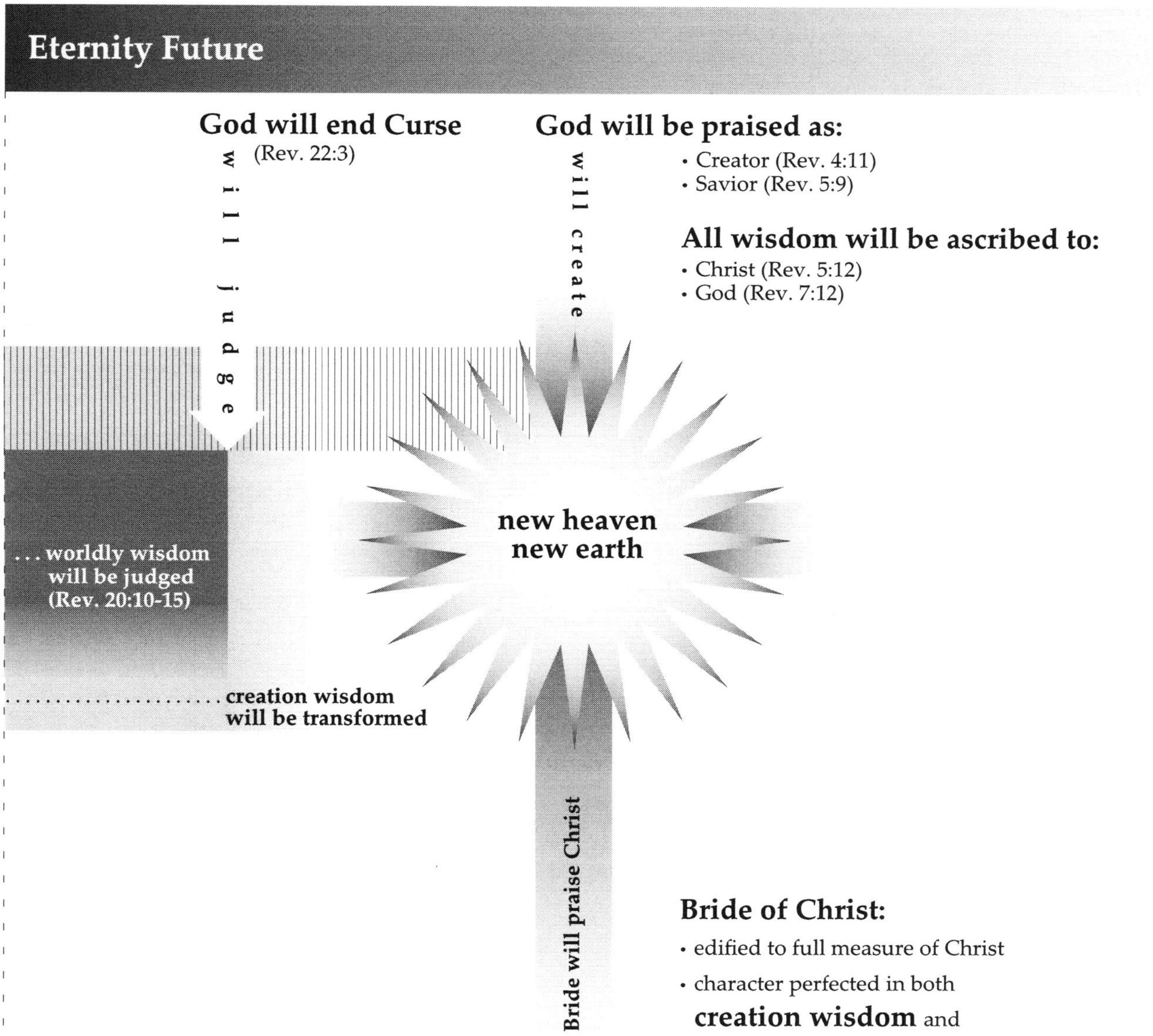
Eternity Future
God will end Curse
(Rev. 22:3)
will judge
God will be praised as:
• Creator (Rev. 4:11)
• Savior (Rev. 5:9)
will create
All wisdom will be ascribed to:
• Christ (Rev. 5:12)
• God (Rev. 7:12)
new heaven
new earth
. . . worldly wisdom
will be judged
(Rev. 20:10-15)
creation wisdom
will be transformed
Bride will praise Christ
Bride of Christ:
• edified to full measure of Christ
• character perfected in both
creation wisdom and
salvation wisdom

2.2C COMMENTARY ON THE THEOLOGY-OF-WISDOM DIAGRAM

OT Wisdom is rooted in man's understanding of creation principles.

OT wisdom is the truth in general revelation (Ps. 19; Rom. 1), and it is framed by reverence for God. It is gained through obedience to the World Mandate and by grace from God—not necessarily saving grace (Ex. 25; Prov.; Is. 29). This wisdom is limited; it cannot save you from your sins. But for this life, it is among the most valuable of all possessions.

The Wisdom Literature of the OT is inspired by God and inerrant, but its viewpoint and methodology are different from the Law and the Prophets. The Law and the Prophets are God's words to man. They reveal God by quoting Him to us. For example, He says, "Do not steal." Proverbs, on the other hand, makes observations such as: *Men do not despise a thief if he steals to satisfy himself when he is hungry; but when he is found, he must repay sevenfold; he must give all the substance of his house* (6:30-31).

The wisdom books express man's viewpoint about the creation and life. Their truth can be characterized in this way. Job says, "This is what it is like to suffer in righteousness." Solomon says, "This is what it is like to be in love." God says, "You have spoken truly about the human experience. Put it in My book. It is part of My record of truth for you."

Solomon, the great OT sage, compiled wisdom and revealed its nature.

Humble enough to ask for wisdom as a young king, Solomon became the wisest man of history through God's gracious gift (1 Kin. 3-13). In jurisprudence (1 Kin. 3:16-28), in artistic ability (1 Kin. 4:32), and in knowledge of the creation (1 Kin. 4:33), Solomon was unsurpassed. Of his 1,005 songs, the erotic love song, Song of Solomon, is considered his greatest. Ecclesiastes is his wise assessment of mortal life on this fallen earth. He also wrote Psalm 72.

Probably no man came closer to fulfilling the Creation Mandate (Gen. 1:26-28) than Solomon. He ruled over nature and nations in a way no other man has. He was well-placed to "report" on mankind's progress in civilization. God did not call Solomon to write prophecy or law; but He did employ him to write and gather wisdom literature—a true and accurate distillation of man's experience on earth.

It is not unreasonable that God gave the wisest of all men insight about the first created thing. Solomon's grasp of gender principles touch love, life, and the whole of creation. They permeate all his work and reach a crescendo in Proverbs 8.

NT Wisdom is rooted in apostolic revelation about the plan of salvation.

Jesus and the Apostles reveal four things not understood and not known about God's plan for saving men:

- The Lamb was slain before the foundation of the world (1 Pet. 1:19-20);
- Christ and His Bride are the model for marriage (Eph. 5:31-32);
- The glory of Christ is to be shared with saints (Eph. 1; 6); and
- We have the mind of Christ! We don't have just the principles, we have fellowship with the Person who designed the principles (1 Cor. 1-3).

NT salvation wisdom is gained through faith in the Person and work of Christ. This wisdom, when received, provides a saving grace from sins for the world to come. The wisdom of salvation is good and wholesome, but it may lead to persecutions in this life. This wisdom offers glory, wealth, and health in the next world.

The wisdom of the Spirit-filled NT believer

The Christian is called to combine the creation wisdom emphasized in the OT and the salvation wisdom emphasized in the NT into one walk. In this, as in almost every other issue, the OT provides the foundation upon which the NT builds.

The basic creation principles emphasized in the OT are: The fear of God, diligence in labor, respect for authority, control of one's tongue, moral purity, family loyalty, and perseverance in hardship. These principles are basic to wisdom and morality worldwide. They are assumed for believers. Indeed the codes of Ephesians 5 and Colossians 3 repeat the basic moral principles in the OT—be good and faithful workers, managers, mates, parents, and children. How regrettable that many Bible-quoters have no credibility or testimony because they are poor workers, mere talkers, or as irresponsible as they are religious (1 Cor. 5:1,11; 1 Tim. 5:8; 1 Pet. 4:14-16).

Worldly wisdom

Worldly wisdom is creation wisdom mixed with sin and not framed by reverence for God. Its prominent sins are pride, rebellion, dishonesty, deceit, and immorality. Satan has led the creation in worldly (or demonic) wisdom (Is. 14:12-14). This demonic wisdom seeks knowledge, life, and power through deception and self-exaltation (Gen. 3:1-6). God has destroyed Satan at the cross and will destroy worldly wisdom in all its pride and sin. He chooses to destroy it with elements of *foolishness*—weakness, suffering, shame, and lowliness (Rev. 17-18).

Christian wisdom

To be wise, Christians will be like unsaved wise people by walking in diligent, respectful, and moral ways. But Christians are different from those who are merely wise in this world in that their focus is the personal Christ who has saved them, loves them, and is preparing them for the true glories beyond. The greatest challenge for the Christian is to discern and walk in true creation wisdom and salvation wisdom without mixing either with sin. When alloyed with sin, creation wisdom becomes worldly wisdom, and salvation wisdom becomes religious hypocrisy.

2.3 A polemic against feminism's goddess

2.3A CATHOLIC AND PROTESTANT GENDER TRADITIONS

The Catholics have had a much more developed and balanced gender universe than the Protestants. They understand that God is our Father, the Church is our mother, Christ is the God-Man, and Mary is His mother. Though their archetypes have been basically right, the Catholics have polluted them with grave errors, foremost of which are:

- **Anti-Semitism**—An archetypal version of mother-hatred. The Catholics have separated Mary from Israel and given her all the glory as God's feminine helper. The "queen of heaven" is actually Israel, not the individual Mary. But Catholics often have hated and persecuted Jews rather than longed for their reuniting with God. Too frequently they have been the proud implants Paul warns against in Romans 10.

- **Idolatry**—Placing the Church above the Word of God, an archetypal version of the Genesis 3:16 curse. The Church is the bride of Christ (Eph. 5), and as His helper-completer on earth, should stand under the Word of God, interpreting and applying it in the world. She should not stand over it to alter or change it.

The Protestants reacted strongly to the over-exaltation of Mary and the Catholic Church's lack of submission to the Word of God. Sadly, Protestants did not repent of anti-Semitism, and the great liberal denominations have shown more disrespect for the Word than Catholics did. In rebelling against the sins of Rome, Protestants threw out some very important gender babies with the bath water—essentially all feminine archetypes, as well as other elements of the Christian faith. Although humanistic in his worldview, Amaury de Riencourt well describes the Protestant imbalance in favor of masculinity:

> The masculine ethos came to prevail completely in Northern Europe and in the American colonies—the male divisive "ego" principle, willful in Luther, rational in Calvin. While Calvin's successful blend of Bourse and Bible was going to generate modern capitalism with its extraordinary force of economic expansion and technological inventiveness, Luther's destruction of the Roman Catholic clergy's countervailing force in Prussia led straight to the modern Bismarkian state. All the colorful, legendary, mythical side of life that had prevailed for centuries gradually disappeared from adult life, to give way to an essentially masculine mode increasingly founded on logic and systematic efficiency—dry, cool, and slightly inhuman. In Protestant lands, all the archetypes of the unconscious which found expression in Catholic symbolism were left without any outlet or form of expression; the anima was thrown back into the unconscious and remained, until our day, as a festering sore, a psychological penalty for the Promethean success of the modern Protestant West.[8]

In its early centuries, Western Protestantism prospered with a powerfully masculine God and masculine spirituality which produced great exegetical study of Scripture (doctrines of salvation, authority of Scripture, and eschatology), scientific study of the world, and capitalistic wealth. However, truth out of balance is like rowing with one ore in the water—eventually one begins to travel in circles. Ironically, Protestants, who first jettisoned the feminine elements of Christianity, are today losing their grip on God's masculinity as well. "Gender-free" Christendom is also losing respect for such classically masculine pursuits as rationality, technology, and the creation of wealth.

Just as Protestants threw out the feminine elements because they were corrupted, now the feminist/humanists are throwing out masculinity because it has been out of balance and corrupted. The masculine God of Scripture is being replaced with a "Spirit who transcends gender" or a "He/She" or merely a "She." Mother Earth and the goddesses are being re-exalted in some circles. Truth and rationality are being thrown out in favor of mysticism and even witchcraft.

We must hold on to both the masculine and feminine archetypes and roots in our faith. Feminists will want us to over-emphasize the feminine elements; "old" Protestants will resist any feminine archetypes as smacking of Catholicism. But we must have both in Biblical balance. Imbalances and reductionism eventually will distort our knowledge of God, His will, and ourselves, leaving us to be tossed to and fro in faith and practice.

8. Amaury de Riencourt, *Sex and Power in History* (D. McKay Co., New York, 1974), 263.

2.3B THE GODDESS AND THE WOMEN WHO MAKE HER

Feminist spirituality is a wide and diverse subject representing the varying beliefs of many different people. In general, feminist spirituality begins with a rejection of patriarchy, Western civilization, and its Judeo-Christian roots. It recognizes no external spiritual authority, but looks to personal experience and feelings for standards and guidance. It is highly eclectic, borrowing heavily from Eastern, ancient Greek, Roman, and Native American religions, New Age thought, psycho-therapy, psychology, and the occult. Consider four characteristics of feminism and its spirituality freely admitted by its advocates.

Rebellion

Feminist thought begins with rejection of and rebellion against patriarchy. Susan Cady defines patriarchy this way:

> Patriarchy is that interlocking system of oppressions—racial, sexual, political and economic—which aims to subjugate and control the earth, the poor, females, people of color, feeling, and spontaneity. Patriarchal spirituality is the extension of that system into our hearts and minds. It is a demonic aspect of classical western spirituality, a system of images, beliefs and practices which has glorified and entrenched power-over in western culture and in Christianity. By patriarchal spirituality we mean everything that wars against our realization of connectedness with one another and the rest of reality, and, as a corollary of this, everything that wars against our experiencing and feeling deeply in our own bodies.[9]

Please notice the last sentence. Feminists are at war with everything that contradicts "their experiencing and feeling." Feminist thought and spirituality are based on the personal feelings and experience of women. They do not believe objective truths or accept external spiritual authorities. They experience things. Thus, their rebellion is truly autonomous. They do not reject one authority to embrace another outside of themselves. They reject God in order to embrace their own feelings. Their autonomous experience is their standard and thus becomes their god(dess).

Self-exaltation

The goals of feminists are to destroy patriarchy and to empower women. It follows that they do not believe in any transcendent God. Rather, they are pantheists who are quick to make divine claims for themselves and all women. Cynthia Eller, a feminist, quotes several other feminist thinkers to this point:

> As Lynn Andrews says, I'm always amazed when people come to me and talk about the Goddess as if I'm not one! Who do they think the Goddess is? She's you! She's me! These women emphasize the divinity of human women, and they worry that attention to some external or greater-than-human goddess will diffuse that emphasis. Sonia Johnson, eager to avoid what she sees as the pitfalls of patriarchal religions, is particularly diligent in keeping the focus on human women. She explains: Goddess worship is not really worshiping the goddess, it is really worshiping women and ourselves, and saying we're peers, we are what creates everything, we are the creator and the created. Hallie Austen Iglehart is

9. Susan Cady, *Sophia* (Harper & Row, 1986), 7.

somewhat more tolerant of an externalized goddess, but only as a transitional stage in the progress toward a more perfect deification of human selves: Ultimately...to be truly whole, we must recognize that there is not goddess beyond ourselves in the rest of creation. We are part of that great natural whole. It may be helpful in our movement to wholeness to refer to a female divine force, but only if we remember that it is a step in our process of reclaiming our own divinity as part of the vastness of the natural world.

The notion of self-as-goddess is further strengthened by widespread spiritual feminist belief in reincarnation. Because spiritual feminists are continually reincarnating, they are not narrow beings confined to the limits of a particular life, but [are] at least semi-divine, if not fully divine beings.[10]

Eclecticism

Having rejected the Judeo-Christian tradition and its Western manifestations, feminist spiritualists turn to all the other cultures and religions of the world. (These are the pagan and idolatrous religions fought and rejected by both Jews and Christians for centuries.) They do not embrace these religions as such, but pick and choose pieces and images from them as they suit their tastes and purposes.

Apart from neo-paganism, the most significant source for spiritual feminist ideas and practices has been the New Age movement.... New Age has taken over where counterculture left off, setting a name to the impulse to explore non-Western religions, occult practices, and innovative forms of psycho-therapy freely and indiscriminately, apart from any commitment to a single religious institution.[11]

Feminists freely borrow and intermingle modern psychology and self-help therapies with the religions of ancient Greece and Rome, the Far East, and Native Americans.

Non-rationality

Feminists make no attempt to systematize or categorize their beliefs. In fact, they largely view striving after logical goals, such as consistency and non-contradiction, as vain masculine pursuits to be avoided.

...spiritual feminists are iconoclasts: they love to flout the rules of the theological discipline, to challenge the categories usually used to think about the sacred. They don't think most of these categories apply to what they experience anyway. Or rather, they think all of them apply indiscriminately, even those categories that were originally set up to be mutually exclusive. Do spiritual feminists believe in one goddess or in many goddesses? Both, they answer, both at the same time. Is their goddess within them, a part of them, or is she completely outside of them, looking in? Both, they answer, both at the same time. Does this goddess exist independently of human beings or did spiritual feminists invent her? Both, they answer, both at the same time.

10. Cynthia Eller, *Living in the Lap of the Goddess* (Crossroads, New York, 1993), 142.

11. Ibid., 64

On the face of it, talking thealogy (sic; the way feminists wish to spell the word theology in order to make it mean goddess-study) with spiritual feminists sounds unrewarding, kind of like trying to play Monopoly with someone who doesn't see why she can't put a hotel up on Boardwalk just because Park Place is mortgaged to the bank. But spiritual feminists are actually very competent players of the theological game. They are surely not the first to suggest that deities are so far beyond the constraints of human intellect that it is an insult to them to pretend that they must adhere to human rules.[12]

2.3C CONTRASTING CHRISTIANITY AND FEMINIST SPIRITUALITY

While the study of modern paganism helps arm us against feminist religion, no one will be able to master all the crazy quilt of its bizarre ideas, beliefs, and practices. However, with a thorough understanding of the foundational tenets of Christianity, we will be able to recognize error when it appears no matter what its guise, because it will contradict what we know to be true. Those armed with a knowledge of truth will discern the counterfeit.

DOCTRINE	CHRISTIANITY	FEMINIST SPIRITUALITY
Trinity	God is personal. God is transcendent. God is masculine.	Patriarchy is evil. No personal, transcendent, or masculine God exists.
Creation	Made by God, but is not God. Reveals God. Feminine in roles.* To be wondered at, not worshiped.	Nature is god(dess). Feminine force (and individual women) are divine; to be worshiped. Pantheistic. Ecology is worship.**
Incarnation	Transcendent God, united with creation in Jesus, the God-Man.	No need for Incarnation, because everything is already goddess. We need only "realize" the goddess in ourselves.
Evil	Evil is real. A violation of God's nature, abnormal. Begun by rebellious creature. Death an enemy.	Evil is an illusion, and is normal. Evil always has been, always will be. Death is the other side of life and rebirth.
Salvation	Life in the Father made possible because Christ paid for sin, met God's standard, and overcame death.	"Salvation" is autonomous freedom and self-worship. Attained by transmigration, reincarnation; Western ideas of scientific evolution are amalgamated with Eastern ideas of the evolution of human spirits. There is no need of a savior.
Judgment	Works done in flesh are judged by a transcendent God. History and evil end. Life for those in Christ is individual and eternal.	There is no Judge. There is no judgment.

* It is not wrong to speak of "Mother Earth," "Mother Nature," "Lady Wisdom," "Israel, the Wife of God," or the "Church, the Bride of Christ," as long as we understand: 1) These are personifications of things and groups—useful and true because of the created roles and relationships they share; 2) These feminine entities are not persons and are not to be worshiped; and, 3) As feminine archetypes, they should be valued and can be understood only in relationship to God, the masculine Person who made them.

** Christians should be conscientious stewards of creation. However, we should be mindful that much of the popular ecology movement is driven by goddess-theology, which holds as a basic tenet that humans should not rule nature, but rather, should coexist with it as peers. This is a profound contradiction to God's command for man to rule the earth for Him (Gen. 1:27-28).

12. Ibid., 130-131

2.3D CONCLUSION: MORE THAN COMPLEMENTARIANS

ICGS aligns itself with the Danvers Statement and those Christians who call themselves "complementarians." With them we affirm that:

- The nature and roles of the sexes are equal in value but different in essence;
- Man's headship in the home and church is fundamental to both the created and redeemed order; and
- Woman's anchoring roles in the private domains are essential to civilization and godliness.

These tenets are clearly taught in the Old Testament and are delineated in the commands of the New (e.g., 1 Cor. 11:1-16; Eph. 5:22-33; 1 Tim. 2:8-15). To ignore or disdain these passages is an assault on God's design for men and women. At a more fundamental level, it is a rejection of the authority of Scripture as the standard for faith and practice.

However, ICGS and *Aspects* courses go one step further than most complementarians go. We believe that the Scriptures not only provide the commands which order the home and the church, they also reveal the everlasting patterns of a gendered universe in which our deepest souls may find their identity.

The masculinity of God is the anchor of the gender universe. God—Father, Son, and Holy Spirit—has created a feminine creation for His good pleasure. He initiates, provides, protects, and leads the entire creation which responds and bears fruit to Him. How much more is this true of Israel, the covenanted people of God, who has been His wife, His helper, and the mother of His Son. Ultimately, Christ and the Church are the pinnacle and original pattern for each man and woman. Adam and Eve were patterned after Christ and the Church, not the other way around.

Finally on the topic of this supplement, Proverbs does not give us the most fundamental of the Bible's gender archetypes. However, the four main characters of the prologue—the seductive "woman" folly, the regal "lady" wisdom, the masculine young fool, and the fatherly sage—are a powerful and vital supporting cast in God's universal gender drama. Knowledge of these entities will greatly enrich our own understanding of masculinity and femininity, and enable us to live as men and women, not only in obedience to His commands, but also in the light of His patterns and plans.

SUPPLEMENT C

The Womanliness of Deborah

Complementarian principles from Judges 4-5

"The Womanliness of Deborah" was first presented by Barbara Mouser as a lecture at the ICGS Conference "Created Male and Female" in Denver, Colorado, in 2003. Available as a booklet from ICGS since that time, it also appeared in "The Journal for Biblical Manhood and Womanhood" (Fall 2006, Vol. XI, Issue 2). It is reproduced here as a supplement to answer one of the most frequently asked questions in discussions about women and leadership, "What about Deborah?" Considering the length and importance of this supplement, it is recommended that study groups devote at least one full week to its content. Study questions have been added to aid in review and group discussions.

1. Preface: Terminology and modern gender controversies

ICGS defends the tenets of "complementarianism" as is clear in the subtitle of this supplement, "Complementarian principles from Judges 4-5." However, as I enter the fifth decade of my participation in this controversy, I believe a review of key terms would be beneficial.

Feminism—The social and political theory that men and women are interchangeable and that no gender-based difference in role, privilege, or responsibility should be recognized or sustained by the state or society. Patriarchy is held to be evil (refer to *FAW—Vol. One*, p. 116-117).

Religious (especially evangelical) feminism; also called **egalitarianism**—Essentially the same view as secular feminists, held by those who claim allegiance to the Bible. In order to make the Bible teach feminism, egalitarians reinterpret passages on male headship and gender-specific roles to negate their meaning or applicability (refer to *FAW—Vol. One*, p. 117-119.) The ordination of women as elders and priests is a central goal of religious feminism. Patriarchy is viewed as an evil antiquity to outgrow and overturn.

Complementarianism—A response to evangelical feminism, arising in late twentieth-century America, affirming that:

- Men are, by God's creation and mandate, responsible to lead the human race with the help, nurture, and counsel of women;
- The sexes are equal in humanity and spiritual worth, but distinctive in sexual nature and roles; and
- Though marred by the sins of both men and women, the headship of man and the complementary relationship of the sexes are restored, not erased, by the redemptive work of Christ.

The faithful Christians who took up the challenge of religious feminism in the latter half of the twentieth century[1] took their stand on Scripture. They defended the equal worth of man and woman as creatures in the image of God, the created headship of man ordained by God, and the different and complementary natures and roles of men and women. They grounded their defense in the careful exegesis of pertinent New Testament passages. From the beginning, these faithful Christians chose to call themselves "complementarians."

> If one word must be used to describe our position, we prefer the term Complementarian, since it suggests both equality and beneficial differences between men and women. We are uncomfortable with the term "traditionalist" because it implies an unwillingness to let Scripture challenge traditional patterns of behavior, and we certainly reject the term "hierarchicalist" because it overemphasizes structured authority while giving no suggestion of equality or the beauty of mutual interdependence.[2]

While "patriarchy" is not explicitly mentioned in the above quote, clearly it was rejected as a standard to defend because of its similarity to "hierarchialism." In the complementarians' view, patriarchy already had been successfully defined as antiquated and oppressive by modern feminist society. In short, it was considered by the complementarians as a word and concept too tainted to defend.

1. Among the most notable of these are the writers of the Danvers Statement in 1987 and the editors and writers of *Recovering Biblical Manhood and Womanhood, A Response to Evangelical Feminism* in 1991.

2. John Piper and Wayne Grudem, eds., *Recovering Biblical Manhood and Womanhood, A Response to Evangelical Feminism* (Wheaton, IL: Crossway Books, 1991), xiv.

As a voice crying in the wilderness, I disagree with modern society and the vast majority of Christians (even those claiming to be Bible-believing) by owning and defending patriarchy. Patriarchy is of God. The Triune God is Himself a patriarchy—a society of masculine Persons ruled by Father. His universe is a patriarchy (1 Cor. 8:5-6; 15:14; Eph. 4:14-15). Father-rule is ordained by God from Genesis to Revelation, and is immortalized for eternity in the names of the fathers inscribed on the New Jerusalem (Rev. 21:12-14). So let us consider again, or for the first time, a "not tainted" definition of patriarchy.

Patriarchy—The rule of fathers; a familial, social, political, and ecclesiastical ordering of human relationships wherein the responsibility for leadership, protection, provision, and governance is laid on the shoulders of men, particularly familial heads.

If the whole world has given patriarchy over to be defined as only **fallen**, we must not acquiesce. We must define and champion patriarchy—**created, fallen**, and **redeemed**. The *Five Aspects of Man*, as summarized on pages 173-179, provides such an outline.[3] Before we dismiss fallen patriarchy (thereby abandoning father-led families, churches, and communities), let us remember that the final and inevitable replacement of patriarchy is totalitarian statism.[4]

ICGS is unwilling to carry on the discussion of manhood and womanhood merely on the ground of man's headship and the difference in the roles of men and women. The universe is bigger than this. The failure to discuss the ultimate and archetypal masculine leaves us without the ultimate and archetypal feminine. But more important, it leaves us without the true revelation of God Himself, without whom we cannot know life, let alone who we are as men and women. **The final answers about our nature as men and women cannot be found apart from the Fatherhood of God, the masculinity of the Trinity, and the femininity of His creation.**

2. Introduction

According to the popular view, God called Deborah to be one of the judges of Israel, to lead men in war, and thus to deliver the nation from oppression. Deborah's leading is considered normal and precedential. If one says that women should not teach men or be ordained, the answer comes back, "Oh, but what about Deborah!" For example, in *Why Not Women?*, Loren Cunningham and David Hamilton write:

> All we need to do to refute this idea—that leadership is male—is to find one woman in the Bible who was a gifted leader. Just one woman, obviously gifted, anointed, and called by God to lead. But as we look at Scripture, we find not one but several, in both the Old and New Testaments. ... Deborah was both a leader and a prophet. She was the head of state, just as Samuel and other prophets were in the days before Israel had a king.[5]

3. Refer to "Ten Biblical Reasons for the Pre-Fall Headship of the Man," *FAW—Vol. One*, pages 96-97. My work, *Knowing God and Understanding Men, A Study of Genesis for Women* (available from ICGS), includes a much fuller discussion of patriarchy, its function, corruption, and God's redemption of it.

4. Ivan the Terrible slaughtered his thousands; statist communism, its tens of millions. The hope inside fallen patriarchy is God's grace, redemption, and work through responsible good men to oppose the bad. Refer to "Building Two Kingdoms," *FAW—Vol. One*, page 99.

5. Loren Cunningham, David Joel Hamilton with Janice Rogers, *Why Not Women?* (Seattle, WA: YWAM Publishing, 2000), 52.

What about Deborah? Does the text teach that Deborah is the leader of the nation and its military deliverer? Does Deborah provide an historical precedent which overturns the principle of male leadership in the home and nation? Is Deborah a judge, a head of state, and thereby a poster girl for egalitarianism? Or has she been misrepresented?

Judges 4-5 is a complicated and unusual passage. However, close examination will reveal that Deborah is not a military leader, a head of state, or an advocate for egalitarian principles. To be sure, she is a great Israelite, a prophetess, and the most noble person in the book of Judges. But she is also a womanly woman, and a strong woman in a day of weak men. Deborah's glory is that she uses her strength to strengthen men so that God is glorified and the nation is freed.

The book of Judges takes place between the founding of the nation under Moses and Joshua and the rise of the kings. With God as Israel's only King, and governmental bureaucracy at a minimum, this should have been a time of great freedom and prosperity. However, because of idolatry, it was instead a dark time of oppression, civil and religious chaos, as *"every man did what was right in his own eyes."*

The book of Judges traces the following cycle six and a half times:

- The people turn away from the Lord to idols;
- God chastens them with oppressors;
- The people repent and call out to God for salvation; and
- God raises up a deliver who militarily defeats the oppressors, restoring freedom for a time. These deliverers are called judges.

3. The prose account of Judges 4

Judges 4-5 relates the third cycle of the six and a half cycles presented in the book. Chapter 4:1-3 covers the first three parts of the cycle—*And the people of Israel again did what was evil in the sight of the Lord after Ehud died. 2 And the Lord sold them into the hand of Jabin king of Canaan, who reigned in Hazor. The commander of his army was Sisera, who lived in Harosheth-hagoyim. 3 Then the people of Israel cried out to the Lord for help, for he had 900 chariots of iron and he oppressed the people of Israel cruelly for twenty years.*

Usually at this point in the cycle, God raises up or calls a military deliverer to save the people. This is perfectly in accord with the definition of a judge given in the introduction of the book of Judges 2:16, 18—*Then the Lord raised up judges, who saved them out of the hand of those who plundered them. Yet they did not listen to their judges, for they whored after other gods... 18 Whenever the Lord raised up judges for them, the Lord was with the judge, and he saved them from the hand of their enemies all the days of the judge.*

According to Judges 2:16, 18, a judge was a person whom God raised up to deliver the people militarily from oppressors—judges saved *out of the hand of those who plundered them*; they *saved from the hand of their enemies.* Secondly, Judges 2:16 mentions that they (the Israelites) *did not listen* to their judges. Clearly this indicates that the judges did have some teaching or exhorting function. However, in this definition and in the presentation of the actual judges in the book of Judges, the military-deliverer aspect is the overwhelming emphasis.[6]

6. I find no clear example in the book of Judges of a judge teaching the people or addressing them except to muster them for war (e.g., Judg. 7:24). The one passage that could be called preaching or teaching is uttered by a prophet, not a judge (vv. 6:7-10). By way of contrast, Samuel, the last judge and founder of "the school of the prophets," carried on an extensive speaking ministry, as is recorded in 1 Samuel (chaps. 3, 7, 8, 12, etc.).

3.1 Who was Deborah?

Judges 4:4-5—*Now Deborah, a prophetess, the wife of Lappidoth, was judging Israel at that time. 5 She used to sit under the palm of Deborah between Ramah and Bethel in the hill country of Ephraim, and the people of Israel came up to her for judgment.* When we come to Judges 4:4-5, we are presented with a variation in the cycle. We are not presented with the call or rise of a warrior. Rather, a woman is introduced and a state of affairs is described. Deborah is the only significant character in the book of Judges whose call **is not** described[7] and who is not said "to arise"—the formulaic description of a deliverer judge (Othniel–3:9; Ehud–3:15; Gideon–6:14; Tola–10:1; Jair–10:3).

Deborah was a prophetess.

The first thing the text tells us about Deborah is that she was a prophetess. A prophet was one who received and communicated words directly from and for God (Ex. 4:15-16; 7:1). There were true and false prophets (e.g., 1 Kin. 22), faithful and unfaithful prophets (Num. 24:12-13; 31:16; 1 Kin. 13), and lifelong and temporary prophets (Num. 11:24). Simply being a prophet does not tell us much about a person's role or even his character. Some prophets appeared, delivered a message, and were not heard from again. Others were towering figures. Except in a few cases, like Moses and Samuel, they were not the rulers of the nation. Most often prophets came to the king with messages from God of warning, guidance, or judgment. Even David, who was a prophet as well as a king, received this kind of ministry from Nathan and Gad.[8] Whatever the particulars, in the Old Testament a prophet of Yahweh spoke God's words as His agent and mouthpiece.

Prophetesses are extremely rare in Scripture. There are 470 mentions of the words *prophet/prophets* and only nine mentions of *prophetess/prophetesses*. Of these nine, two are false prophetesses. This leaves only Miriam, Deborah, Huldah, and Isaiah's wife[9] as legitimate Old Testament prophetesses. The New Testament prophetesses function in a different era with a different kind of prophetic gift, and so are not included here.[10]

That Deborah was a prophetess means that God sometimes spoke through her. By itself, this information does not tell us anything about her role in the nation or even about her character. God chooses whom He will, and usually we do not know why. Isaiah tells us that the rule of women is a sign of degeneracy, not liberation (Is. 3:12). Certainly the time of the Judges was a dark time in Israel's history. Those who seek to extrapolate doctrine or practice from Deborah need to remember that Judges 4-5 is the historical report of a very rare circumstance in a far-from-ideal setting. These chapters were given for our edification, but should not be seen as precedents, or used to overturn other clear commands of Scripture.

---

7. Gideon's and Samson's supernatural calls are described in detail (Judg. 6:11-26; 13), as is the rise of Abimelech and Jephthah by the agency of men (9:1-21; 11:1-11). Unfortunately, *The Women's Study Bible*, usually an excellent and conservative commentary, calls Deborah, "A Distinguished Judge," speaks of her as "elevated to high political power," and extrapolates "God's call" for her from Judges 4:4. Dorothy Kelley, general editor, *The Women's Study Bible* (Nashville, TN: Thomas Nelson Publishers, 1995), 389, 392.

8. Refer to 2 Samuel 7:3-17 for the difference between Nathan speaking for himself to David, and as the mouthpiece of God.

9. Likely, Isaiah is using *prophetess* in Isaiah 8:3 only as a title for his wife (i.e., Mrs. Prophet) rather than a reference to her as God's spokesman. The context is clearly conjugal, and there is no record of Isaiah's wife speaking for God.

10. John Piper and Wayne Grudem, *Fifty Crucial Questions About Manhood and Womanhood* (Wheaton, IL: The Council on Biblical Manhood and Womanhood, 1992), 25-26. Question 23 explains the difference between Old and New Testament prophecy this way: "Prophecy in the worship of the early church was not the kind of authoritative, infallible revelation we associate with the written prophecies of the Old Testament. It was a report in human words based on a spontaneous, personal revelation of the Holy Spirit (1 Cor. 14:30) for the purpose of edification, encouragement, consolation, conviction, and guidance (1 Cor. 14:3, 24-25; Acts 21:4; 16:6-10). It was not necessarily free from a mixture of human error, and thus needed assessment (1 Thess. 5:19-20; 1 Cor. 14:29) on the basis of the apostolic (Biblical) teaching." For further information: Wayne Grudem, *The Gift of Prophecy in 1 Corinthians* (Washington: University Press of America, 1982), and "Prophecy—Yes, But Teaching—No: Paul's Consistent Advocacy of Women's Participation Without Governing Authority." To download a copy, see Articles section of CBMW Resources: www.cbmw.com/resources.

Deborah was married.

No details are given about Deborah's husband or marriage. She is simply described as the wife of Lappidoth. However, the fact that she is identified as a wife (4:4) and later identified herself as a mother (5:7) who ministered from a particular place (4:5), warrants the understanding that Deborah's ministry did not negate her life as a conventional homemaker.

Deborah was judging (adjudicating).

Next we are told that Deborah *was judging Israel at that time.*[11] The word ***shaphat*** (to judge) is a broad and general word which means judge, adjudicate, decide, govern, deliver, pronounce judgment, or execute judgment. Fortunately the text does give a little more contextual information to help us understand what Deborah was doing.

Clearly Deborah was not providing military deliverance under her palm tree. While the text is not specific, it is most likely that she rendered verdicts in lawsuits and gave divine guidance. 1 Samuel 9:6-10 provides an example of this practice. The future king, Saul, sought a prophet or "seer" when he lost his donkeys. In 1 Samuel 9:6, Saul said to this servant, *"Behold, there is a man of God in this city, and he is a man who is held in honor; all that he says comes true. So now let us go there. Perhaps he can tell us the way we should go."* Three things are said about the seer (prophet) whom Saul sought: He was known to be a man of God; he was held in honor; and all that he said came true.

Undoubtedly the same could be said of Deborah. She was not merely wise or insightful; she was actually a prophetess—she spoke the words of God. Second, Deborah was a woman of integrity, loyal to God and dependable. Whether she dealt with issues such as "should I marry Sue or Jane?" or "Pete stole my pig, make him give it back," the text simply does not say. Whatever the details, we know that her judging provided adjudication or guidance counseling, not military deliverance from oppressors. In this sense, she was "judging," but she was not a "judge" in the sense the book of Judges defines this role.

The question arises, where were the elders and priests whom God had appointed to judge the people (Ex. 29:9; Num. 11:16-25)? The only priest mentioned in the book of Judges was apostate (Judg. 17-18). The elders after Joshua's time were corrupt or foolish (Judg. 2:7, 10; 8:14-16; 21). Likely, the people resorted to Deborah because she had both the Word of God and personal integrity, a rare combination in those days.[12]

Deborah was under her palm tree.

One detail about Deborah's style of ministry is mentioned. She stayed put, under her palm tree, and the people came to her. Years later, Samuel also judged at Ramah (1 Sam. 7:15-17). Unlike Deborah, he walked a circuit. Deborah's habit was to minister at home. This is a detail; nevertheless, home-based work is classically feminine.

---

11. The New International Version's translation of Judges 4:4—*Deborah was leading Israel at this time*—is an unfortunate and unnecessary egalitarian interpretation.

12. The priesthood must have been no better in Deborah's time than in the time of Samuel under Eli and his sons. As Daniel Block puts it, "The silence of the priesthood in the book of Judges is deafening." A. R. Millard, James K. Hoffmeier, David W. Baker, editors, "Deborah Among the Judges: The Perspective of the Hebrew Historian," *Faith, Tradition, and History, Old Testament Historiography in Near Eastern Context* (Winona Lake, IN: Eisenbraums, 1994), 252.

3.2 The deliverer-judge Barak

Call and command

Judges 4:6-7—*She sent and summoned Barak the son of Abinoam from Kedesh-naphtali and said to him, "Has not the Lord, the God of Israel, commanded you, 'Go, gather your men at Mount Tabor, taking 10,000 from the people of Naphtali and the people of Zebulun. 7 And I* [the Lord] *will draw out Sisera, the general of Jabin's army, to meet you by the river Kishon with his chariots and his troops, and I [the Lord] will give him into your hand'?"* Whatever the nature of Deborah's judging ministry, something provoked her to summon Barak (v. 6). From the context, we know the following: 1) The northern tribes were suffering a harsh oppression (vv. 4:2-3; 5:6-7); and 2) They had cried to the Lord for help (v. 4:3).

Whether God initiated the message to Deborah to commission Barak in response to the people's cries to Him, or whether the people petitioned Deborah and she sought the Lord for His Word, we do not know. What we do know is that God's prophetic Word was to call and command Barak to engage Sisera, the enemy general, with a sure promise of victory. Again, demonstrating her preference for ministering from home, Deborah sent for Barak. His coming a distance of some 75 miles indicated his respect for the Lord and for His prophetess. Deborah's words to Barak made at least three things clear: 1) She did not speak from her own wisdom or because of her popularity with the people, she spoke on the authority of the Word of God alone; 2) Barak was and had been the military leader of the tribes—*Go, gather* ***your*** *men*; and 3) Barak was here commanded to be the deliverer-judge as described in Judges 2:16, 18.

Deborah framed her message to Barak as a question: *Has not the Lord, the God of Israel, commanded you...?* It was a question that demanded an affirmative answer, putting the greatest possible emphasis on the fact that it was Yahweh who commanded and who would win the battle Himself. What more could any general ask? God not only told him what to do and where to go, but what the outcome would be—certain victory. Nevertheless, instead of marching off speedily to execute the will of the Lord, Barak issued his own condition to Deborah and thereby to God.

Condition and accommodation

Barak was the commander of the army; the people had cried out for salvation, and yet no deliverer had arisen. It was likely that God had commanded Barak previously to go forth,[13] but he had refused to go. If this was the case, Deborah was repeating a command Barak had already heard, but refused to obey. (God often sent prophets to warn and command errant leaders.[14]) Whatever had happened in the past, Barak next issued a clear condition for his obedience to God. Verse 4:8—*Barak said to her, "If you will go with me, I will go, but if you will not go with me, I will not go."*

Why Barak did not obey the Lord straightway we do not know. Perhaps he thought the people did not trust him as much as they trusted Deborah; perhaps he feared they would not answer his muster; perhaps he trusted Deborah's physical presence as an assurance of God's help more than God's own promise. Whatever the reason, Barak's issuing a condition to God was not a good or admirable thing (as some have tried to make it[15]). Both Deborah and God were displeased with this response from Barak as we see by their responses to him.

---

13. The divine warrant for the extermination of the Canaanites was given in Moses' day (Deut. 7:1-5); yet because of Israel's failure to obey completely, the Canaanites remained among them as a snare (Judg. 2:1-4).

14. Examples of prophets counseling kings: Samuel to Saul (1 Sam. 13:8-14); Nathan to David (2 Sam. 12:1-15); and Jeremiah to Zedekiah (Jer. 37:1-10). Many more examples could be given.

15. Daniel Block argues that Barak is righteous, and that "the request to be accompanied by the prophet is a plea for the presence of God." Daniel I. Block, *The New American Commentary, Vol. 6, Judges, Ruth* (Nashville, TN: Broadman & Holman Publishers, 1999), 199.

Condition and judgment

Judges 4:9-10—*And she said, "I will surely go with you. Nevertheless, the road on which you are going will not lead to your glory, for the Lord will sell Sisera into the hand of a woman." Then Deborah arose and went with Barak to Kedesh. 10 And Barak called out Zebulun and Naphtali to Kedesh. And 10,000 men went up at his heels, and Deborah went up with him.* Willing to accommodate Barak's weakness, Deborah agreed to go; but she was not pleased or honored. Apparently, she would have preferred for Barak to go do his job and leave her under her palm tree to do hers. She saw the demand that she go to the battle as unnecessary. God saw it as shameful, and pronounced through Deborah a divine judgment against Barak, the warrior. It was the duty of ancient commanders to meet their enemies of equal rank and standing. That Sisera, Barak's "opposite number," would be vanquished by a woman would be a shame to both Barak and Sisera (e.g., Judg. 9:52-54).

Upon first reading, some might imagine that Deborah was the woman who would slay Sisera, but God had another woman in mind. Verse 4:11 is included at this point to prepare the way for Jael's appearance later in the chapter—*Now Heber the Kenite had separated from the Kenites, the descendants of Hobab the father-in-law of Moses, and had pitched his tent as far away as the oak in Zaanannim, which is near Kedesh.*

3.3 The battle: Deborah exhorted; Barak went forth; God triumphed.

> Judges 4:12-16—*When Sisera was told that Barak the son of Abinoam had gone up to Mount Tabor, 13 Sisera called out all his chariots, 900 chariots of iron, and all the men who were with him, from Harosheth-hagoyim to the river Kishon. 14 And Deborah said to Barak, "Up! For this is the day in which the Lord has given Sisera into your hand. Does not the Lord go out before you?" So Barak went down from Mount Tabor with 10,000 men following him. 15 And the Lord routed Sisera and all his chariots and all his army before Barak by the edge of the sword. And Sisera got down from his chariot and fled away on foot. 16 And Barak pursued the chariots and the army to Harosheth-hagoyim, and all the army of Sisera fell by the edge of the sword; not a man was left.*

After Barak and Deborah returned to the north, Barak called out the troops and went to Mount Tabor as commanded. However, when God drew Sisera out as He had promised, Barak was again slow to act. Deborah commanded Barak with the same sort of language she used in their first encounter. She exhorted him to act, using once again the form of a rhetorical question to emphasize that God Himself was the One who went forth to destroy the enemy; *"Does not the Lord go out before you?"* Thus encouraged, Barak went forth, the men followed him,[16] and God routed Sisera's army.

3.4 A surprise ending for Sisera

> Judges 4:17-21—*But Sisera fled away on foot to the tent of Jael, the wife of Heber the Kenite, for there was peace between Jabin the king of Hazor and the house of Heber the Kenite. 18 And Jael came out to meet Sisera and said to him, "Turn aside, my lord; turn aside to me; do not*

16. Sarah Sumner writes, "Deborah is commended for leading ten thousand men into a battle against King Jabin and his army." Sarah Sumner, *Men and Women in the Church* (Downers Grove, IL: InterVarsity Press, 2003), 109. Leading the army into battle is what Barak did, not what Deborah did.

be afraid." So he turned aside to her into the tent, and she covered him with a rug. 19 And he said to her, "Please give me a little water to drink, for I am thirsty." So she opened a skin of milk and gave him a drink and covered him. 20 And he said to her, "Stand at the opening of the tent, and if any man comes and asks you, 'Is anyone here?' say, 'No.'" 21 But Jael the wife of Heber took a tent peg, and took a hammer in her hand. Then she went softly to him and drove the peg into his temple until it went down into the ground while he was lying fast asleep from weariness. So he died.

Hospitality with a hammer

The Kenites were descendants of Moses' brother-in-law, Hobab, who had acted as a guide for Israel in the wilderness (Num. 10:29-32). They later settled among the tribe of Judah in the south. Heber, Jael's husband, had moved to the north, away from his relatives, where he was on good terms with Jabin, the Canaanite king. Probably it was for this reason that Sisera trusted Jael's invitation and entered her tent for sanctuary. At first Jael was the perfect hostess, inviting the exhausted general into her tent and serving him lavishly. In response, Sisera commanded her to stand guard and protect him from pursuing Israelites. However, when Sisera was asleep, Jael killed him with the skill and common implements of a Bedouin wife. She drove a tent peg through his temple with a hammer. Thus, the Canaanite general came to a surprising and ignominious end—exactly in accord with God's prediction through Deborah.

Barak pursued what he could not attain.

Judges 4:22—*And behold, as Barak was pursuing Sisera, Jael went out to meet him and said to him, "Come, and I will show you the man whom you are seeking." So he went in to her tent, and there lay Sisera dead, with the tent peg in his temple.* Just as Barak did not obey God's command to go to battle without condition, neither did he accept God's limitation on his glory. After the battle, Barak pursued the fleeing Sisera, apparently determined to seek what God had expressly forbidden him—the glory of slaying Sisera. Barak probably assumed that the woman prophesied was Deborah. When Deborah did not go to the battle, Barak may have thought he could triumph after all. But God's possibilities and resources are limitless. Barak did not know that God had another woman living right in Sisera's path of retreat who would be more than able and willing to kill this wicked man.

Thus, the historical prose record of this episode concludes in a most satisfying statement, emphasizing the work of God, the final Deliverer-Judge, and the work of the people in faithful obedience. Judges 4:23-24—*So on that day God subdued Jabin the king of Canaan before the people of Israel. 24 And the hand of the people of Israel pressed harder and harder against Jabin the king of Canaan, until they destroyed Jabin king of Canaan.*

4. The poetic account of Judges 5

The cycle of Deborah and Barak is unique in Judges in that it is presented twice—once in the factual prose account of chapter 4, and a second time in the dramatic and poetic account of chapter 5. Probably in obedience to God's command in verse 12 to awake and sing, Deborah writes this vivid account of the events as only an eyewitness could. It is considered one of the oldest and finest examples of Hebrew poetry. While Barak sings this song with Deborah, she is its author, as is indicated by her first-person references in verses 7 and 13.

4.1 Why Deborah sings

> Judges 5:1-5—*Then sang Deborah and Barak the son of Abinoam on that day: 2 "That the leaders took the lead in Israel, that the people offered themselves willingly, bless the Lord! 3 Hear, O kings; give ear, O princes; to the Lord I will sing; I will make melody to the Lord, the God of Israel. 4 Lord, when you went out from Seir, when you marched from the region of Edom, the earth trembled and the heavens dropped, yes, the clouds dropped water. 5 The mountains quaked before the Lord, even Sinai before the Lord, the God of Israel."*

Deborah praises God for two things.

Deborah praises God that His people moved out in obedience to fight for Him—officers led and men followed. Secondly, she praises God as the ultimate Warrior who brought His people from Sinai and who triumphs over the Canaanites with supernatural power.

The beginning of oppression's end

> Judges 5:6-8—*"In the days of Shamgar, son of Anath, in the days of Jael, the highways were abandoned, and travelers kept to the byways. 7 The villagers ceased in Israel; they ceased to be until I arose; I, Deborah, arose as a mother in Israel. 8 When new gods were chosen, then war was in the gates. Was shield or spear to be seen among forty thousand in Israel?"*

Deborah describes the oppressive conditions created by the Canaanites. Travel, commerce, and village life had ceased. People stayed home or crept about in fear of assault, rape, and theft. And yet, the root cause of the problem was not the Canaanites; it was the Israelites themselves who had *chosen new gods*. Without God, they were prostrate and disarmed before their technologically-superior foes.

This was the situation until, *I, Deborah, arose as a mother in Israel.* While God is clearly the Deliverer of His people, this short verse reveals Deborah as the human hinge of the story. When oppression and slavery seemed the immovable state of affairs, Deborah arose as a mother. Through her, deliverance is given birth; *the noble remnant comes forth* (v. 13).

Deborah's joy in "opening the door"

Deborah is best understood as one of the significant Biblical women "who open the door" on great historical developments. Women sometimes initiate great events; but, as we shall see, men must walk through the doors women open in order to complete and execute what the women have begun. This is not a contradiction of the basic gender pattern in which men initiate and women respond. Rather, this represents an example of the "interdependence" principle laid out by Paul in 1 Corinthians 11:8-12.[17] Scriptural examples of this pattern of women initiating great events and men completing them are:

- Eve opens the door of sin;
  Adam walks through and brings the curse on mankind.
- The midwives reject Pharaoh's tyranny;
  Moses is born and grows up to crush Egypt.

17. For more on interdependence and counterpoint, refer to pages 76-79 and 156-157.

- Rahab opens the door of Canaan to Israelite spies;
  Joshua comes through to conquer the land.
- Hannah opens her life to God in a corrupt day;
  Samuel comes forth to establish the kingdom.
- Ruth insists on coming to Bethlehem;
  God, through Boaz, plants the Messianic line.
- Mary opens her spirit and body to God's call;
  Christ comes through her to save the world.
- Deborah exhorts and supports Barak in battle;
  Barak and his men defeat the Canaanites.

How do we know these actions are gender "counterpoint" and not a deliberate overturning of patriarchy? Deborah identifies herself as a mother—not a revolutionary title for a woman. Is she referring to the fact that she is a biological mother, or is she implying a motherly attitude and posture to the whole nation? Both are completely warranted from context. She describes her motivation, not as a judge or even as a prophetess, but rather, as a mother—one concerned for the life and well-being of God's children.

Praising men and God

Judges 5:19—*My heart goes out to the commanders of Israel who offered themselves willingly among the people. Bless the Lord.* In verse 9, Deborah's *heart goes out*—she is full of admiration for and pride in the Israelite men who came forth to lead Israel. An officer corps answered the muster of Barak, enrolled, and took charge of the enlisted volunteers. For these commanders, without whom no army would exist, Deborah praises God. Had not these men followed God, Deborah's initiating would have availed nothing. She continues in 5:10-11—*"Tell of it, you who ride on white donkeys, you who sit on rich carpets and you who walk by the way. 11 To the sound of musicians at the watering places, there they repeat the righteous triumphs of the Lord, the righteous triumphs of his villagers in Israel. Then down to the gates marched the people of the Lord."*

Judges 5:3 is a call to the defeated Canaanite kings (vassals of Jabin, who served under Sisera), to worship the true God. Judges 5:10 is apparently a second such call to the Canaanite enemies, this time to the wealthy merchants who prospered through Jabin's oppression. These men are also commanded to tell of the triumphs of God and Israel.

Gender-specific commands

Judges 5:12—*"Awake, awake, Deborah! Awake, awake, break out in a song! Arise, Barak, lead away your captives, O son of Abinoam."* Deborah's song presents a staccato series of scenes, full of energy and rich imagery, but often with little context. Verse 12 may represent a summary of God's overall commands to Deborah and Barak for the whole operation—Deborah, you prophesy; Barak, you go to war. More specifically, these directives fit the situation after God routed Sisera. Deborah is to sing—lead the response of praise for the victorious warriors. (For other examples of this practice, see Miriam in Ex. 15:1-18, 20-21, and the women of David's day in 1 Sam. 18:6-7). Barak is to finish what remains of the military operation by leading away the captives. In either case, these commands are classically gender-specific: Deborah is to respond with praise; Barak is to go and do.

4.2 The roll call of honor and shame

> Judges 5:13-18—*Then down marched the remnant of the noble; the people of the Lord marched down for me against the mighty. 14 From Ephraim their root they marched down into the valley, following you, Benjamin, with your kinsmen; from Machir marched down the commanders, and from Zebulun those who bear the lieutenant's staff; 15 the princes of Issachar came with Deborah, and Issachar faithful to Barak; into the valley they rushed at his heels. Among the clans of Reuben there were great searchings of heart. 16 Why did you sit still among the sheepfolds, to hear the whistling for the flocks? Among the clans of Reuben there were great searchings of heart. 17 Gilead stayed beyond the Jordan; and Dan, why did he stay with the ships? Asher sat still at the coast of the sea, staying by his landings. 18 Zebulun is a people who risked their lives to the death; Naphtali, too, on the heights of the field.*

The faithful and unfaithful tribes

In verse 13, Deborah returns to her introductory theme—praise for God's people rising up to follow Him in holy war. In the verses that follow, she identifies by name the tribes that answered God's call and are thus worthy of praise: Ephraim, Benjamin, Machir (alternate name for Manasseh), Zebulun, and Issachar. On the other hand, Reuben, Gilead (alternate name for Gad), and Dan are singled out for shame. They heard the call of God, but tarried with the daily affairs of flocks and fleets. Deborah, as a true glory-of-man woman (1 Cor. 11:7), gives herself wholeheartedly, not only to the praise of God, but also to the praise of worthy men. Following the patterns of wisdom, she is a full-orbed woman of wisdom, speaking lifegiving counsel and praising the righteous (Prov. 4:7-9; 8:13:21), while scorning and rejecting the dishonorable (Prov. 1:24-33). In verse 18, the highest praise is awarded Zebulun and Naphtali. These tribes not only answered God's call, they risked their very lives in the fiercest part of the battle.

God who wins the battle

> Judges 5:19-22—*"The kings came, they fought; then fought the kings of Canaan, at Taanach, by the waters of Megiddo; they got no spoils of silver. 20 From heaven the stars fought, from their courses they fought against Sisera. 21 The torrent Kishon swept them away, the ancient torrent, the torrent Kishon. March on, my soul, with might! 22 Then loud beat the horses' hoofs with the galloping, galloping of his steeds."*

In verses 19-22, Deborah moves from outlining the faithful and unfaithful deeds of men to describe that which actually turns the battle—the work of God and angels. Sisera's 900 chariots would ordinarily be highly effective in the plain of the Esdraelon Valley where this battle was fought. However, just as Sisera comes forth in his might, God supernaturally sends a torrential downpour to cause the usually-tiny Kishon river to turn into a flood. The chariots are caught in a quagmire, the horses break loose in a frenzy, and Sisera's troops are left in rout. Almost certainly "the stars fighting from heaven" is a reference to the angelic forces who battled demons in order to fulfill God's command to send this unusual rain storm. The similarity between the victory at the Red Sea and this victory is apparent. God is the almighty God of nature. The strongest weapons of man are no match for Him. The Canaanite god, Baal—supposedly the god of rain and lightning—is shown to be as impotent as his servants.

The strongest curse

Judges 5:23—*"Curse Meroz, says the angel of the Lord, curse its inhabitants thoroughly, because they did not come to the help of the Lord, to the help of the Lord against the mighty."* Deborah has been writing her song in the words of God under the inspiration of His Spirit, but now in verse 23 she quotes the Lord directly. "The angel of the Lord" is the Ultimate Warrior who has brought the Israelites from Sinai, through Sier, and into the land under Joshua (Ex. 23:20-33). Now He, the preincarnate Christ, utters a curse on the town of Meroz.

Apparently Meroz was a town in or near the Esdraelon Valley; it is unknown and unfound, a reasonable expectation given this curse. Meroz's curse is more severe than the shame put upon the other slackers. Perhaps the men of Meroz were near the line of retreat and had special opportunity to help with the pursuit and slaughter of the enemy, but did not. The Lord curses them thoroughly because they did not **help Him**. As we have seen, God does not need men. He will win the battle sovereignly, whatever the details. However, God desires to work with, in, and through His people. Their response to His commands does not determine the outcome of the battle; it determines the outcome of their own lives. Judges 4-5 presents a microcosm of all history. All of the ages encompass a holy war between God and His servants against Satan and his servants. In the end, the record will be clear—who came to serve, who did not, who served with highest distinction, and who were cowards of greatest ignominy.

Jael, the blessed Bedouin

> Judges 5:24-27—*"Most blessed of women be Jael, the wife of Heber the Kenite, of tent-dwelling women most blessed. 25 He asked water and she gave him milk; she brought him curds in a noble's bowl. 26 She sent her hand to the tent peg and her right hand to the workmen's mallet; she struck Sisera; she crushed his head; she shattered and pierced his temple. 27 Between her feet he sank, he fell, he lay still; between her feet he sank, he fell; where he sank, there he fell—dead."*

What a contrast between Meroz and Jael! Israelites who had every opportunity and reason to serve God did not, and thus received the harshest curse. Jael, a non-Israelite with apparently no opportunity or capacity, became the heroine of the battle! Truly God uses the weaker things of this world to overcome the mighty.

Who was Jael? Why did she do what she did? She was of the Kenites, descendants of Moses' in-laws, friends of the Jews. But she was not a Jew. In addition, her husband, Heber, had moved away from the Judahites in the south, choosing to live in a land of Canaanite oppression. Heber and Jabin were on friendly terms; but as becomes clear, Jael and Sisera were not. Jael bears strong resemblance to Rahab in Joshua 2. Rahab was a non-Jew, who lived in the midst of Canaanites; indeed she was one. She, like they, had significant knowledge of the God of Israel; His mighty deeds had been shaking the nations for decades (Josh. 2:8-13). But unlike the other Canaanites, Rahab chose to repent of her idolatry and seek the mercy of Yahweh. Jael lived among Canaanites, but she was a loyal worshiper of Yahweh. When her opportunity came to strike a literal blow for God and freedom, she did it without hesitation.

The phrase *most blessed of women* brings to mind Mary, the mother of Christ, though it seems hard to imagine two women more different than Jael and Mary. Jael is the most blessed of *tent-dwelling women*. She is here honored as the greatest Bedouin woman ever to live. Mary, on the other hand, is the greatest woman of all generations. However, Jael and Mary share a similarity which is the foundation of their greatness. Both are on the Lord's side, utterly committed to Him. Both love Him first with heart, mind, and soul. Both are willing to do whatever He needs or wants done—be it slaying a wicked general or bringing the Son of God into the world. They are both the "handmaids of the Lord."

4.3 A defeated champion in the combat of mothers

> Judges 5:28-30—*The mother of Sisera wailed through the lattice: 'Why is his chariot so long in coming? Why tarry the hoofbeats of his chariots?' 29 Her wisest princesses answer, indeed, she answers herself, 30 'Have they not found and divided the spoil? A womb or two for every man; spoil of dyed materials for Sisera, spoil of dyed materials embroidered, two pieces of dyed work embroidered for the neck as spoil?'*

In the last scene of Deborah's song, we move from the tent of Jael to the house of Sisera's mother, where this well-to-do woman impatiently waits the return of her son from the battle. Not considering defeat possible, she and her attendants speculate about what is keeping the general. Their answer—rape and pillage. Deborah could not have portrayed the Canaanite culture more effectively than this![18] When the "cultivated" matrons of a people deliberately and enthusiastically rear sons for the military, economic, and sexual oppression of their neighbors—such a society is revealed as corrupt, root and branch.

Deborah is a modest and humble woman. She does not dwell on herself or her role in events. However, by closing her song with Sisera's mother, she casts herself without words as the victorious champion of mothers in the battle between light and dark, good and evil, between Yahweh and those who hate Him. Deborah's God has triumphed over Baal; her technologically-inferior culture has defeated the corruption of Canaan; her man, Barak, will come back from the battle to enter the roll call of faith (Heb. 11:32-34), while the tyrant Sisera lies dead with a tent peg through his head. Many Israelite men have been faithful, while the hosts of Sisera have been swept away by flood and sword. Deborah has reason to rejoice. Her God has brought great triumph, and she has been the mother of it. Thus, we have in Judges 5:31 the glorious conclusion of her song: *"So may all your enemies perish, O Lord! But your friends be like the sun as he rises in his might." And the land had rest for forty years.*

5. Complementarian principles from Judges 4-5

Having reviewed the text of Judges 4-5, let us return to our original question. Does the cycle of Deborah and Barak support egalitarianism? Does Deborah's ministry refute the whole principle of male leadership as some suggest?

5.1 The womanliness of Deborah

Deborah is not an example or justification for women's usurpation of men's offices or roles. Rather, as a strong woman, she deploys her strength by disciplining its use in womanly ways in order to strengthen men and glorify God.[19]

---

18. Sisera's mother refers to the Israelite women—who supposedly will be raped—with a crude and demeaning term.

19. It would be easy to develop a complete presentation of the "five aspects of woman" using Deborah. She ruled her domain at the palm tree in a way that reached the whole nation; she helped Barak become the leader he needed to be; she gave life as a mother to her country; she exhorted, reproved, and praised the wise and the foolish as a true lady of wisdom; and she exulted in glorifying honorable men and the God who led them.

Deborah is not a judge.

In the sense that the book of Judges defines a judge, Deborah is not a military deliverer.[20] Rather, she is a prophetess, and as a prophetess, she commands and exhorts Barak with God's own words and authority.

Deborah accommodates and cooperates.

Deborah works with Barak in ministry. She goes with him to the muster and shares with him the song she writes. She does not see Barak as a "sensitive" man who is opening equal opportunity for women on the battlefield. Barak's weakness irritates her; nevertheless she works for his success.

Deborah is a wife and mother.

Staying under her palm tree, Deborah expects people to come to her to receive her ministry. Her womanliness encompasses and informs her ministry; her ministry does not obliterate her womanliness. Her competitor is not Barak, or even Jabin or Sisera; by implication she presents Sisera's mother as the champion she bests.

Deborah does not lead or fight in the battle.

War is the work of men. Nowhere in the Bible are women mustered for battle. To be killed by a woman was dishonorable (Judg. 9:52-54). Women always have played a significant role in war as spies, informants, and anchors on the domestic front (Num. 32:1-27, especially vv. 26-27; Josh. 2–Rahab, the informant; 2 Sam. 17:17-20). On rare occasions, they kill. But, according to the Bible, it is not normative, desirable, or glorious for women to go to battle with men.

Deborah arises as a mother, not as a judge or warrior.

Because Deborah uses her prophetic gift in the context of integrity and womanliness, she becomes a powerful wisdom figure for the nation. Her strength is used to motivate men, and when they act, she is the first to praise them. When they are lazy or cowardly, she is the first to scorn them. What women want in society is usually what they get. Sisera's mother approved of rape and theft; Deborah wanted freedom and the glory of God.

Deborah is commanded to sing, not take captives.

Deborah's song praises God for the victory and eulogizes the men who fought willingly. Deborah is a great "glory of man" woman. Of the 31 verses in her song, seven explicitly praise the righteous and courageous men who came forth to fight (vv. 2, 9, 11, 13, 14, 15, 18).

---

20. Daniel I. Block, *The New American Commentary, Vol. 6, Judges, Ruth* (Nashville, TN: Broadman & Holman Publishers, 1999), 193-194. Daniel Block poses an impressive series of questions challenging the idea that Deborah is presented as a savior or deliverer:

- Why is she not introduced as one whom Yahweh had raised up?
- Why is there no reference to her inspiration and empowerment by Yahweh's spirit?
- Why does she need Barak to accomplish the deliverance?
- Why is the verb *yasa*, "to save," never applied to her?
- Why does she say, "Yahweh will sell Sisera into the hands of a woman," instead of "into my hands?"
- Why does the author observe that "she went up with Barak" (4:10) but avoid placing her at the head of the troops?
- Why does Deborah announce to Barak, "This day Yahweh has given Sisera into your hands," (4:14) rather than into "my hands?"
- Why is she absent from the description of the actual battle (4:15-17), and why does she never meet Jabin or Sisera?
- Why did the poet prefer the title "mother in Israel" (5:7) over "savior of Israel?"
- Why does the poet avoid the root *qum*, "to rise," and does not refer to Yahweh as the causative subject, when he speaks of Deborah's rise? (The word translated *arose* in 5:7 is what Block calls "an awkward variant," not the typical verb. p. 226.)

If Deborah had been egalitarian

The final test for determining whether a woman is complementarian or egalitarian is to look at the results of her life and work. Women standing on patriarchy strengthen men as leaders, providers, and protectors. Egalitarian women seek to replace men in these roles. The most convincing evidence that Deborah was a womanly woman, "complementarian" in belief and practice, is to look at the results of her life. If Deborah had been egalitarian, her goal would have been to take Barak's job, not exhort him to do it. Her goal would have been to arise as a deliverer, not as a mother. She would have exploited Barak's invitation to the battlefield, not reproved it. She would have battled for equal opportunity for Israelite women in armed combat, not praised a homemaker. She would have filled her hymn with her own achievements, not those of men at arms. Her goal would have been to have her name in Hebrews 11, not Barak's. In short, her goal would have been to replace the men, not make them strong.

Deborah is a woman who opens the door.

Exhorting and going forth as a companion to Barak, Deborah is the catalyst that rouses the faithful remnant of the nation. The result is victory and glory for God, honor for the men who served willingly, shame for slackers, and great renown for two women who stood in the gap in extraordinary ways. A great lady of wisdom, Deborah exhorts, reproves, condemns, and praises in the pattern of wisdom herself. She is a life-giving mother and a "glory of man" to men who are the glory of God. Her purpose is to exalt men into their proper roles, praising all who come forth.

5.2 What Barak does

Barak is a weak man who does the will of God when paired with a righteous and wise woman. He does the job of deliverer-judge, makes the roll call of faith, but suffers a loss of glory because of his lack of zeal and obedience. For clarification, let us review the deeds of Barak for good and ill. On the negative side, Barak knew his job as commander, but did nothing to save the people in their bondage. When Deborah commands him, he hesitates, demanding that she go with him. On the day of the battle, Deborah again must "push him out the door" with command and exhortation. Finally, Barak, unwilling to pursue when commanded, then pursues when forbidden. He attempts to pursue Sisera, even though God has said he will not slay him. On the positive side, Barak does go when Deborah says "Go" and when she accompanies him. He does call out the men, go to Mt. Tabor, and lead 10,000 men down the mountain. He does behold God rout Sisera before him, and he does pursue the Canaanite chariots and army.

One of the clearest statements that Barak, not Deborah, is the judge of this cycle is his listing with the other judges in 1 Samuel 12:11[21] and Hebrews 11:32-34—*And what more shall I say? For time would fail me to tell of Gideon, Barak, Samson, Jephthah, of David and Samuel and the prophets—33 who through faith conquered kingdoms, enforced justice, obtained promises, stopped the mouths of lions, 34 quenched the power of fire, escaped the edge of the sword, were made strong out of weakness, became mighty in war, put foreign armies to flight.* Certainly Barak well fits the description, *were made strong out of weakness, became mighty in war, put foreign armies to flight.*

---

21. The ESV and NIV render the second judge listed in 1 Samuel 12:11 as *Barak,* in accord with some Septuagint and Syriac manuscripts. The NASB and NKJV render him *Bedan,* according to the Hebrew manuscripts. (Refer to NIV's note in the margin on 1 Sam. 12:11.) In all likelihood, the Hebrew is a scribal error since there is no other record of a judge named *Bedan* in the OT and because of the consonant similarity in *Barak* and *Bedan* in Hebrew.

5.3 Standing in, not taking over

Women taking men's roles is an abnormality, not a freedom.

Women were never anointed to be kings, priests, warrior judges, apostles, or elders. On rare occasions they were prophetesses. There is no precedent in Deborah for matriarchy or women's ordination. To use rare and exceptional women as a fulcrum for overturning the gender standards of Scripture and nature is as pervasive today as it is aberrant. Because women are gifted, smart, competent, or visionary is not an excuse for giving them the offices and duties of men. To do so is a final judgment on men and a displacement of the women which will prevent them from deploying their strengths in their natural and most effective framework. By her words, Deborah considers it more desirable to arise as a mother than as a judge or even as a prophetess.

It is a curse on a people when women and children rule over them, not because women and children are inherently evil, but because it represents a breakdown of God's created order whereby men lead and protect while women help and nurture for the glory of God and the benefit of all.

Women who "stood in"

In the case of dead or absent men, God allows women to stand in for—but not take over—male roles and duties. Zelophehad's daughters provide a clear case study of the "no men" problem. Zelophehad had no sons, so God said that his daughters might inherit his land (Num. 27:1-11). In this case, God approves the idea of women standing in the gap where there are no men to provide the natural male leadership. However, in Numbers 36, we see that stand-ins can quickly create a problem. The tribal elders come back to Moses and point out that if the women marry outside their tribe, then the lands of Zelophehad will be transferred to another tribe, thus diminishing the God-appointed heritage of their tribe. In reply, God says the women may marry whomever they please, but the men must be from their tribe in order to assure that the tribal inheritances be preserved.

Stand-ins must have limitations; otherwise stand-ins become take-overs, and the fabric of society is destroyed. Today our society is in tatters from take-overs, rooted more in gender confusion and rebellion than in any other cause. Some women do need to work outside the home. However, when feminist doctrine establishes that all women **should** work outside the home for their own self-respect and independence, women become take-overs in the workplace. Men are displaced in their primary role as providers, and children are deprived of their primary caregiver. Working women have taken over from far too many men; divorce has taken over from life-long monogamy; and alternate forms of childcare have taken over from motherhood. Men are weakened and displaced; women are exhausted and frustrated; children are neglected and abused. We have taken the principle of Numbers 27, added sin to it in many cases, and completely neglected the truth of Numbers 36. A great deal of the genius of Deborah is that she did stand in, but she limited herself even as she did so. Therefore, God was glorified, and men, women, and children were strengthened by her life and ministry, not weakened.

5.4 Strengthening or enabling weak men?

Accommodating weak men

Accommodating weak men, or a man who is weak at the moment, is not an exact science, but rather, an art requiring much wisdom. When women coddle and cover for weak men too much, they exacerbate their weakness. However, as in the case of Deborah, sometimes exhortation or encouragement, coupled with going the second mile in support, will enable an otherwise passive man to do his duty. How far should a woman go in such a case? When does helping a weak man strengthen him? When does it only enable him to be more irresponsible, thus augmenting sin?

Deborah chose to go to the battle and to tell Barak when to go; she did not fight the battle for him. They shared the victory together (they sang her song together). Yet she refused to give him the glory as the champion he was not. He is mentioned only once in the song of victory, and that in praise of Issachar, not Barak (v. 15).

Factors to consider

When trying to discern the difference between strengthening men and enabling them to be weak, consider:

- **Motive:** Deborah clearly had the glory of God and the good of His people foremost in her mind; her life was not about exalting or advancing herself.

- **Method:** Deborah did her ministry in "the style" of a woman—she stayed home. When telling Barak the Word of the Lord, she put it in a form to emphasize the authority of God, not her own. In recording events, she put emphasis on the actions of God and men, not her own.

- **Short-term result:** Deborah had encouragement along the way. After she agreed to go with Barak, he actually went! He mustered the troops. After she told him to go fight, he went and fought.

- **Long-term result:** Is a woman a stand-in for absent or weak men, or is she a take-over? What is the long-term effect of her work? What does she seek to perpetuate? Deborah did not found a school of prophets for prophetesses, nor did Jael start a paramilitary academy for girls. Godly women use every means at their disposal to get men to do their jobs, not to take their jobs.

Office and gifts are appointed; glory is earned.

God's Word upholds gender-specific offices and roles. This does not mean that incompetence is called competence, that failure is honored as success, or that disobedience is honored with glory. God is not mocked, justice is justice. Glory will finally go to those who earn it. Men must be actual men, or they will not be glorified. The question is, will we be actual women? Glory, divine approval, and usefulness to the Kingdom belong to the faithful, whether they are man, woman, or child, in a tent, under a palm, or at the head of the troops.

6. Conclusion

The most honorable character in the book of Judges, Deborah becomes the catalyst and impetus for great good. Because of her, God is glorified as the Deliverer-Judge. Many men rise up and fight bravely. Jael is honored as an extraordinary believer and servant of God. Barak does his job, is honored for his faith, although his glory is diminished. Canaanite evil is defeated, and the northern tribes gain peace for 40 years. Through subsequent millennia, saints have been edified by this great story of faith and Deborah's war hymn glorifying God and those who came to fight for Him.

Deborah did all this as a womanly woman. She was not a military leader, a head of state, or an advocate for egalitarian principles. Deborah was a wife, a mother, a prophetess, a singer, a patriot, and a great lover of God. Deborah was strong and she was a prophetess. What really makes her remarkable was that she used her strengths and prophetic gift in their most effective framework—the created channels of her own womanliness.

7. Study questions for review and discussion

a. Contrary to popular belief, this supplement argues that Deborah was not a deliverer-judge of Israel. What Scriptural evidence is provided that Barak was, in fact, the judge of Judges 4-5, and that Deborah was the prophetess who exhorted him?

b. Explain the concept of women who "open the door." Give examples from Scripture. Can you give other examples of this dynamic from secular history or from your own experience?

c. What is the difference between a woman who "takes over" from men and one who "stands in" for them? Contrast motives, methods, and results as completely as you can.

d. Explain what this means: "Office and gifts are appointed; glory is earned." How can an understanding of this principle give one peace about the injustices of this life? In God's economy, do credit and blame finally go to their rightful owners?

e. What have you learned from Deborah's example and the analysis in this supplement that help you distinguish between "taking over" work designated for men and "opening doors" for the glory of God?

f. Who was the deliverer-judge of Judges 4-5?